Sport and Society

Series Editors
Benjamin G. Rader
Randy Roberts

A list of titles in the series appears at the end of this book.

FRITZ
POLLARD

FRITZ POLLARD

PIONEER IN RACIAL ADVANCEMENT

John M. Carroll

UNIVERSITY OF ILLINOIS PRESS
Urbana and Chicago

The author has quoted from an unpublished chapter from *Education for Freedom* by Horace Mann Bond with the permission of Mrs. Horace Mann Bond, all rights reserved.

© 1992 by the Board of Trustees of the University of Illinois
Manufactured in the United States of America
C 5 4 3 2 1

This book is printed on acid-free paper.

Library of Congress Cataloging-in-Publication Data

Carroll, John M. (John Martin), 1943–
    Fritz Pollard: Pioneer in racial advancement / John M. Carroll.
        p.   cm. — (Sport and society)
    Includes bibliographical references and index.
    ISBN 0-252-01814-1 (acid-free paper)
    1. Pollard, Fritz.   2. Football players—United States—Biography.
3. Afro-Americans in business—Biography.   I. Title.   II. Series.
GV939.P66C37   1992
796.33'092—dc20
[B]   90-25556
                                                                                CIP

For Charlotte

CONTENTS

PREFACE

This book would not have been possible in its present form without John Francis "Jay" Barry, whom I first met in 1962 after a Brown University football game in Princeton, New Jersey. A half-scared sophomore, I was included on the Brown traveling team to make passes to the punter because the regular center was having difficulty with the long spiral passes. At the rear of the Brown bus after our defeat at the hands of the Tigers, Jay, who seldom missed a Brown game home or away, sat down next to me, complimented me on my perfect snaps, and predicted that I would be a fine player for Brown one day. He was wrong on the latter point, but I appreciated his kind words and was surprised that he knew where I was from and who I was. That, I came to find out, was just Jay's nature. He cared about Brown, Brown athletics, and people. Jay was kind and considerate and took the time to seek out and chat with even the second- and third-team members of the Brown eleven. For many of us, Jay Barry was "Mr. Brown Football."

A lifelong resident of Warren, Rhode Island, Jay developed a strong interest in sports before entering Brown University. After graduating from Brown in 1950, Jay worked for many years at the *Brown Alumni Monthly*. During this time, he became an expert on Brown athletics, especially football. Jay first met Fritz Pollard in 1954 at the time Fritz was inducted into the National Collegiate Football Hall of Fame. Beginning in the late 1960s, Jay and Fritz began to collaborate on a biography of Pollard. With a heavy work schedule at the university, Jay spent his precious free time doing interviews and collecting materials for the book. By the early 1980s, he had assembled three large boxes of research materials, including a number of long interviews with Pollard and other Brown football players of the World War I era. As was Jay's way, he gladly put aside his own work on Pollard when university officials asked him to produce two important books on Brown history. I talked with Jay at times during those years, usually seeking a favor, and he always responded in a kind and efficient manner to my requests for photographs or research materials. Several years ago, I was shocked and greatly saddened to hear that Jay Barry had died. The Brown University community lost one of its most loyal and devoted employees and alumni. I hope that this book will in some small way be a tribute to his often-unheralded dedication.

In addition to Jay Barry, numerous individuals have helped me in researching and writing this book. Ella Barry generously allowed me to use Jay's materials on Pollard. Jay Barry's classmate at Brown, Wheaton Holden, was encouraging and provided me with important information and leads. The staff at the Brown University Archives, especially archivist Martha Mitchell and Gayle Lynch, was extremely knowledgeable and efficient. Martha Mitchell went beyond mere courtesy in making my research at Brown both enjoyable and profitable. Pollard's children, Leslie Keeling, Eleanor Towns, and Fritz Pollard, Jr., kindly granted interviews and patiently answered follow-up questions. Fritz Pollard III also took time from a busy schedule to talk with me about his grandfather. Andrew Buni was helpful in explaining the importance of Narragansett Pier as a networking system for young black students. Wardwell Leonard and Watson Smith, Brown graduates of the classes of 1918 and 1919, respectively, were generous in sharing their memories of Brown in that era. I would also like to thank archivist Kenneth C. Cramer of the Dartmouth College Library, as well as the staffs at the Schomburg Center for Research in Black Culture and the Rockefeller Family Archives, for providing useful information. Archie Motley of the Chicago Historical Society took a personal interest in the project and aided my research considerably.

Bob Carroll of the Professional Football Researchers Association proved to me that he is one of the best-informed people in the country on the subject of professional football. He provided me with materials, answered numerous questions, and saved me from a number of errors in interpretation and fact. Pearce Johnson of the

Providence Steam Roller organization, an eyewitness of the early pro game, was encouraging and provided important insights about Pollard. Joe Horrigan of the Pro Football Hall of Fame was generous in sending me materials and giving me the benefit of his knowledge on early pro football. H. N. Young was helpful in telling me what he knew about Pollard's years in Hammond, Indiana. Concerning Pollard's seasons in the Coal Region, I am indebted to Bill O'Brien and John Sullivan for welcoming me to Shenandoah and Mahanoy City and providing many insights on Coal Region football. Joe Zagorski also sent along some important information on Pollard in the Coal Region.

I would also like to thank Dale Wright for putting me in contact with people who knew Pollard in New York during the 1930s and 1940s. I am grateful to St. Clair T. Bourne, Sr., Joseph Mahood, Pat Patterson, Major Robinson, James E. Booker, Sr., Mable Abrams, Mary Jennings, and Evelyn Cunningham for granting interviews.

The staff of the Lamar University Library was helpful in providing research assistance, especially Mary Frances Sherwood, Juanita Weisel, Linda Dietert, Helen Dupre, Sharon Kelley, Norma Jones, Corinne Freeland, and Mark Asteris. Lamar History Department secretaries Dee Sherrill and Randy Landry and their staffs were helpful with typing and photocopying. Graduate students Burton Middleton and Joseph Poole ably assisted me in microfilm research. Dean John Idoux and my department chair Adrian Anderson were encouraging and helped to expedite my research and writing. My colleague JoAnn Stiles generously provided some research assistance at the Library of Congress. I would also like to thank Lamar University for awarding me a Faculty Development Leave, a research mini-grant, and an organized research grant which facilitated research and writing.

William J. Baker, Gerald Gems, David Wiggins, Randy Roberts, and Benjamin Rader read some or all of the draft chapters and saved me from many factual or interpretational errors. Lawrence J. Malley has been most supportive throughout the project, as has Richard Wentworth. Ray and Nancy Carroll were hospitable in providing room, board, and encouragement during two summers of research in Rhode Island. Most of all, I cannot express enough gratitude to my wife Charlotte for skillfully assisting in conducting a number of oral interviews, as well as for her love, patience, and support.

Prologue:
"A Genuine Unknown Hero"

The temperature was in the mid-fifties and there was a threat of rain as nearly forty thousand fans began to file into the newly refurbished Yankee Stadium on the evening of September 23, 1978, to watch Grambling State University oppose Morgan State in an intercollegiate football game. The annual event, which featured two of the nation's top black collegiate football powers, had been sponsored by the New York Yankees and the New York Urban League for the past seven years. In conjunction with the game, the New York Urban League would present the 1978 Whitney M. Young, Jr., Memorial Award to Frederick Douglass Pollard during a halftime ceremony. Promoters of the game were elated about the relatively large crowd because the nation's largest city was under a partial news blackout. Since August 10, when the New York City Pressmen's Union went on strike, the city's major newspapers had ceased publication, and the bitter labor dispute continued.[1]

Relying on television and radio broadcasts and the few out-of-town-newspapers still distributed in the city, many New Yorkers were still able to keep up with national and world events as well as sporting news. President Jimmy Carter's rating in public opinion polls had recently climbed by sixteen percentage points as a result of his summit meeting with Egyptian and Israeli leaders at Camp David, Maryland. The New York Yankees, who had seemingly knocked their archrivals the Boston Red Sox out of the American League Eastern Division title chase by beating them six straight times in late August and early September, had seen their lead slip to one game over the resurgent Bosox in what would be one of the most memorable major league baseball races in recent years. Those fans who had heard the afternoon football scores knew that Bear Bryant's number one-rated Alabama team had been upset by the University of Southern California, and that Bo Schembeckler's Michigan Wolverines had defeated Notre Dame by two touchdowns in the first meeting between the two schools in thirty-five years. Many of the African-American fans, who made up a majority of the spectators that evening, were still buzzing about Muhammad Ali's one-sided decision over Leon Spinks in New Orleans the previous weekend. Incredibly, the thirty-six-year-old heavyweight champion became the first man to win the title three times. Fewer of the football patrons had probably read or heard that a federal judge had cleared Alex Haley of charges that he had stolen parts of his prize-winning novel, and later popular television series, *Roots* from another author.[2]

As the stadium began to fill, Fritz Pollard was being honored by Urban League officials and guests at a dinner in the Yankee clubhouse. Nearly eighty-five years old, Pollard had been born in a different century, when Grover Cleveland had presided over a country supposedly enjoying the "Gay Nineties." For Pollard and other African Americans of that era, the nineties and the beginning of the new century were years of struggle. Lynching was a frequent event in the South, race hatred was intensifying throughout the nation, and opportunities for blacks were few. Pollard's life had been influenced more by the first black heavyweight champion, Jack Johnson, than by any of the others who followed. As a youth, Pollard gave up a promising career in baseball because he and his race were barred from the established leagues. However, he was one of the lucky few of his race fortunate enough to attend college and be in a position to challenge some of the imposing racial barriers that stood in the way of African-American progress.

With tears in his eyes, Pollard rose slowly from his seat to accept a plaque (which he would receive again at the official halftime ceremony) making him the twelfth recipient of the Whitney M. Young, Jr., Memorial Award. The plaque was inscribed: "To Fritz Pollard In Honor of His Courage, Determination, and Accomplishments, as a pioneer in collegiate and professional football during the early years of the 20th century and for his contributions and inspiration to the Black community." Pollard joined a select circle of athletes, entertainers, humanitarians, and civil rights advocates who had previously garnered the award. Rosa Parks, who ignited the Montgomery, Alabama, boycott movement in 1955 when she refused to step to the rear of a city bus, received the first award in 1971, and in 1977, the Urban League made the presentation posthumously in honor of Jackie Robinson. Pollard was honored to be associated with such historic names, but he was most pleased to join his former gridiron opponent, later teammate, and long-time friend Paul Robeson, an Urban League selectee in 1972. In summing up his feelings that night, Pollard later told a reporter, "I couldn't ever ask for anything more."[3]

As Pollard, Urban League officials, and their guests made their way to seats near midfield, the highly touted Grambling Tigers were struggling with the Morgan State Bears in a scoreless first-half tie. Before the evening was over, Grambling would score three second-half touchdowns to win the contest and push coach Eddie Robinson one game closer to his eventual record-setting mark for victories by an intercollegiate football coach. Pollard was familiar with the struggles of a black college coach because exactly a half century earlier he had begun his coaching career at Lincoln University. During his three-year tenure at the black Pennsylvania college, he had fought unsuccessfully for interracial competition with white colleges. A little more than a decade later, after the National Football League (NFL) had raised a color barrier against African-American players, Pollard recruited heavily from black colleges to build and coach a powerful all-black professional team, the Brown Bombers, in order to demonstrate that Negro players were capable of competing at the highest level of play.[4]

After the halftime whistle blew and some of the fans had finished mildly booing the favored Grambling team for its lackluster performance, Urban League and New York Yankee officials made their way to the center of the field to conduct a brief ceremony honoring Pollard. As he emerged from the sideline amid a ripple of applause and walked slowly toward the assembled dignitaries near the fifty-yard line, few in the crowd who were not familiar with his career would have suspected that this small, elegantly dressed man had accomplished so much both on and off the gridiron. Just over five feet seven inches tall and well above his playing weight of 165 pounds, Pollard walked with a purposeful gait and might have passed

for a man ten years younger. His life had been one of achieving
"firsts" for African Americans. He had been a pioneer in interracial
relations in an era before many people spoke in terms of a civil
rights movement. Many of his racial breakthroughs have been forgotten amid the accelerating pace of the civil rights movement in
the second half of the century, but in terms of breaking down racial
barriers, Pollard's accomplishments were self-evident. In 1916, he
became the first man of his race to be named to a backfield position
on the mythical All-America team named by Walter Camp. At the
time, the former Yale coach called Pollard "one of the greatest
runners these eyes have ever seen." Some football expects, including
Wallace Wade, Pollard's former teammate and later a successful
collegiate coach, ranked him ahead of Red Grange as a college
halfback. The winter before his All-America season, Pollard had
been the first black to play in the Rose Bowl. As a professional,
Pollard was instrumental in integrating what by 1922 would become
the National Football League. Those in the crowd who had heard
Pollard's name mentioned in recent years perhaps knew that he was
the first black head coach in the NFL. Few remembered that he
was the first of his race to play quarterback in the now well-estab-
lished professional football league. During his playing days, he also
organized and coached the first all-black professional team and later
returned to coaching in an unsuccessful effort to thwart the segregationist policy adopted by NFL owners in the 1930s. In 1954,
Pollard was the first black named to the National Collegiate Football
Hall of Fame, but inexplicably had been denied entrance into its
professional counterpart in Canton, Ohio. Although the list of athletic firsts was impressive, few in the crowd in September 1978 could
begin to appreciate the courage and determination it took for a
young African American to confront and surmount racial barriers
in a less tolerant America more than fifty years before. Racial slurs,
physical abuse, and the humiliation of being denied dressing quarters,
hotel accommodations, and access to restaurants and transportation
had awaited Pollard at every turn. Although he had often understated
the extent of the racial harassment he had endured, Pollard in later
years admitted that he had been "niggerized" throughout his athletic
career.

Yet, Pollard's pioneering endeavors did not end when his playing days were over. In the 1920s, he established what may have been the first all-black investment securities company in the country. The following decade Pollard ran the first African-American tabloid in New York City. In conjunction with his brother Luther, he had an early involvement in the making of all-black films during the World War I era. By the 1940s and 1950s, Pollard was one of a handful of African Americans who continued to produce black films. At the same time, he established himself as a leading black booking agent and was responsible for integrating scores of nightclubs that had previously barred African-American entertainers. During the 1940s, his Suntan Studios in Harlem was a training ground and springboard for scores of young black artists who sought careers in the entertainment world.

Pollard had accomplished much in eight-and-a-half decades, but most of the fans who saw the small, elderly man accept the engraved plaque knew little of Fritz Pollard or his courage and determination. The New York newspaper strike had curtailed advance publicity of the 1978 Young Award and seemed certain to limit national coverage of the award ceremony the following day. A few months earlier, the nationally syndicated sportswriter Jerry Izenberg had described Pollard as "a genuine unknown hero," lamenting that it was "a shame and a scandal" that "young people do not even know his name." Izenberg explained the oversight by pointing out that each generation regardless of race acts as if it "invented the games we play, the barriers we break and the hurdles we clear." Those who had seen Pollard play, however, never forgot the small, shifty halfback. John Sullivan, who as a teenager in the 1920s watched Pollard play for Gilberton in the rough and tumble Pennsylvania Coal Region, recalled that he was the fastest player he had ever seen, and opponents "did everything to injure him" because he was a college star and the only black man in the league. "He was a real pioneer," Sullivan concluded, "just like Jackie Robinson." Richard Lechner remembered that at age twelve or thirteen he would scale the fence and melt into the crowd at League Park in Akron, Ohio, to see the small but magical Pollard lead Akron against the legendary Jim Thorpe and the Canton Bulldogs. More than fifty years later, Lechner could still close his eyes and see the "Titanic struggles" between the two men as if they happened yesterday. He also remembered the rampant racial prejudice in Akron and praised Pollard not only for his superb football skills, but also because "he was able to endure and not be bitter."[5]

Despite his considerable accomplishments, Pollard's life was far from idyllic. Like many African Americans of his generation who were fortunate enough to attend college, Pollard often found himself torn between black America and white. White America offered greater opportunity for advancement and success but often demanded varying degrees of subservience. Black America represented tradition, family, and solidarity but also meant segregation and more limited opportunity. More often than he liked, Pollard was forced to make concessions to white racial prejudices. To his generation, these compromises with the prevailing racial code were survival skills that allowed success in a world that was primarily hostile. Perhaps because he mastered these skills so deftly, he developed the reputation of being something of a con-man and financial operator; more than once he overstepped the line of propriety and had minor brushes with the law. As an educated man and celebrity, Pollard was part of the elite of black America. Although he had little regard for money or material comfort per se, Pollard expected—and generally managed—to live in the fast lane. Unfortunately, his determined pursuit of athletic and business success and the high expectations he set for himself sometimes had deleterious effects on his family.

That Pollard's multifaceted, pathbreaking career sometimes resulted in the neglect of his family was one of the ironies of his life. Above all, he attributed his own success to the values, determination, and pride instilled by his parents, brothers, and sisters. To be sure, Pollard's son and daughters greatly admired their father and agreed that he was a kind and loving parent when present and an important role model even when absent. All too often, however, he was off pursuing his athletic career or one of his numerous other ventures. His daughters Leslie and Eleanor, who were raised by their mother, Ada Pollard, sometimes suffered the additional indignity of inadequate financial support when one of their father's business schemes failed to bear fruit. The Pollard children were not embittered by their father's parental shortcomings, however, because he, as well as their mother, provided them with an important legacy. They were part of a family that had been in the vanguard of black progress in America since the Civil War and before. Their maternal great-grandfather, Daniel Laing, Jr., was a Dartmouth College graduate and one of the first black medical doctors in the United States. On their father's side, the Pollards of Chicago had been on the cutting edge of racial advancement for more than two generations.

Pollard's more casual, easy-come-easy-go approach to money, and sometimes life, contrasted with the more strict precepts he absorbed as a youth in Chicago. Several generations removed from slavery, John William and Catherine Amanda Hughes Pollard set high standards for their children, reinforced by the family's solid record of achievement in the difficult years of adjustment after the Civil War. In almost every interview he ever gave, Pollard traced the source of his own strength and courage in challenging the formidable racial barriers that stood before him to the inspiration and guidance he received while growing up in this remarkable family on Chicago's North Side. It was, according to his reckoning, the pioneering spirit of his family that enabled him to sustain indignity and humiliation, rebound in the face of adversity, and achieve what he did. Pollard must have known, however, as he raised his plaque and walked slowly off the Yankee Stadium field in 1978 that the politely applauding fans had little appreciation of the obstacles he had faced or the struggles he had encountered, beginning in Chicago more than eight decades earlier.

THE REMARKABLE POLLARDS

1

Frederick Douglass Pollard was born in the Rogers Park section of Chicago on January 27, 1894, the seventh of eight children born to John William and Catherine Amanda Hughes Pollard. He was named after the famed abolitionist and civil rights leader Frederick Douglass, whom his parents had seen give a stirring oration at Chicago's Columbian Exposition the preceding year. Family members originally called the youngest Pollard Fred, but the large number of German and Luxembourg immigrants who resided in Rogers Park nicknamed him Fritz, a name that had stuck by the time he entered public school.

The Pollards had moved to Chicago in 1886, living first in the Edgewater section and quickly resettling in the all-white, relatively affluent village of Rogers Park on the shores of Lake Michigan about ten miles north of the Loop. At a time when most African Americans faced a life of grinding rural poverty and an emerging racial caste system in the South, the Pollards were relatively affluent and well educated and had moved northward from Missouri in search of even a better life and more opportunity for their children. In almost every interview he ever gave, Pollard proudly recounted how his family, going back several generations, had survived and prospered through the slavery era and the troubled postwar decades by a combination of hard work, persistence, courage, and a pioneering spirit. He firmly believed that his family's pioneering heritage gave him the motivation and courage to challenge the formidable racial barriers of another century.[1]

According to a family history compiled by Fritz's older brother

Luther, John William Pollard's ancestors were Virginia slaves. In the last year of the Revolutionary War they were freed, and John Pollard's grandparents and parents became free black yeomen farmers in Culpepper County, Virginia. John Pollard was born there in a free Negro community in 1846. A few years after his father was killed in a lumbering accident, their mother sent John, then eight, and an older sister to Leavenworth, Kansas, to be raised and educated. This was done, according to the family account, because of a rash of incidents in Virginia in which children of free blacks were kidnapped and sold into bondage by proslavery zealots.[2]

The Kansas Territory—referred to at the time as "Bleeding Kansas"—was the center of a national controversy provoked by the passage of the Kansas-Nebraska Act of 1854, and focusing on the question of extending slavery into the western territories. John Pollard grew up amid the turmoil and irregular combat between pro- and antislavery forces. After the Civil War began, the recently admitted state, at the urging of its new U.S. Senator James H. Lane, took the lead in recruiting black Union troops. Under his direction, two regiments, the First and Second Colored Kansas, were formed. John Pollard was among the first wave of African Americans to join the Union military cause when he enlisted in the Second Colored Kansas Regiment as a private in 1862 under the alias Jackson Ridgeway, most likely because he was underage. The following year the regiment, under the command of Colonel Samuel J. Crawford, was one of the first black regiments mustered into federal service as the 83rd United States Colored Infantry.[3]

The 83rd Colored Infantry performed well in combat, especially during the Arkansas campaign of 1864. At the Battle of Jenkins' Ferry it repulsed a larger Confederate force, captured a battery, and reportedly shot all rebel prisoners. This last act was in retaliation for a Confederate massacre of African-American soldiers of the First Colored Kansas Regiment a short time before. Life was doubly difficult for the first black combat troops because most Confederate officers refused to take black prisoners, usually executing those who attempted to surrender. Little is known about John Pollard's service in the regiment except that he was a drummer and that during his idle time he established a reputation as a boxer. By the end of the war, according to the family account, he was lightweight boxing champion of the 83rd, setting a standard of athletic achievement that all of his children would attempt to emulate.[4]

Fritz Pollard later recalled that when his father was mustered out of the Union Army, "he knew the angles and was mixed up with some pretty wealthy men." Returning to Leavenworth, John Pollard learned the barber trade from a white man, also named Pollard, and completed what education he was able to obtain. He studied at a school organized by Hiram Revels and Blanche K. Bruce, who would later become the nation's first two black U.S. senators and represent Mississippi during Reconstruction. Pollard was impressed with these men and determined to further his own education. With their encouragement, he set out for Ohio in 1866 with the hope of studying law at Oberlin College but got only as far as St. Louis, where he contracted smallpox. Although the illness ended his dream of becoming a lawyer as well as his formal education, Pollard had learned from Revels and Bruce that education was an important avenue toward black progress and would instill this idea in each of his children. When he recovered from the smallpox, Pollard polished his barbering skills by working at an exclusive private hotel in St. Louis before returning to Leavenworth. Restless for adventure and greater economic opportunity, he soon migrated to Mexico, Missouri, a jumping-off point for wagon trains heading west. He worked in a leading barbershop there and gained a reputation as a master barber; in the early 1870s he opened his own shop, with five chairs and a bath, located near the beginning of the Santa Fe trail.[5]

It was in Mexico that Pollard met Catherine Amanda Hughes, who had come to the Missouri frontier town to further her education. Little is known about the Hughes family except that Amanda was born in Paris, Missouri, in 1856 and that her mother was of mixed Negro and Indian blood and her father was a white man, probably of French descent. Amanda, who was light-skinned, completed her education and was soon being courted by John Pollard. They married in 1874, purchased a home in a desirable section of town, and began to raise a family. Three children were born in Mexico: Artissmisia, who was called Artie, was born in 1875, Luther in 1878, and Willie Naomi in 1883. When Artie became of school age, the Pollards refused to send her to the segregated public school and instead hired tutors and a governess to educate her and the other children. Despite the fact that he owned a successful business as well as real estate in Mexico, the unsatisfactory educational opportunities there, as well as the deteriorating racial climate in the state in the aftermath of Reconstruction, prompted the Pollards to move in 1886. Fritz later recalled that his father chose to relocate the family in the Chicago area because "he could be assured of a good education for his children as well as bringing them up in a desirable environment."[6]

Having sold his business and most of his real estate in Mexico at a sacrifice, John Pollard expected to settle his family in the North Shore suburb of Evanston, Illinois. Instead, he decided to locate in Rose Hill, now Edgewater, in the northeastern section of Chicago about four miles south of Evanston. A short time later, the Pollards moved again to Rogers Park just to the north of Edgewater. The decision to settle in all-white Rogers Park, then not part of Chicago, rather than in Evanston may explain something about John and Amanda's outlook. The growing university town of Evanston in 1886 had a small but significant population of blacks, most of whom were of the lower socioeconomic class, whereas Rogers Park had no African American residents at all. One can speculate that the Pollards considered themselves in the upper strata of African American society and believed that they would face less discrimination and realize greater opportunity in an all-white town. The Pollards were proud of their racial heritage, to be sure, but given the prevailing prejudices of the time may have realized that their children would encounter fewer racial restrictions and enjoy greater educational advantages in Rogers Park. Like many African Americans of the era, the Pollards walked a tightrope between racial solidarity on the one hand and the obvious benefits afforded by white society on the other. In this case, they appear to have opted for the advantages offered in an all-white community. Nearly all the Pollard children seemed to take pride in being raised in an all-white environment. Fritz Pollard reflected some of the family elitism when he recalled proudly many years later that "the Pollard family was kind of independent a little bit, financially. My folks have had money all their lives, and we didn't need to ask, beg for anything. My father had a successful business, owned his own home, this was back in 1886."[7]

John Pollard bought a home on East Ravenswood Avenue and opened a three-chair barbershop in an adjacent building directly across from the Chicago and North Western Railroad Station where businessmen awaited trains for their commute to the Loop. A second son, Leslie, was born in 1886 and was soon followed by Ruth, Hughes, Fritz, and Frank. By the time of Fritz's birth, Rogers Park, with 3,500 residents, had been annexed by Chicago but remained a suburban village relatively isolated from the Loop to the south and Evanston to the north. For 27 cents, the Chicago and North Western Railroad provided the only efficient transportation downtown until a trolley line was built in 1892. Even then, however, a number of years passed before many residents felt comfortable using the new trolley. Fritz's brother Luther recalled that the northern section of Chicago was quite rural until about the turn of the century; during the winter months he and his friends would skate along a ditch on the frozen prairie all the way into the north branch of the Chicago River. With few social activities available in Rogers Park during the 1890s, Luther Pollard recalled, residents usually gathered at the "two local gossip centers, Carpenter's Cigar Store and Pollard's Barber Shop." Despite the proximity of Evanston, most Rogers Park people sought outside entertainment, did their marketing, and conducted other commercial business in the Lake View section of the city about five miles to the south. The fact that Rogers Park as well as Evanston was dry as a result of a "four-mile limit" prohibiting the sale of alcoholic beverages in the vicinity of Methodist-run Northwestern University helped foster ties between Rogers Park and the more lively township of Lake View. The Pollards, therefore, were one of the few black families in the northeastern section of Chicago and were largely insulated from the small African-American population in Evanston and the larger black settlement to the south of the Loop.[8]

The majority of Chicago's twenty thousand black residents in 1894 lived on the South Side just below the Loop. Primarily employed as unskilled laborers, waiters, and domestic servants, the African-American population supported twenty churches, a dozen fraternal lodges, several social and cultural clubs, and three newspapers. In theory at least, Illinois was quite liberal with regard to the treatment of black citizens. As early as 1874, the state assembly passed a law forbidding segregation in public schools. School officials were subject to a fine if they excluded children on the basis of race, as were citizens who used intimidation to prevent black attendance.

Illinois also had a state civil rights act. The 1885 statute "forbade discrimination in restaurants, hotels, theaters, railroads, streetcars, and other public accommodation and entertainment." In practice, however, most black Chicagoans lived in clearly defined sections of the city and were frequently subject to violations of their civil rights. The Pollards were fortunate to have been able to purchase property in the mid-1880s in a previously all-white community, and likely would not have been allowed to do so a decade later when racial tensions began to rise in Chicago. The fact that John Pollard was a skilled barber and a veteran of the Union Army, as were many of the native-born residents of Rogers Park, may help account for the Pollards' relative acceptance there.[9]

Many years later Fritz Pollard agreed that his family was generally accepted in Rogers Park, but also noted that there were problems with some of the neighbors and visitors to the community. "They had to come to my dad's barbershop because there weren't any others," he said, "but we had our troubles around there." The Pollards faced occasional threats and harassment from local residents. Fritz's mother, for example, never answered the front door without slipping a handgun into her apron pocket. As a boy Fritz recalled being denied the privilege of sitting down with his friends and having a soda at the corner drugstore, at least until his father visited the store and set the proprietor straight. At the Rogers Park Beach the Pollard children were taunted occasionally with racial insults and attacked by youths from outside the neighborhood. However, Pollard concluded, "the majority of people around there who would have caused trouble were afraid of my father." Nevertheless, the sting of racial discrimination and prejudice touched young Pollard deeply. When asked many years later about the first time he remembered being the victim of racial discrimination, Fritz simply replied, "the minute you're born."[10]

Fritz's father was one of more than seventeen thousand black barbers in America in 1890 which according to the census report of that year was the second most popular profession for African Americans. At the time, barbering was largely a black trade "beneath the dignity of whites," and African-American barbers routinely worked, if not lived, in white communities. According to family lore, John Pollard was no ordinary barber, however. By the 1870s he was widely recognized as one of the best barbers in Missouri, and later settled in Rogers Park in part because he was encouraged to open a shop by local businessmen who had heard about his skill with a razor and scissors.[11]

Above all, Fritz remembered his father as a strict disciplinarian; he "didn't allow any of us to smoke or anything like that." If the boys did get out of line, "he'd take that razor strop and strap us before we could get to the corner. He'd give us that strap and fan us and then make us go in the barber shop and sweep up all the hair and wash all the spittoons." Although in later years Fritz usually made light of his father's harsh punishments, it is clear that the strict discipline made a deep impression on him and that he was probably somewhat afraid of his father. John Pollard was a little aloof from the family, demanded and received the children's respect, and, when inclined, imposed an exacting system of discipline within the family — all traits that Fritz would later exhibit with his own children. However Fritz clearly admired his father and described him as a "crackerjack" who "could tell all kinds of stories to kids and everything. He would take us out in the back yard and kid us to death" and tell tales about the Civil War and his other adventures.[12]

John Pollard also taught his sons how to avoid unnecessary confrontations with whites. These tense situations often arose when strangers to the neighborhood came into the barbershop and made insulting racial remarks. Fritz remembered that his father instructed the boys on "how to handle these situations without losing our heads and using our fists." He also recalled, however, that his father taught each boy in turn how to box and defend himself, a skill Fritz sometimes found useful in future years. His father's message, which Fritz internalized and lived by throughout his career, was that to succeed in the white world a black man had to know how and when to roll with the tide of racism as well as how and when to protect his dignity by fighting back. Although the Pollards lived in a white neighborhood and represented the elite of black Chicago, they were not immune from the necessity of emphasizing how important self-control was in surviving an acutely racist society.[13]

The elder Pollard insisted that all the boys learn the barber trade and work in his shop. They started by sweeping the floor and shining shoes, and when they had mastered every procedure each in turn was given his own chair. Fritz recalled that his father told each one of them that "when you go out in the world you can have any job you want but you'll never be broke. You can always go back to being a barber" and gave each boy a barber kit before he left home. John Pollard had high aspirations for his sons but knew from experience that the road to success for a black man in white America was difficult. Fritz had no interest in becoming a barber and practiced the trade only twice during his career; he did learn from his father valuable survival skills and the practical necessity of scrambling to make a living.[14]

Amanda Pollard was a tall, beautiful woman who, as the daughter of a white man, had fair skin in contrast to her dark-skinned husband. In turn-of-the-century America and for many years thereafter, skin color was an important fact of life for African Americans. Light-skinned blacks had a higher standing among some elements in African-American society, and whites in general had a higher opinion of African Americans of lighter pigmentation. Some of the largest black-owned businesses were cosmetic firms which provided skin-bleaching and hair-straightening products that purported to make African Americans look more like whites. Some light-skinned blacks were "passable" or accepted in white society as white. Although none of the Pollards were passable or known to have used skin-bleaching products, they, like all black Americans of the era, were aware of the advantages of light skin color. According to family lore, the eldest son Luther, who had light skin like his mother, was allowed to compete in athletics at Lake View High School in the 1890s because he "passed" as an Indian. Although some of Fritz's features reflected his Indian ancestry, he had dark skin like his father and was aware at an early age that his acceptance in white society would be more difficult. He once tried to pass himself off as an Indian in a semipro football game, but few of the fans or opposing players were fooled.[15]

Fritz did, however, take after his mother in many ways: he was aggressive and had an effluent personality, high aspirations, and a good head for business. According to her granddaughter Leslie Keeling, Amanda "was the dominant one and she ruled the roost." Fritz remembered that his mother had a lot of personality and was a go-getter. She was considered a "very high-class seamstress," and such big downtown Chicago stores as Marshall Fields and Chas. A. Stevens would send her women's dresses to tailor at home. Like her husband, she was strict with the children and would whip their legs with a switch if they stepped out of line. Fritz Pollard, Jr., recalled that his grandmother was progressive and had a sharp mind for business. "You talk about women's rights," he said. "Grandmother could do anything; she handled all the business. She had accounts in all the stores when women didn't have accounts. Whenever the kids were getting into trouble she was the one who went to court and talked to the judges to get them off."[16]

Amanda was a progressive woman and had high aspirations for her children, but she was no radical. A conflict between her and the third-eldest son, Hughes, resulted, according to family accounts, in the teenager either leaving, or being forced to leave, home. Although family members were unsure about the nature of the dispute, they agreed that Hughes was the most unusual of the Pollard brothers, a young man who sometimes flaunted social and racial customs and often got away with it. One might speculate that Amanda objected to Hughes's ostentatious behavior; she, as well as her husband, no doubt felt somewhat conspicuous in an all-white community and expected her children to conform to some of the more basic racial conventions of the day. Although Fritz never publicly mentioned the dispute between his mother and Hughes, which took place when Fritz was about fifteen, it undoubtedly made an impression on him. Like his mother, Fritz was bright, innovative, and certainly not a conformist, but throughout his life he was always conscious of the fine line which white society drew demarcating acceptable and unacceptable behavior for African Americans.[17]

Fritz's older sisters and brothers set a standard of achievement in education, music, athletics, and other areas that was admirable by any measure, but truly remarkable given the racial barriers they faced. All of the children attained at least a high school education, were exceptional athletes, and, with the exception of Luther, played at least one musical instrument. Artie, the eldest, eventually went on to study nursing and became the first black registered nurse in Illinois. Willie Naomi was one of the first black women to graduate from Northwestern University (1905) and, according to family lore, was denied election to Phi Beta Kappa only because of her race. She became a school teacher in Oklahoma and later taught for many years at Wilberforce University in Ohio. Fritz recalled that "she was a brilliant woman." Ruth, who died young, was a champion sprinter at Lake View High School and according to Fritz could beat him in running contests until he was in high school. Pollard maintained that his sisters influenced him in many ways while he was growing up, most of all by insisting that he study. Although he was not an overly enthusiastic student, family members, especially his sisters, firmly demanded that he apply himself, and his grades were better than average. He recalled that "my mother and father and sisters just made us study, because they were all high school graduates, you know, and if I came home and anything was wrong they'd take a strap to me."[18]

The older Pollard boys, Luther, Leslie, and Hughes, also set high standards of achievement and served as role models for Fritz as well as his mentors in athletics, their major interest. Luther was a star athlete at Lake View High School in the mid-1890s and may have been the first African American to compete in interscholastic athletics in Chicago. He was a halfback on the football team and reputedly one of the decade's finest pitchers. According to Fritz, Luther developed a pitch called an in-drop (probably like a screwball) and hoped to play in the major leagues. Failing to convince scouts that he was a full-blooded Indian and thus surmount the color barrier in organized baseball, Luther played for many years on the Rogers Park town baseball team. He was instrumental in convincing Fritz to concentrate on football, which seemed to offer greater opportunity for outstanding black athletes. In later years, Luther became a successful businessman in Chicago; he was a pioneer in producing some of the first all-black films during World War I, operated an African-American newspaper in the 1920s, and later established a successful advertising agency. Fritz Pollard, Jr., summarized Luther's impact on his father when he said: "Luther was the oldest boy and they all halfway looked up to him and kind of copied after him. Luther did some strange things. I mean, Luther was the only black that had an office downtown. Right down on Michigan Boulevard. He was a real enterpriser. And that's where they got their business sense from. They were all influenced by him."[19]

Leslie, who Fritz considered the outstanding athlete in the family, had the greatest impact on his brother's future career in athletics. In the early 1900s, Leslie attended North Division High School, where he was a standout halfback in football and a superb shortstop on the baseball team. He played on a powerful football team that featured Leo De Tray and future University of Chicago All-America quarterback Walter Steffen. In 1908 Leslie enrolled at Dartmouth College, where he had a short but spectacular football career. He helped lead Dartmouth to a 10–6 upset victory over Princeton at the Polo Grounds in New York, a game which Princeton nearly refused to play because of the presence of a black on the Dartmouth squad. Fritz remembered that "they didn't want to play against my brother because he was black, but Dartmouth insisted and he went on and played anyway and I think that broke down one of the barriers where Princeton was concerned." Leslie dropped out of school that year, became a sportswriter for a black weekly newspaper in New York City, and was the first secretary of the Urban League in the city. He also coached football for four seasons at Lincoln University in Pennsylvania before his untimely death in 1915. When Leslie broke into big-time football in the East, Fritz, an impressionable teenager, could talk of little else. He was determined to follow his brother east and play at one of the white colleges that dominated college football, preferably Dartmouth. Following in his brother's footsteps, Fritz did go east to play college football and later coached at Lincoln University.[20]

Hughes, who was two years older than Fritz, was the most unique of the Pollard brothers. Fritz's son remembered Hughes as "a man above everybody! Got away with murder! I mean he could do no wrong. Hughes was into everything. He was just crazy. But, everybody loved him." Fritz later described Hughes as "the biggest and toughest of all of us" and at times "a big bully." He was a star halfback at Lane Technical High School as well as head drum major in the band and leader of the school orchestra.[21]

In 1909 when Fritz was an eighty-nine-pound sophomore trying out for the Lane Tech football team, it was Hughes who saw to it that his younger brother got a chance to play. As Fritz related the story, Lane Tech was to play the powerful Hyde Park High School team in its first game. Hughes went to the Lane principal, William Brogan, and the coaches and said, " 'Listen, if my kid brother can't play, I'm not going to play.' That did it," Fritz said. "I got my first chance. He was just one of those kind of fellows." After the Hyde Park game, Hughes gave up football, with the exception of one appearance in a championship game at the end of the season. He went back to the band and the orchestra and let Fritz become prominent in athletics. After he left home as a result of the dispute with his mother, Hughes went on to become an outstanding musician and led a popular Chicago jazz group, the "Melody Four." During World War I, he went to Europe and served with the French army on the Western Front, where he was gassed. Before and after the war, he performed in Australia, England, and France and was recognized as one of the world's leading trap drummers. According to Fritz, Jr., he married two white women, one in France and one in Australia, both of whom attended his funeral. Hughes died in Chicago in 1926 as a result of complications from being gassed during the war. Of all his older brothers, Fritz had the least to say about Hughes and perhaps had mixed feelings about his most flamboyant sibling.[22]

Throughout his career Pollard often referred to his family's background and history in answering questions about his specific achievements or commenting on his pioneering efforts in challenging racial barriers. When responding to queries about being the first black halfback selected to Walter Camp's All-America team, Fritz typically began, "it all goes back to Luther." On other occasions, he mentioned his parents or his older brothers and sisters and their successful surmounting of racial constraints and other obstacles. Pollard's son and daughters were equally aware of the family heritage; as Fritz, Jr., said, "They had a lot of know-how. That's what stuck me. I thought about it many times. They pioneered, there's no question about it. And all of us have followed that heritage."[23]

In the Pollard household, Fritz learned lessons and skills that would serve him well. His parents taught him how to cope with the racial problems that he would encounter. They impressed upon him the importance of being confident and aggressive as well as knowing when to compromise with prevailing racial mores and when to fight back to protect his dignity. Much of this was simply part of the Pollard legacy dating back several generations. The whole family, especially his mother and sisters, stressed the importance of a sound education. His father taught him a valuable trade in his barbershop, and his mother and brothers encouraged him to learn how to play the piano and the sliding trombone, skills that would be important for his survival and success in years ahead. The older Pollard boys honed Fritz's skills as an athlete, paved the way for him, and taught him how to deal with the racially motivated abuse he would encounter again and again in athletic competition.

Although he was fortunate to grow up in a stable, highly motivated, and reasonably affluent family far removed from the South's grinding poverty and the suffocating racial oppression which most African Americans of his generation faced, Pollard encountered other kinds of difficulties. Being raised in a white neighborhood had certain advantages, but it also created pressures. Fritz Pollard, Jr., raised by his grandparents in Rogers Park a generation after his father, stated that "growing up in an all-white neighborhood made you an overachiever." He meant that all white eyes were on you, and your success or failure had distinct racial overtones. Part of the Pollards' high aspirations and considerable achievements were connected with the neighborhood in which they chose to live. For Fritz, the white environment combined with his older brothers and sisters' record of success provided opportunity as well as an extraordinary amount of pressure to achieve. He once said that because of his brothers "things were perhaps a little easier for me than for someone else, although I got kicked and boxed around too, you know." Pollard may have had in mind his hard knocks on the athletic fields, but one suspects that he was also referring to the great pressures to succeed that the white environment and his family put upon him. The combined pressures made Pollard an inveterate overachiever who came to play the role well, but it also created an inner tension which caused him to rebel sometimes against the discipline and high standards needed to attain those goals.[24]

As a youth, Pollard's most noticeable features were his small size, light weight, and dark skin. In summing up his father's difficult road to success, Fritz, Jr., remarked, "Dad had all kinds of problems. First, he was small, he was very dark. And his brothers were all robust. He had to fight his way through everything." As a high school sophomore trying out for the Lane Tech football team, Fritz was four feet, eleven inches tall and weighed only eighty-nine pounds. Hughes, by contrast, was over six feet and weighed more than two hundred pounds, and the other brothers were only slightly smaller. In later years, Fritz made light of his small stature, explaining that he just swelled up his chest and tried to emulate his older brothers. But even given the superb athletic tutoring which his brothers provided and Fritz's natural skills of speed and agility, he was at a distinct disadvantage. He was also aware at an early age that his brothers and other family members would not accept excuses that he was too short or too light, and that he would have to measure up to his more robust brothers. To compensate for his physical shortcomings, Pollard developed an exterior personality best described as assertive and aggressive, even cocky. If he stood tall and tried to act like his larger, more confident brothers, perhaps he would be accepted as they were and could even duplicate their athletic feats. Underneath this outer layer of confidence and assertiveness that most people came to associate with Fritz Pollard, however, was a sensitive, more fragile person aware of the difficult task of living up to the Pollard tradition. On a number of occasions during his career, Pollard shed that outer protective shell and revealed, sometimes rather emotionally, a more delicate inner being racked by the strain of trying to succeed at all costs.[25]

By today's standards, Pollard's dark skin would not necessarily represent much of a handicap. In the early part of the century, however, most white Americans, even those who considered themselves liberal on the race issue, tended to believe that light-skinned Negroes, presumably of mixed blood, were more intelligent and thus more acceptable than those with darker complexions. In athletics as well as in other endeavors, many African Americans who made breakthroughs in white society and gained a limited degree of acceptance were light-skinned. Nearly all the first blacks to attend and play football at predominantly white colleges, for example, had light complexions; a few were "passable" and thus not even listed among the early black players. Thus, Pollard's dark features represented a considerable disadvantage for him in challenging contemporary racial barriers in white America. As Fritz Pollard, Jr., pointed out, his father was like Jackie Robinson because neither man could ever be mistaken as being anything other than black.[26]

Despite the handicaps he faced, Pollard would develop a driving willpower to overcome obstacles and match his family's record of success. He drew upon that tradition of achievement, as well as the confidence and independence that was part of the Pollard heritage, to launch an athletic career that would make him a pioneer in challenging the racial caste system of twentieth-century America. "Jackie Robinson got all the due," Fritz Pollard, Jr., reflected, "but Dad was really a pioneer."[27]

LEARNING TO SURVIVE

2

Fritz Pollard grew up in Chicago during a period of rapid transition in the city's racial makeup. Between 1890 and 1915, the black population of Chicago increased from less than fifteen thousand to more than fifty thousand. Although this growth rate would be dwarfed by the massive wartime influx of southern blacks, it represented a significant increase. African Americans were still a small segment of the city's population, but much more conspicuous than they had been in earlier years. When Pollard was a boy, the majority of black Chicagoans lived in an area near the stockyards on the South Side, the "black belt." Before the turn of the century, African Americans lived, for the most part, interspersed among whites, even in neighborhoods on the South Side. By the eve of World War I, however, an all-black ghetto had emerged on the city's South Side, with strictly segregated housing patterns.[1]

The rapid increase in Chicago's African-American population, with an accompanying competition for jobs and housing between blacks and whites, led to a noticeable rise of racial tensions in the city by the early 1900s. In the Hyde Park section to the south of the Loop near the University of Chicago, for example, white residents formed a protective organization in 1908 to restrict blacks to specified residential districts. The Hyde Park Improvement Protective Club used vandalism, intimidation, and economic boycotts to force African Americans out of proscribed neighborhoods. It advocated segregation in the Chicago public schools and attempted to segregate such public facilities as parks and playgrounds. The Hyde Park episode of 1908–9 was typical of the growing racial animosity in Chicago in the early twentieth century.[2]

Despite the enactment of the Illinois Civil Rights Act in 1885, black Chicagoans faced numerous incidents of discrimination throughout the city. The historian Allan Spear has concluded that in the early 1900s "a Negro could never be certain of what awaited him when he entered a store, restaurant, saloon, or hotel outside the black belt." A similar situation existed in the public schools. Although the 1874 Illinois law integrated public schools, frequent incidents of racial friction occurred in the Chicago schools. Most problems originated with white students and their parents; by the early 1900s, white students who were transferred to predominantly black schools staged a number of riots and boycotts. In 1912, for example, the Chicago *Tribune* described one such incident at the racially mixed Wendell Phillips High School as "a miniature race riot."[3]

In areas of the city distant from the black belt, including the North Side, the few black residents in white neighborhoods reported a more harmonious racial climate. Most African Americans on the North Side were native Chicagoans or long-time residents, middle-class and representing only a tiny fraction of the overall population in the area. In the wake of the violent 1919 race riot, the Illinois Commission on Race Relations interviewed a few black North Side residents who reported that in general they had been accepted by their white neighbors when they had moved into the area, usually in the 1880s or 1890s, but that racial tensions had increased in the early twentieth century. Although most maintained that they were still accepted by whites in their neighborhoods, they also complained about "minor expressions of antagonism," particularly when they attempted to buy property.[4]

The Pollard family's experience as the only black residents of Rogers Park reflected these inconsistencies in the racial climate of the city at the turn of the century. Pollard often maintained that his family was accepted by the people of Rogers Park but would just as quickly recount any number of slights, insults, or incidents of discrimination which he and other family members had experienced. The Pollards were a solid middle-class family that posed no apparent threat to their neighbors, but they were also victims of the prevalent racism which infected American society in the early twentieth century. For example, just after World War I, George Jean Nathan and H. L. Mencken wrote *The American Credo*, which listed 435 beliefs commonly accepted by Americans. Among the truisms whites held about blacks were that Negroes' votes may be readily bought for a dollar, that educated Negroes refuse to work and become criminals, that all Negroes who show any intelligence are two-thirds white and the sons of U.S. senators, and that as soon as Negroes get $8 they go to a dentist to have a front tooth filled with gold.[5]

For the Pollards, life in Rogers Park was full of contradictions. As Fritz, Jr., concluded, "there were just so many inconsistencies about the whole racial business." He recalled that although the family was generally accepted in the community, it was subject to discrimination, particularly in the area of buying property. His grandfather, moreover, was welcomed as a Sunday school teacher by the well-to-do congregation at the local Lutheran church, but the family was still harassed.[6]

Fritz Pollard grew up in such an environment in the late 1890s. He remembered his home life as being strict but generally happy. According to his recollection, Rogers Park was a wealthy suburb with "a lot of fine people there in the community." One of Fritz's closest childhood friends was Charles "Chick" Evans, the future golf great. They caddied together at a local golf course, swam at the beach, and played on the same neighborhood baseball and football teams. Fritz once boasted that as a youth he could beat the future U.S. Open champion in a round of golf. Both boys attended Eugene Field Grammar School, which Pollard described as "a rather high-class school which turned out some very smart boys." He remembered studying algebra as early as the fourth grade, but admitted that he disliked history and did not like to read. Most of his time and energy was devoted to the numerous athletic contests that were a focal point for the neighborhood youngsters.[7]

Some of Fritz's fondest childhood memories were of football games, which usually included his older brothers and neighborhood friends, played in his backyard. When there were too few youngsters for a game, those available would kick the ball up a large sand hill at the back of the Pollard lot, scramble after it, and seize it before it rolled down. The principal hazards were being knocked into mud puddles in the alley behind the yard or temporarily losing the ball when it was inadvertently kicked into one of the uncovered wagons which frequently used the back alley. "You know my brothers," Pollard said, "they were kind of idols to we youngsters. They taught me how to fall and roll the shoulders, and protect yourself with your hands, and with your feet; principally with your feet." As a boy, Pollard realized that he was much faster than most of the other children his age and possessed a certain shiftiness that was to his advantage in backyard football games. When later asked about his elusive style of running, he said, "I think it was born in me. It was just one of those natural things and my brothers taught me the rest of it."[8]

Like other communities in the Midwest and around the nation at the turn of the century, Rogers Park supported a variety of town athletic teams, with the greatest emphasis given to baseball and football. Although Rogers Park had fewer than four thousand residents when Pollard was growing up, three town teams competed in baseball and football. The senior baseball team competed in the North Shore Baseball League against teams from Evanston, Wilmette, Winnetka, and communities to the north, while the football squad played teams from various sections of Chicago. The county fair was also a focal point for athletic competition among communities in the region. Pollard recalled that "in our community the North Side of Chicago, Rose Hill, Edgewater, and Hyde Park and all those places, they used to have these town teams, different age groups, and even when the big fellows finished college they came back and played that Thanksgiving Day game. The little children would play in the morning, the intermediate kids played at noon, and the big team took the field at two o'clock." Pollard remembered that on Thanksgiving Day the "county fairgrounds was a pistol and it was a whole lot of fun."[9]

Pollard's earliest recollection of playing organized football was when he was ten and played for the Jed Colts. The team was sponsored by Jed Jewell, who ran a newspaper and cigar store in Rogers Park. Fritz recalled that Chick Evans was the quarterback and that he played center because he was so small. "I'll never forget those little green suits, green and white," he said. "Oh, gee, they were the cutest little damn things, thinking about it now. And we used to play Edgewater and Evanston and all the various teams." Following in his brothers' footsteps, Pollard was an avid and talented baseball player. At one point or another, he played on all the Rogers Park teams and developed into a top-flight shortstop. He also played on the Eugene Field Grammar School baseball and football teams. It was at Eugene Field that he was first recognized as a promising sprinter and at the age of thirteen ran in an event at the University of Chicago Relays. Pollard recalled that in local track events, usually held at the fairgrounds on the Fourth of July, he was often given a ten- or twenty-yard head start in the sprint races because he was so little. He would then proceed to outdistance his rivals by about double the original handicap.[10]

Pollard did not lack boyhood heroes or role models to inspire him to great athletic achievement. First, he patterned himself after his older brothers because as he put it, "they were stars to us." He was most impressed by Leslie because he had played football in the East at Dartmouth. Beyond that, he idolized some of the local college stars who had played with Leslie at North Division High School; Walter Steffen, for example, became a 1908 Walter Camp All-America quarterback at the University of Chicago. Pollard recalled going to a number of games at nearby Northwestern University. "We'd go out to the games in a Tally-Ho wagon," he said, "and watch the games because we just admired all of them." Pollard remembered seeing Northwestern play the University of Chicago and the Carlisle Indians. "I had a lot of visions in athletics before I even got old enough to run," he concluded.[11]

By 1909, Pollard and other aspiring black athletes had another sports hero and role model to consider: Jack Johnson, the new heavyweight boxing champion of the world. In late 1908, Johnson defeated Tommy Burns in Australia to win the championship. Within a year the black champion had successfully defended his title against a series of white opponents. The novelist Jack London began a movement to draft Jim Jeffries, the former and undefeated heavyweight champion, as "the hope of the white race" to come back and "remove the golden smile from Jack Johnson's face." By 1910, Johnson was more than just the black heavyweight champion, he was a symbol of black rebellion against the distinctly inferior role which white society had designated for African Americans. He flaunted the norms of conduct to which whites expected blacks to adhere and liked fast cars, white women, and flashy clothes. He also had a sharp and disrespectful tongue. When Johnson defeated Jeffries in a much ballyhooed fight on the Fourth of July in 1910, white frustration and anger burst forth in nationwide rioting directed against jubilant blacks. Johnson's biographer Randy Roberts has noted that "never before had a single event caused such widespread rioting. Not until the assassination of Martin Luther King, Jr., would another event elicit a similar reaction." Coming in the wake of the violent Springfield, Illinois, race riot of 1908, which touched off racial conflict in Chicago, Johnson and his spectacular victory over Jeffries were major topics of discussion in the Pollard household.[12]

Johnson's achievement as well as his flamboyant behavior and life-style provided both an inspiration and warning for the Pollards, as well as for many African Americans. The black champion had reached the pinnacle of success in a sport many Americans considered a test of prowess and had demonstrated the fitness and potential of their race. Through his achievement Johnson showed the heights to which black athletes might rise in American society. Yet, his accomplishment was marred by a concerted reactionary impulse from white America. The white press seemed as much disturbed by Johnson's aggressive behavior, provocative life-style, and his hero status among millions of oppressed African Americans as it was by the fact of Johnson's holding the championship. During the next few years, Johnson was harassed by authorities and convicted of a violation of the Mann Act, fight films of the Johnson-Jeffries match were banned in the United States, and Johnson slipped away to an exile in Europe to avoid imprisonment.[13]

Fritz Pollard, Jr., emphasized that his father and uncles followed Johnson's career closely. The Pollard brothers "keyed on Jack Johnson. They were very much aware. We all were," he said. "They talked to me about Jack Johnson when I was coming along. Luther and Dad. Anybody that knew what was going on. If they thought that you were going to go any place. I mean this was the background. You had to understand. You had to play within certain perimeters." Johnson's rise and then his later exile provided a clear message for Fritz Pollard. Black athletes could succeed in the white-dominated athletic world, but only if they abided by an unwritten code of conduct both on and off the playing field. To a large degree, Pollard's career would be guided by Jack Johnson's experience; to seek the heights of athletic achievement, but also to stay within those "certain perimeters" of conduct that might ensure lasting success.[14]

In September 1908 at age fourteen, Pollard entered high school, where he would test both his mental and athletic fitness. He attended the recently constructed Albert G. Lane Technical High School, which was closer to the Pollard home than North Division High School from which his brother Leslie had recently graduated. Hughes would also attend Lane Tech to begin his junior year. Lane Tech, one of the first large manual training high schools in the country, had the goal of educating "foremen and superintendents whose future plans didn't necessarily include further education." The new building at the corner of Sedgwick and Division streets on Chicago's North Side could accommodate more than 1,800 students.[15]

Pollard was a member of the first graduating class at Lane Tech. His high school transcript indicates an overall four-year average of C plus. He took a wide spectrum of courses, ranging from black-smithing and foundry and patternwork to such standard subjects as English, algebra, and chemistry. He graduated with only a half year of a foreign language, a deficiency which proved to be a major obstacle for his future academic and athletic aspirations. Given the number of extracurricular activities in which he participated, it is a wonder that Pollard did as well as he did in his studies. According to the senior class issue of the *Tech Prep*, Pollard participated in both outdoor and indoor track and played in the orchestra for four years, played football for three years, was a member of the outdoor baseball team for two years and the indoor nine for one year, and participated in inter-room debates for two years. He also played trombone in the school band when he was not otherwise occupied on the athletic field.[16]

In 1908 Fritz and Hughes were the only African Americans enrolled at Lane Tech. Before Fritz graduated, several other blacks would attend Lane, including Virgil and Nat Bluett, who later be-came star athletes in Chicago. Fritz had many fond memories of his high school years but also pointed out emphatically that "Lane Tech wasn't any beauty spot, at all."[17] On the basis of his record in extracurricular activities alone, one might conclude that Pollard was accepted by the students and faculty at Lane. This was only true to a degree. A cartoon featuring Pollard in the March 1910 issue of the *Tech Prep* indicates prevailing racial attitudes. Above the caption "Fritz as Mercury" appears a sketch of a Negro in a track suit which shows the runner as having exaggerated protruding lips and thick, kinky hair, features which hardly applied to young Fritz Pollard.

Although Chicago public schools had been legally integrated for thirty-five years when Pollard entered high school, incidents of discrimination and interracial strife had increased since the 1890s. By the early 1900s, as Allan Spear has noted, racial tension was a major problem in the public schools. "In 1905, a group of white children rioted when they were transferred to a predominantly Negro school, and in 1908, over one hundred and fifty students stayed home when they were transferred to a school attended by Negroes. A year later, two Negro children, enrolling in a previously all-white school, were insulted and beaten by their classmates." The Chicago school board frowned on the interracial disturbances, but concluded in 1912 that the "color line is a source of continual strife."[18]

The racial climate the African-American athlete faced in interscholastic athletics was inconsistent. A 1922 study by the Illinois Commission on Race Relations reported that "there seems to be no feeling between the white and Negro members of a school team, but the Negro members are sometimes roughly handled when the team plays other schools." Black athletes, the report stated, were generally accepted on high school teams, and their white teammates would usually protect them if they were assaulted or harassed by the opposing team or its fans. The study did note, however, that a few years earlier there had been some friction between black athletes and white on integrated teams. The best evidence indicates that the few African-American athletes who participated in Chicago interscholastic sports in 1908 and before were better accepted than those who competed after World War I, but that they too usually encountered trouble when playing against all-white teams.[19]

The outstanding African-American student athlete in Chicago before Fritz Pollard made his mark at Lane Tech was Samuel "Sammy" Ransom, who had played for Hyde Park High School from 1900 to 1903. Ransom, the only black to compete for the South Side Chicago school, played right halfback on some of the most powerful interscholastic football teams of the era. Playing in a backfield that included future three-time University of Chicago All-America quarterback Walter Eckersall, Ransom, Eckersall, and the Hyde Park eleven demolished its high school opposition and defeated several college teams, including the University of Chicago. The 1902 squad won the first national interscholastic championship by defeating a Brooklyn, New York, high school 105–0. Both Ransom and Eckersall made the Chicago *Tribune* all-city team three years in a row. Ransom, an equally good if not better baseball player, was a star catcher and pitcher for the Hyde Park nine. Of even greater interest, he was elected captain of the Hyde Park baseball team in 1902 and 1903.[20]

Ransom, who had a dark complexion like Pollard, seemingly gained a degree of acceptance from his Hyde Park teammates that would be unusual for a black man less than a decade later. Interestingly, Pollard never mentioned Ransom in any of his later interviews recapping his boyhood days. Brief season summaries that appear in an informal history of Hyde Park High School sports indicate that Ransom was a highly esteemed athlete and that few racially motivated incidents were instigated by opponents because of his presence on the playing field. After graduation, Ransom was recruited to play football by University of Chicago coach Amos Alonzo Stagg (who a few years later would bar blacks from his teams) but opted to attend Beloit College in Wisconsin, where he became an outstanding athlete. The fact that Ransom was an exceptional athlete and one of only a handful of blacks competing in Chicago interscholastic sports at the time may help account for his unusual degree of acceptance. By the time Pollard entered Lane Tech in 1908, Chicago's black population had increased significantly and the number of African-American scholar athletes, while still small, had increased with it. As an African-American athlete, Pollard felt the effects of the city's gradually increasing racial tensions.[21]

During his freshman year, Pollard participated in indoor and outdoor track and played in the orchestra and band, but did not play football. According to his often-repeated account, his high school gridiron career began in a game against Hyde Park. In fact, Pollard had already played in a "try out" game against Thornton High School the previous week, scoring a touchdown in a 16–0 Lane victory. It is probable that Pollard did not play in 1908 because he was considered too small to try out or that he failed to make the team. Hughes's dramatic intercession with the principal and coach in 1909 suggests that Fritz might have been cut from the 1908 squad.[22]

Pollard no doubt remembered the Hyde Park contest as his first game because it was Lane's first league match that year and an early turning point in his gridiron career. "We weren't supposed to win against the great Hyde Park High School," he recalled. They had "a fellow by the name of Butch Scanlon who later became coach at the University of Chicago. I'll never forget him, big and rugged and tough. He was playing tackle and I was playing end. And oh boy, he was kicking me around something terrible." As Pollard remembered the scene, his brother Hughes went over to Lane quarterback Artie Wagner and said, "Artie, see that big fellow out there kicking my kid brother around. Well, give me the ball and let me take it through there; I'll fix him." Wagner called the signal and Hughes blasted through left tackle and laid Scanlon "straight out on the field." In Pollard's account, Hughes then turned to Fritz and said: "From now on, you just learn to take care of yourself. I'm all through. I'm not even going to play anymore." The *Tech Prep* recorded that Hyde Park defeated Lane 28–11, but noted that "the game, although not very clean, was a royal one and even in defeat the boys deserve a great deal of credit for their splendid playing." Fritz scored one touchdown, and Hughes made the conversion.[23]

Pollard's parablelike account of the Hyde Park game in later years seems suspect, especially because he sometimes had Lane winning the contest. In one interview, he recalled that when he and Hughes got home after the game, one of his older brothers said, "If you ever get hurt, don't ever come back home. Now your brother taught you what to do and how to take care of yourself, so just don't get hurt or don't come home." Even allowing for the embellishment of the story over the years, Pollard's initiation into interscholastic football was apparently traumatic. Telling an undersized fifteen-year-old sophomore not to come home if he got hurt on the gridiron was indicative of the high standards set in the Pollard household.[24]

It was, of course, vital that Pollard learn to protect himself. He was a natural target for the bigger and stronger white boys on the opposing teams because of his size and skin color. In later years, Pollard usually shrugged off questions pertaining to attempts of high school players to injure him by saying, "It was pretty rough with Hyde Park and Englewood and Crane Tech during those days." Accounts of Lane games in the *Tech Prep* indicate that he was singled out for especially rough or unfair treatment by some opposing players and referees. Beyond this, football as it was played in the early twentieth century was excessively brutal. Several major efforts were made to ban the game on both the high school and collegiate levels because of the large number of serious injuries and deaths that resulted from unsportsmanlike conduct and the straight-ahead style of play. In 1906, the Intercollegiate Rules Committee revised the existing rules, in part because of the intervention of President Theodore Roosevelt, supposedly to curb the use of the dangerous mass plays. However, the rules changes, the so-called "Revolution of 1906," had little effect in reducing the number of deaths and serious injuries. In 1909, thirty men died on the nation's gridirons, half of them high school players. Further rules changes, urged by midwestern college coaches, were made in 1910 and 1912 in an effort to open up the game and make it less brutal and more exciting to watch. The most important of these had to do with the more liberal requirements for using the forward pass, which had been legalized in 1906.[25]

It was fortunate for Pollard that he began his high school football career during a period which saw a radical transformation in the game. To the extent that they did open up the game, the rules changes made from 1906 to 1912 certainly favored the small, swift, and elusive Pollard. Until 1906, football was primarily a contest of brute strength, with teams plunging forward in mass formations to make the required five yards for a first down. With all twenty-two players congregating around the ball, pile-ups, roughing, and mass mauls prevailed. The 1906 rules established a scrimmage line or neutral zone between the offensive and defensive teams, restricted linemen from dropping back on offense, and increased the first-down distance to ten yards in three tries in the hopes of encouraging end runs and open play. Forward passing was also legalized, but was so restricted that it became virtually a desperation measure. According to William J. Baker, "A ball had to be thrown across the line of scrimmage downfield into a ten-yard-wide alley, five yards on either side from the point at which it was snapped. Chalk lines running up and down as well as across the field assisted officials in detecting infractions, making popular a new term for the field of play: the gridiron." Given the limited usefulness of the forward pass and the increase in yardage for a first down, the 1906 changes had a minimum impact on either opening up the game or eliminating mass play.[26]

With the rules changes, it was hoped that football would gain more spectator interest and thus greater financial return. The subsequent rule changes in 1910 and 1912 discouraged mass formations and promoted forward passing. As the historian Benjamin Rader has noted, "They wanted a game that featured long runs, more scoring, and the greater likelihood of upsets."[27]

Pollard's third high school game against Northwestern Military Academy played at Lake Geneva, Wisconsin, is indicative of the kind of open football that was catching on in the Midwest. Lane defeated Northwestern by a score of 29–17 in a game that featured passing, end runs, and long punt returns. The *Tech Prep* reported that "F. Pollard's work on the offensive was brilliant; after catching a punt on our twenty-yard line he ran ninety yards for a touchdown through his knowledge of dodging and twisting." At the age of fifteen Pollard was making his mark as a budding star in Chicago interscholastic football.[28]

The highlight of the 1909 season came on October 16, when Lane played Crane Tech for the technical schools championship of the city. One of the students at Crane was George Halas, a fourteen-year-old, 110-pound freshman. Over the years, Pollard would develop a bittersweet relationship with Halas, ultimately accusing him of being instrumental in imposing racial segregation in the National Football League. During his high school days, Halas played for four years on the Crane lightweight football team and thus did not compete against Pollard, who played on the Lane heavyweight team. They did, however, oppose one another in track meets and indoor baseball.[29]

The football contest was considered the "big game" because Crane Tech was the only other large technical school in the city, and as the *Tech Prep* put it, "naturally we were out looking for their scalps." Hughes Pollard returned from his self-imposed exile in the band to spark Lane to a 17–6 triumph over Crane for the technical schools championship. He ran for one touchdown and a kicked a field goal to assure the Lane victory. After the game Hughes hung up his football uniform for good and gave his full attention to the band and orchestra. In the game story, Fritz was cited for his defensive play and several long runs around end. Lane went on to win two of its last five games, finishing the season with a record of five wins and four losses, a respectable achievement for a team in only its second season in the competitive Cook County high school league.[30]

The Lane band and orchestra helped foster a lifelong interest in music which would be of great value to Pollard in terms of personal enjoyment, making contacts, and providing a source of income when the Great Depression put him in dire financial straits. Fritz played slide trombone in both organizations and was reputedly a fine musician. His participation in the band was sporadic, however, in that he was almost constantly engaged in athletic contests at which the band played. He undoubtedly marched in the "Taft Day" ceremonies in September 1909 when the Lane band marched downtown to greet President William Taft in what the 1910 yearbook described as a "noisy demonstration" to which the band contributed its share.[31]

A school reporter in the April 1911 edition of the *Tech Prep* indicated the magnitude of Pollard's athletic activities when he wrote that " 'Fritz' who also ran in the Cook County meets despite the fact that he was catching on the indoor team at the time, has been one of the mainstays of school athletics, as he is on almost every team." In fact, Pollard competed in both indoor and outdoor baseball as well as in indoor and outdoor track, at least to the extent that the events did not conflict. He was a first-rate sprinter and hurdler and clearly had Olympic potential. One can only speculate about how good he might have been had he devoted his full energy to track. During the course of four years, he competed in more than fifteen different running events for Lane Tech. As a high school junior and senior, he usually ran the one hundred yard dash in 10.1 seconds. "Once or twice I got under ten," he said. "I was just fast enough not to beat the champion, but I'd run second and third all the time." In the hurdles contests, his strongest events, he was rarely defeated. Pollard ran the 220-yard low hurdles in just over twenty-five seconds, and his best time in the 110-yard high hurdles was 15.3 seconds. In his senior year, Pollard was Cook County champion in both the low hurdles and the half-mile run.[32]

During the indoor and outdoor track seasons, Pollard managed his time carefully in order to play as much as possible on the Lane indoor and outdoor baseball teams. Indoor baseball was a popular sport in early-twentieth-century Chicago. It was played in school gymnasiums during the winter and had rules similar to the outdoor game. A large, lightweight ball and a long, thin bat were used to minimize damage to the indoor facility. The playing area was, of course, smaller and the defensive positions were realigned to include right- and left-side fielders similar to the short fielders in modern slow-pitch softball. The positions of shortstop and center field were eliminated. When he was available, Pollard played catcher on the indoor team. Lane had a strong indoor team and usually only Crane Tech, which featured George Halas as a star pitcher and right-side fielder, defeated Lane in league play. On the outdoor team, Pollard played shortstop, his best position. According to the Lane Tech box scores, he was an excellent all-around baseball player who batted over .300, hit with power, and committed few errors. After the 1912 season, Pollard was selected All-Cook County shortstop.[33]

While Pollard set high standards of achievement in a number of sports, his favorite game was football. While on vacation in Chicago during the summer of 1910, Leslie instructed Fritz on the finer points of the game as it was played by the eastern colleges. During his last two football campaigns at Lane, Fritz would benefit from Leslie's instruction as well as the rules changes and demonstrate that open football featuring end runs and forward passing was exciting to watch. By 1910, Pollard was shifted to right halfback and often played tackle on defense. He now weighed between 135 and 140 pounds and found it easier to contend with linemen who then averaged about 160 pounds. Pollard averaged just under one touchdown a game for the 1910–11 seasons and had at least six long touchdown runs called back because of penalties. Before the 1910 season, the *Tech Prep* described Pollard as "gritty and nerveless. He is a born football player, clean, and decidedly tricky."[34]

Pollard played a role in transforming the Chicago student game from a usually slow-moving clash of mass formations to a more wide-open contest featuring long runs and more scoring. The *Tech Prep* indicated his impact in a game report of a 1911 contest between Lane and Wendell Phillips High School, which Fritz missed due to an injury. "With Pollard out of the game," the school reporter noted, "the Wendell Phillips game was not as spectacular as usual, being more of the old style football variety." Pollard led Lane Tech to two successful seasons in which it placed second and third in the northern division of the Cook County League, with impressive triumphs over Englewood, University High, Wendell Phillips, and

St. Rita's College. Perhaps Pollard's most spectacular game, however, was his last away game against Detroit Central High School played on Thanksgiving Day 1911. Lane lost the game 6–0, but there was little doubt in the mind of the *Tech Prep* reporter that the officials were responsible: "The game was one such as has been rarely witnessed in Detroit. Pollard was the feature of the game, bringing the grand stand to its feet time and again. He made several touchdowns, which did not count, however, as we were heavily penalized at such times."[35]

Although game accounts emphasize his spectacular long runs, Pollard was by no means a one-dimensional player. He was an excellent defensive player and was particularly adept at making open-field tackles, a skill that football experts would note throughout his career. He was also a good kicker. During his senior year, Pollard did the punting for Lane, drop-kicked points after touchdown, and converted three fairly long field goals. The *Tech Prep* gave some indication of his all-around abilities when it stated that "his spectacular playing has been the feature of most of the games for he is a demon both in offense and defense. Although not a star kicker his booting has been steady and consistent more than can hardly be hoped for from a high school man."[36]

Being a high school football hero was heady stuff for young Pollard, but his life was not all touchdowns and glory. As one of the few black players in the Chicago interscholastic league, he received more than his share of verbal and physical abuse. Most opposing teams singled him out as a target for rough play, piling on, and outright illegal acts aimed at injuring him. Although his teammates did their best to protect him, they did not always succeed. After a 1911 road game against Rockford High School, the *Tech Prep* noted that "they were laying for Pollard up there, but they missed him." To combat the dangerous situation, Pollard used a unique tactic that during the course of his career became one of his trademarks and discouraged would-be ruffians intent upon maiming him. When tackled, he would roll over on his back, cock his legs, and flail them bicycle-style to prevent piling on. Despite this technique and the training his brothers had given him, Pollard sustained several injuries during his senior year, at least one the result of dirty play. In an account of a game against University High, the *Tech Prep* reported curtly that "Pollard went out of the game after a kick in the back" and would miss the next game. Pollard later admitted that he was roughed up many times in high school games and maintained that he was also the target of racial slurs. "In the beginning they were pretty rough," Pollard said, "but I had been taught to take care of myself and maybe I didn't realize exactly how rough they really were."[37]

In 1970 when Pollard was asked if he had experienced any racial discrimination when he played at Lane Tech, he replied emphatically, "There were problems. There were problems." He seemed most incensed by incidents in which his coach and teammates became accomplices in acts of discrimination. One such episode occurred as a result of a non-league game against a team in southern Illinois. Coach R. F. Webster told Pollard to report to the train station at a certain time on a Saturday morning, but the team had departed by the time Fritz got there. As Pollard related the story, "another train came in and I took the train. They said it didn't stop at this particular place, and I got off about eight or ten miles down and I walked all the way back to where we were playing. And I found out when I got back that it was done on purpose because this team down in southern Illinois didn't want to play against me and they had no way of telling me no, so they pulled that stunt on me." When asked if he meant that his own team had pulled the stunt, Pollard replied, "yes, my own team." Even the intervening years had not fully soothed the hurt and disappointment Pollard felt because his coach and teammates had let him down on that autumn Saturday some sixty years before.[38]

Pollard remembered a similar incident that occurred in November 1910 when Lane journeyed to Wisconsin to play against St. John's Military Academy. A group of St. John's cadets greeted the Lane eleven at the railroad station and escorted them to the campus. Pollard recalled that a couple of the cadets threw their arms around him, guided him around the military compound, and took him to dinner. The next day when Coach Webster picked the team to go out and play, he went up to Fritz and said, "Pollard, this is a practice game, I think we'd better save you." At the time, Pollard recalled, "I didn't have any more sense than believe him." After the game, however, several of the cadets who had treated him royally the day before told him, "Nigger, we did all that to keep you out of the game." Pollard was outwardly calm about the incident at the time, he later said, because "my brothers and my dad had taught me to handle those things and I never lost my head about it. I just figured it was another thing that came along."[39]

There is little reason to doubt the accuracy of Pollard's recollection. The *Tech Prep* game account states that "with many of the substitutes in the line-up, Lane lost 40–0 to St. John's Military Academy. . . . The absence of many of our regulars and the fact that St. John's team greatly outweighed ours accounts for our defeat." Coach Webster may have had several reasons for keeping many of the regulars out of the lineup that day. Perhaps he was conducting some form of protest against the refusal of the St. John's players to compete against a team including a black player. Another explanation might be that he was resting most of his regulars for the following weekend's championship contest against Oak Park High School at Chicago's Phipps Field. The crux of the matter was that Pollard was subjected to racial taunting from some of the St. John's cadets and naturally assumed, given his previous experience, that his benching was a result of the race issue. Being one of the few blacks in Chicago high school football at the time, Pollard carried additional burdens which few others could understand.[40]

In June 1912, Pollard graduated from Lane Tech and could look back proudly on a record of success and achievement. He had maintained a better than acceptable academic average and had participated in more extracurricular activities than anyone else in his class. Moreover, he had twice been named to the all-Cook County football squad as a halfback and had garnered all-county honors in both track and baseball. Pollard was not overly enthusiastic about going to college, however; his main and sometimes sole interest was sports. He realized, however, that limited athletic opportunities existed for African Americans beyond the local amateur or semipro level in either track or baseball, especially since the color line remained as firm as ever in the latter sport. As for football, serious competition existed only at the college level.[41]

During the summer of 1912, family members encouraged Fritz to consider furthering his education and athletic interests by attending college. Pollard had a vague and perhaps romantic notion of attending Dartmouth College where his brother Leslie had played football. Leslie, however, encouraged Fritz to attend the all-black Lincoln University in Oxford, Pennsylvania, and Willie Naomi was equally adamant that her younger brother receive his higher education at Northwestern, her alma mater. Northwestern was one of the few schools in the Western Conference, later known as the Big Ten, which permitted blacks to play football. The universities of Illinois, Michigan, and Chicago, for example, allowed African Americans to matriculate, but by 1912 had unwritten rules prohibiting their participation in football. As he whiled away the summer playing semipro baseball in Rogers Park and communities along the North Shore, Pollard made a tentative decision to give Northwestern a try; it was close to home, and many of his friends were going there. He would report to the Evanston campus for football practice in early September.[42]

THE TRAMP ATHLETE

3

At the turn of the century, it was fairly common for so-called "tramp athletes" to wander from campus to campus, offering their football talents to the highest bidder. Most of these athletes only vaguely posed as students and often played for many years, sometimes at a number of different colleges. When Fritz Pollard set out for Evanston to attend freshman football practice at Northwestern in September 1912, he had little idea that he would begin a sojourn that would be remarkably similar to that of a tramp athlete. His primary reason for going to Northwestern "was the thought of playing four more years of football."[1]

Pollard began freshman football drills with some trepidation because he knew that big-time college football was a white man's game. He later recalled that "the coaches were white, the players were white, and the fans were white. No complaints at this stage of the game, sixty years later. That's just the way it was. There just weren't that many colored men attending college in the first decade of this century, let alone competing with the white man on the athletic field." Most of Pollard's football heroes were white players such as quarterbacks Walter Eckersall and Walter Steffen of the University of Chicago and the great halfback Willie Heston of Fielding Yost's "point-a-minute" University of Michigan team of 1902. At that time Pollard knew little about the African-American athletes who had been standouts at the major white football schools and almost nothing of the star players at black colleges. The Chicago newspapers, including the *Defender*, gave little coverage to such black stars as William Henry Lewis, Harvard's All-America center in 1892 and 1893, William Clarence Matthews, an outstanding Harvard end of 1904, or the great Minnesota wingman Robert Marshall, who made Walter Camp's second team All-America squad in 1905.[2]

Pollard received little encouragement to attend college or to play football from anyone outside of his family. As he described the situation, "there were no college scouts pounding on the Pollard door offering free scholarships or maybe a new horse and buggy for my father. There was no money being offered under the table. In fact, there wasn't even any money on the table. And here I was a kid with the reputation of being a pretty good athlete and a very good football player." He knew that "beyond the Pollard family, there was probably no one in the United States who gave a damn where Fritz Pollard went to college, or even whether or not he did go to college."[3]

Arriving on the Northwestern campus two weeks before classes were set to begin, Pollard drew a football suit and started practice with the freshman team. He had not applied for admission, and no one knew that he was coming. Looking back to that time, Pollard thought it funny that "no one asked any questions—not the trainer, the freshman football coach, or anyone else." He enjoyed the practice sessions, however, and met some fine fellows on that freshman team. When school opened, Pollard went to see the dean about registering for classes—just a formality, or so he thought. Pollard remembered walking into a stuffy-smelling office, books piled to the ceiling along all four walls. "I guess it was an impressive place by the standards of the period," he recalled, "but I was a pretty cocky kid then and I wasn't about to be intimidated by a stuffy office and a lot of books." The dean immediately asked him why he had come to Northwestern. Pollard remembered that he was so impressed with himself at the time that "my first thought was one of disappointment. I was disappointed that the dean didn't congratulate me on having made All-Cook County halfback the previous fall. So, like a damn fool I said, 'Why, I came here to play football, of course.'" The dean looked over his spectacles at Pollard for a long moment and replied, "Well, Northwestern isn't the place for football players, Pollard. This is a place for students. I don't think you belong here." That was the end of both the interview and Pollard's career at Northwestern.[4]

Recalling the incident many years later, Pollard had mixed feelings about his quick exit from Northwestern. He believed that he would have grown to like the place, but he admitted that the dean was right and that he had been terribly naive. "Hell, I had absolutely no conception what it was like to get into college," he said. Northwestern, however, was probably not the right place for Pollard to showcase his football talent. Although the school had built a new thirteen-thousand-seat stadium in 1905, the trustees dropped football the next year during the "football crisis," when many college administrators became alarmed by the number of serious injuries and deaths that resulted from the game. The sport was revived in 1908, but Northwestern struggled in Western Conference play during the next four seasons with an overall 3–11–1 record. From 1888, when the sport was introduced on the Evanston campus, until 1922 when things took a turn for the better, Northwestern was known as the "graveyard of college coaches." Fourteen had come and gone during the period, eleven of them lasting only one season. The football historian Howard Roberts has suggested that Northwestern's problems on the football field probably reflected its administration's negative attitude toward the game. For example, Abbott Fletcher, a Northwestern football star around 1910, had an A taken away by a professor who became angry when Fletcher refused to give up football and concentrate solely on his studies. Northwestern simply was not noted for its prowess on the gridiron.[5]

When Pollard returned home from Evanston, Willie Naomi "raised holy heck around the house" and tried to convince Fritz to go back to see the Northwestern dean, but Fritz decided to steer clear of the place, the embarrassment was too great. By that time it was too late to register at another school. As Pollard later recalled, his thought at that point was to attend Dartmouth, where Leslie had played, or Harvard, where he could expect to play big-time football and also get a good education. He decided to wait until January 1913 when the second semester would begin and then head for New Hampshire and Dartmouth College. Meanwhile, Pollard was still determined to play some kind of competitive football that fall. There were a number of good pro and semipro teams around Chicago; practically every community fielded a team. Loyalties were strong and local pride was fierce; most teams would gladly welcome a shifty halfback, regardless of his color. On the semipro teams, the better players were paid a small sum per game, but many of the men received nothing and played for the sheer fun of it. Semipro football was extremely rough and somewhat informal. Star players regularly jumped from one team to another from Sunday to Sunday, depending on who offered the most money.[6]

Leslie, who had played some semipro football himself both before and after attending Dartmouth, thought it was a fine idea for Fritz to get his feet wet playing against some older and more experienced players. It could only help as a preparation for the day when Fritz would play college football. Pollard's parents and Willie Naomi were less enthusiastic. They supported Fritz's objective of playing college football but were dubious about this latest venture, believing that if he got involved in playing football for money it might somehow sidetrack him and cause him to lose interest in attaining a higher education.[7]

Despite the warning, Pollard signed on with a team in Evanston and played about eight games that season. He ran into few racial problems when playing at home because he was well known as a local high school football star. As the only black on the Evanston team, Pollard did experience occasional problems when the team went on the road. Some fans would chant, "Nigger, Nigger," he recalled, point their fingers at him, and scream that the home team was going to lay him out cold. But there was little of this sort of reaction, and almost none from the players on the other teams. Semipro football was a Sunday afternoon diversion, primarily for the working men who made up most of the teams and for the few hundred spectators who attended. Few cared whether an African American played or did not play.[8]

Pollard remembered playing in games against the Decatur Staleys, who later became the Chicago Bears under the direction of George Halas, and the Racine Cardinals, later known as the Chicago Cardinals, both charter members of the National Football League. Most of all, he recalled that "the players were mean. They played a rough game and usually on a dirt surface that left you with a nose full of dust after a tackle. The players were out there working off the frustrations of putting in a sixty hour week at the local sweat shop—for about twenty cents an hour."[9]

The crowds were not large, usually four to five hundred. At some point during every game, the team manager of the home team would take up a collection from the crowd, usually after his team had made an outstanding play. A full hat did not always mean that the teams ended richer than they started; "the money," Pollard recalled, "had ways of disappearing. The managers always had to be on the lookout for the quick con job. One trick was for a fan to pull out a ten dollar bill and ask for nine dollars change. When the manager put the derby down to make change, a kid who was a plant would snatch the hat, leap the nearest fence, and be gone. That trick used to work at least once a year in every ball park."[10]

Like the other star players in semipro ball, Pollard occasionally jumped to another team when "the expenses" were right. On one Sunday he was recruited by a Wisconsin team which featured an all-Indian lineup. The Wisconsin players convinced Pollard to pose as an Indian so that he might play in an important game against a rival team from Minnesota. His name for the game was Charlie Lone Star. As Pollard later recounted the story, the Minnesota team had a great drop-kicker, George Capron, who had attended the University of Minnesota a few years before. "Early in the game Capron booted a beautiful field goal from 40 yards out and they led us, 3–0," Fritz recalled. "But not for long. I ran the next kickoff back for a touchdown and we won the game, 6–3." Capron was upset after the game, and Pollard went over to see him. "I remember we both sat on a wooden fence near the field, dirty and sweaty," Fritz said, "and we talked for a long while. He a white man and me a black posing as an Indian. He got a kick out of finding out that I wasn't an Indian after all. While we talked, my teammates—the real Indians—were sitting in a circle in the end zone and celebrating the victory by circulating a couple of large jugs that it's safe to say did not contain lemonade. We became good friends and kept in touch down through the years." Besides Capron, not many of the opposing players or the fans were taken in by Pollard's attempt to disguise himself as an Indian, but few of them complained; it was the nature of semipro football during the second decade of the century.[11]

During that fall Fritz's mother began a campaign to encourage her son to attend Brown University, a Baptist college in Providence, Rhode Island. For some years, Mrs. Pollard had done seamstress work for one of Chicago's largest department stores, Chas. A. Stevens & Co. One of the owners, Elmer T. Stevens, was a 1904 Brown graduate and familiar with Fritz's football exploits at Lane Tech. Hearing about his difficulties at Northwestern, Stevens recommended

Brown as a small college where Pollard would not get lost in the shuffle. He regaled Mrs. Pollard with stories about Brown and its fine football tradition. Pollard recalled that throughout the fall his mother would break into the dinner conversation and switch the topic to Brown University. "She'd start rattling off the names of some of Brown's great football players as if she'd seen them play and knew all about them." By wintertime, some of his mother's enthusiasm began to rub off on Fritz and the rest of the family. As the weeks passed, Pollard found himself telling friends that he would be attending either Dartmouth or Brown during the upcoming spring semester.[12]

In late January 1913, Pollard boarded a train bound for Boston, his final destination being Dartmouth College in Hanover, New Hampshire. As a concession to his mother, and partly to satisfy his own curiosity, he agreed to stop off in Providence and take a look at Brown. Pollard did not send in an application to either of the colleges. "Maybe some kids did in those days," he later explained, "but nobody told me what to do. I just packed my bags, jumped on the train, and headed east." When he arrived in Providence, Pollard hailed a cab which took him to the Brown campus on the city's East Side. As Pollard remembered many years later, "the cab driver took me up this steep hill, which I found out later was College Hill. And right straight ahead of me at the top of the hill were those big, beautiful iron gates leading to the campus. It was a cold, clear January day and the late afternoon sun was shining directly on the gates, making them sparkle. Oh, boy. I got a lump in my throat."[13]

After spending the night with Johnny Cromwell, whom Leslie had met at Dartmouth and told his brother to contact, Pollard made an appointment to see the college dean about admission. Dean Otis Randall informed Pollard that Brown did not accept students at midyear, but given the circumstances, he suggested that Fritz talk with the university's president, William Faunce. As Pollard later described the scene, "Prexy Faunce," as the students called him, "was not much bigger than I but he was a rather stern looking man. He had white hair and a thick white mustache, and his sharp eyes seemed to climb up over his rimless spectacles when he'd lower his head to speak to me." After a short conversation, Faunce leaned back in his chair and uttered a few words that Fritz would not soon forget. "Well, Pollard," he said, "you're too far from home for us to let you go back. If you really have decided that you want to come to Brown, I guess we'll have to let you stay as a special student." Pollard was delighted as he ran all the way back to Johnny Cromwell's apartment. During the spring semester, he studied hard and passed all of his courses, but his troubles at Brown had just begun. Having gone to a technical high school, he still did not have sufficient foreign language credits for admission to Brown as a regular student. After the end of the spring semester, Dean Randall suggested that Fritz attend a six-week summer program at Columbia University in New York to attain the needed credits in French and Spanish. Although summer school posed a financial problem, the Pollard family responded by sending a check to help Fritz with his expenses in New York City.[14]

Early in July Pollard left for New York. Years later he recalled his initial impressions of the nation's largest city in the last full summer of peace before the Great War. "What a city! I'd never seen anything like it," he said. "I've spent the better part of my life in New York City. I love the place. It's home to me. But that first impression is one I'll never forget." Reviewing on old copy of *Variety*, Pollard recalled that Paul Ruben's *Sunshine Girl* was at the Knickerbocker Theater and that Rudolph Friml's *High Jinks* and Victor Herbert's *Sweethearts* were the other hit plays that year. The sixty-story Woolworth Building, heralded as the world's tallest structure, was completed that summer. Arturo Toscanini was making his first American appearance as a symphony conductor at the Metropolitan Opera House. Some of the hit songs were "Peg of My Heart," "The Trail of the Lonesome Pine," and "He'd Have to Get Under, Get Out and Get Under (To Fix Up His Automobile)."[15]

Pollard may have been humming some of those tunes that summer, but he had little time or money to attend the opera or the plays at the Knickerbocker Theater. Staying with his brother, Leslie, he did, however, get to see many of the sights in the bustling city. In his six weeks at Columbia, Pollard completed the equivalent of two years of French and one of Spanish. He was now ready, or so he thought, to tackle Brown University and perhaps a few opposing halfbacks.[16]

When Pollard returned to Providence, he was in for a shock. The university would accept his French credits, but not the ones in Spanish. Pollard protested, but the college dean was adamant. Professor Albert Johnson, head of the Romance Language Department, simply said that no one could possibly learn enough Spanish in summer school to pass an examination. The case was closed. Professor Johnson had spoken, and apparently no one on campus, not even Dean Randall, was about to take issue with him. Despondent and low on cash, Pollard did not know what to do. He did know one thing: he "was afraid to go home and admit defeat." Apparently the high standards set for him by his family were so firmly ingrained in him that he refused to concede failure and ask his parents for further assistance. He decided to stay in Providence and see what he could do about getting into Brown for the second semester. Through his friend Johnny Cromwell, Pollard got a job as a busboy at the Noon Day Club in downtown Providence. Meanwhile, his family back in Chicago thought he was attending Brown. Even some of the people at the university took him for a student because they saw him on campus so often. "I'd made a number of friends there the previous spring," he recalled, "and I'd visit them off and on just to keep up the friendships and to grab an occasional meal on the house."[17]

During the winter of 1913–14, Pollard rented a room on Cushing Street near the Brown campus. At that time the largest concentration of African Americans in Rhode Island lived on Cushing and Meeting streets on the northern edge of the campus, extending westward down College Hill toward Benefit Street. Pollard's landlord was a gardener, Joseph Laing, whose family had once been notable in African-American history. Joseph was the son of Daniel Laing, Jr., one of the first black medical doctors in the United States. At the time Pollard was much more interested in Joseph Laing's seventeen-year-old daughter Ada, described by one of her childhood friends as being "very attractive, sweet, and very bright." Ada was about five-foot-one, had pretty hair, and was regarded by her friends as a "little Indian princess." A childhood playmate, Mable Abrams, recalled that Ada "realized she was somebody. She was very bright, grasped things easily." Pollard remembered that at first he and Ada would "go out to a movie or a dance once in a while . . . by the middle of the year things got real serious between us and I guess my life at that time centered around Ada and my job — in that order. We were finally married that summer."[18]

At the time Pollard was undoubtedly unaware of the prominence of the Laing family. Ada's grandfather, Daniel, had been a practicing physician at the Massachusetts General Hospital as early as 1850, and according to Dr. Martin Delany, attended lectures at the Harvard Medical School that year. During the early 1850s, Laing spent two years in Paris attending lectures and studying under "that great master of surgery, Velpeau." Upon his return to the United States, Laing attended Dartmouth College Medical School and received his formal medical degree in 1854. A specialist on remittent fever, he and his wife, the former Anna Bicknell Parker, spent most of the next decade in Liberia, where Laing worked as a physician for the American Colonization Society. Joseph Laing was born in Monrovia, Liberia in 1860. Stricken with fever in the mid-1860s, Dr. Laing returned with his family to Charleston, South Carolina, where he died in 1869. According to family lore, Dr. Laing was poisoned at a banquet in his honor by whites who opposed his establishment of a medical clinic for blacks in that city. Anna Laing took the family, which then included Joseph and a daughter, Mary, to Providence where she had relatives. From that point on the fortunes of the Laing family declined rapidly.[19]

In the late-nineteenth and early-twentieth century, Providence was not a very hospitable city for African Americans. Although Rhode Island had a liberal heritage in race relations, the massive influx of foreign immigrants in the last half of the nineteenth century contributed to a deteriorating racial climate by the early 1900s. A 1909 study of social and economic conditions in Rhode Island's capital city described the plight of Providence blacks: "Few of the men appear to have steady employment, most of them working at gardening and odd jobs. Scarcely any are to be found in skilled trades or positions of responsibility, or would be welcome if they applied." The author concluded that "for no race is the outlook so unpromising." Mary Jennings, an African American and long-time resident of Providence's East Side, maintained that her husband, a southerner by birth, often stated that Providence in the early 1900s was about as bad as Georgia in terms of progress for blacks. She said that Providence was largely segregated, and that African Americans did not accomplish much there because the more talented among them moved away.[20]

Ada's father, Joseph, grew up in such an environment in the late nineteenth century. After the death of his sister Mary in 1880,

Joseph finished high school but continued to live with his mother on Cushing Street. He was employed as a clerk and later a porter at a firm in downtown Providence. In 1891, he married Lelia Beuzard of East Providence, and they had four children in rapid succession, Ada being the second eldest. After his wife died in the early 1900s, Joseph apparently lost his job downtown and became a gardener. Mary Jennings recalled that after Ada's mother died Joseph married a white woman, and that neither of them paid much attention to the children, who were by then teenagers. It may have been because of Joseph's declining economic fortunes that he rented a room to young Pollard in late 1913. During the spring, Fritz and Ada fell in love and began to talk of marriage. Pollard later reflected that "I guess with all the other problems in my life, getting married in June of 1914 was not the wisest thing to do. But when you're 20 and in love, well, more often than not your heart rules your head." The fact that Ada was pregnant at the time may have had a bearing on the sudden impulse toward matrimony. According to Pollard's daughter Leslie, Joseph Laing disapproved of her father and forbade his daughter to marry him. Mable Abrams remembered that Ada and Fritz eloped and were married, most likely "in one of the northern states." She said that the neighborhood girls, including Ada, used to play baseball in the Abrams's yard on Meeting Street, and that they all "had a fit when Ada ran off with *that* man."[21]

Pollard's irresponsibility toward his family and sexual indiscretion might simply be written off as youthful immaturity. However, there is reason to believe that it was also a form of rebellion against the discipline and high level of accomplishment his family demanded. At various points in his life, Pollard would flee from family pressures and responsibilities, always to return to the quest for achievement and success. For the moment, his major problem was money to support his wife and expected child. To supplement his income, Pollard began a pressing club on the Brown campus. For $1 a month, students could bring in as many items as they chose for Fritz to press and repair. The success of this venture encouraged Pollard to open a tailor shop that summer at Narragansett Pier, an elegant vacation resort in southern Rhode Island, where he and Ada spent the summer months. "The sum and substance of all this," Pollard later recalled, "was that my interest in college had taken a back seat." He had not contacted Dean Randall about making up his

Spanish credits or done anything about getting back into Brown for either the spring or fall semesters of 1914. Pollard was so embarrassed about his failure to make the grade in college—and deceiving his parents in the process—that the only family member he confided in was Leslie. His older brother suggested that in the fall Fritz should head straight for Hanover, New Hampshire, and attempt to get into Dartmouth. The advice sounded good. "Heck," Pollard remembered, "any advice about that time would have sounded good. I was a real mixed up kid."[22]

Leaving Ada behind with relatives in Rhode Island, Pollard took a train to Hanover in September 1914 as German forces retreated northward after their stunning defeat at the Marne River. After arriving in the small, quiet New Hampshire college town, Pollard proceeded to the gymnasium and was pleasantly surprised when he was immediately issued football equipment. When he trotted out to the practice field, he was further relieved to see a couple of friendly faces: Milton Ghee, a 1914 All-America quarterback, and Hank Llewellyn, whom Fritz had played against in the Chicago interscholastic league. The next day Clarence W. "Cupid" Spears arrived. The future Dartmouth All-America lineman had also played against Pollard back in Chicago. Feeling right at home, Pollard got a room, registered for classes, and began to look forward to matching his brother's achievements as a Dartmouth football player.[23]

The Dartmouth coach that year was Frank W. Cavanaugh, later known as the "Iron Major" because of his bravery and heroism in World War I. An 1898 Dartmouth graduate, Cavanaugh was then in his fourth season of a six-year reign that produced a 42–9–3 record for the Big Green. His 1913–15 teams each lost only one game. During the war, Cavanaugh nearly lost his life when shell fragments tore one side of his face apart. After the conflict, he became one of the nation's most respected coaches, with successful teams at Boston College and Fordham. Cavanaugh, six-foot-one, 230 pounds, coached tough, aggressive football and had the respect and admiration of his players no matter where he coached. One of Cavanaugh's traits was his ability to retain and use every scrap of information he had ever heard about any football player. According to Pollard, "Coach Cavanaugh knew I was coming to Dartmouth. To hear him tell it, he knew I was heading north before I knew it myself."[24]

During one of the early practice sessions, Pollard recalled that Cavanaugh took him aside for a talk near a little hill adjacent to the football field. He familiarized Fritz with the Dartmouth system and emphasized, according to Pollard, that "you better know that up here we don't like to lose." Cavanaugh explained that that meant team play and devotion. "The classroom and the practice field. Nothing else counts," Pollard recalled him saying. After Fritz concurred with Cavanaugh's theories about football, the coach raised one final point. "I know you're colored and you know you're colored. The point I want to make, Pollard, is that I have no objection to having you on my team." Cavanaugh went on to say that "some people aren't as open about these things as I am. Some coaches. Some players. They don't want anything to do with Negroes. In the restaurants. On the trains. On the football field." Cavanaugh reminded Pollard that sometimes things were going to get rough. "Think you can keep your head on your shoulders? Think you can keep your ears open and your mouth shut?" Pollard remembered him asking. Fritz was startled for a second, but quickly replied: "I always have so far. There won't be any trouble coach."[25]

There was indeed a lot of trouble ahead for Pollard at Dartmouth. For about a week everything went well for him both on and off the practice field. So well, in fact, that he was making plans to rent an off-campus room and bring his wife to Hanover. Then one morning Pollard found a note in his campus mailbox from the dean of the college requesting that he report to his office for a brief discussion. Pollard later reflected that "in my young life I'd had more experience with deans than most men my age." The dean immediately demanded to know if Fritz had ever attended Brown University. Pollard said that he had, but only as a special student. The dean acknowledged that fact, but pointed out that it would have been better if Pollard had told the truth about his experience at Brown when he registered. He went on to say that there had been more than a few athletes jumping from one college to another recently, and that Dartmouth did not want any part of that sort of thing. "Under the circumstances, Mr. Pollard," Fritz remembered him saying, "I think it would be best if you left. I'm sorry."[26]

That evening Pollard slowly packed his bags, went around campus to say goodbye to Ghee, Llewellyn, Spears, and some other friends, left a note for Coach Cavanaugh, and took a train headed for Boston. Leslie had once told him that if he ever got into trouble and needed a friend, he should see William Henry Lewis, the former Harvard All-America center and recently assistant attorney general under President Taft, who was then a Boston attorney. When he reached Boston, Pollard sought out Lewis at his law office. Lewis took an interest in Fritz's problems and went into action the following morning. Using his connections at Harvard where he had once been a line coach, Lewis arranged for Pollard to have an interview with the admissions officer the very same day. Twenty-four hours later Pollard had been accepted for admission to Harvard, with the stipulation that he make up his Spanish deficiencies the following summer.[27]

Pollard's acceptance at Harvard came on a Friday afternoon and he was scheduled to register officially the following Monday morning. On that Saturday, however, Harvard was slated to open its football season with a game at Harvard Stadium against Bates College of Lewiston, Maine. It happened that Charlie Brickley, the Harvard captain, drop-kicking star, and All-America quarterback, had heard about Pollard through William Henry Lewis. Brickley made arrangements for Pollard to sit on the Harvard bench, in street clothes, for the Bates game. The word *bench* did not adequately describe the situation on the Harvard sideline as Pollard remembered the scene. Harvard had at least a hundred players suited up for the game, and at least seven or eight benches were needed to accommodate them all. "I remember I took a seat way down at the end of the bench," Pollard said. "Six inches more to my left and I'd have been in one of the water buckets."[28]

The Crimson coach, Percy Haughton, made a lasting impression on Pollard. Before Haughton arrived at Harvard in 1908, the Crimson had suffered through a number of lackluster seasons under the coaching of nonsalaried Harvard graduates and team captains, who had adhered closely to the amateur standards of the English collegiate tradition. What was worse, "Harvard annually served as a doormat on which Yale footballers wiped their feet." Haughton became Harvard's first full-time professional coach soon after his arrival in 1908, and between then and 1916 when he retired, Harvard enjoyed winning football, defeating archrival Yale eight times and at one point going thirty-three games without a loss. Harvard also won three mythical national championships during those years. Pollard remem-

bered Haughton that day as pacing cooly along the sideline, a newspaper clenched tightly in his hand as he sent in team after team of
Harvard men in the 44–0 rout of Bates. He did not say much while
the game was in progress, but on the occasions when he did speak
his deep Groton-trained voice rang out all over the field. Pollard
recalled that "he was an impressive figure of a man but I had the
feeling that maybe he lacked warmth."[29]

While walking across the field after the game, Pollard was startled
to meet a man he had played against in the semipro leagues around
Chicago. The man was then a coach at Bates, and he immediately
began talking to Fritz about leaving Harvard and attending the small
college in Maine. He told Pollard that he was crazy to think about
going to Harvard. Had he not seen the four or five talented teams
that Haughton had run on and off the field in the romp over Bates?
Did Fritz really believe that a small, black freshman would get any
kind of real chance to play at Harvard? Besides, the coach added,
Pollard would really have to hit the books at the Cambridge school.
Was that what Fritz wanted? Pollard recalled that his "friend made
some good points about Harvard and then he did a selling job for
Bates." He told Pollard what a nice small school Bates was and how
beautiful the foliage was in Maine during the fall. Despite his football
training and experience and his outwardly confident demeanor, Pollard clearly felt insecure about himself and his chances of breaking
into big-time football at Harvard. As Pollard recalled, "one thing
led to another and I got on the train with the Bates team and left
for Lewiston, Maine. No thank you to William Henry Lewis. No
goodbyes. No nothing. I just up and left."[30]

Pollard's sojourn in Maine was brief and unhappy. He was
admitted to Bates as a student, but he was not allowed to play
football. Bates College regulations stipulated that a transfer student,
in this case from Harvard, had to sit out a year before becoming
eligible for intercollegiate athletics. Pollard attended classes and
cooled his heels. Before long, the beautiful fall turned into the
unrelenting Maine winter. As Pollard remembered Lewiston, "it's
eighteen million miles from home and it's cold. I nearly froze to
death that winter." He also missed his wife. One day when Pollard
was walking across campus in a light snow storm he ran into the
college president, who inquired how he was doing at Bates. Pollard
told him that he was not doing well at all and that he hated the

cold weather. After a brief conversation, the president agreed to lend him $10 to buy a train ticket back to Boston, and he left the next day. Pollard later recalled that his stay in Maine was "a brief but sad period in my life."[31]

After he arrived in Boston, Pollard was initially too ashamed to go back and see William Lewis. He did, however, because he had nowhere else to turn. That night, Lewis and some of Leslie's other friends in the Boston area, including the former Harvard football player Clarence Matthews, met with Fritz and gave him a stern lecture. They told him, according to Pollard's account, that he was becoming nothing but a tramp athlete and that if he did not straighten himself out he would be a disgrace to himself and his family. The men suggested that the best thing for him to do was to go back to school, clear up his language deficiencies, and then reapply to Brown. Leslie's friends then took up a collection to help Pollard make a new start. One of the men, a Dr. Robinson, even allowed him to sleep on the operating table in his office to save Pollard the cost of a room. The next day Lewis proposed that Fritz attend high school as a special student in Springfield, Massachusetts, where Lewis had spent some time and had many friends. Lewis contacted William C. Hill, a Brown alumnus, who was principal of Springfield Central High School. He explained Pollard's situation to Hill and suggested that if Fritz could pick up the necessary credits at the Springfield high school, then he would probably be admitted to Brown in the fall of 1915. Hill agreed to accept Pollard as a special student and admit him immediately even though the school year was already underway.[32]

Pollard quickly returned to Providence, where he was reunited with Ada. They packed hastily and said their goodbyes to friends and relatives. In early December, as British and French armies faced the German invaders in crudely constructed trenches across a span of France and Belgium that became known as the Western Front, Fritz and Ada left for Springfield. They rented a small apartment, adjusted to the new life, and awaited the birth of their first child. Frederick Douglass "Fritz" Pollard, Jr., was born in February 1915. With the added responsibility of being a father, and realizing that this might be his last opportunity to get into college and make something of himself, Pollard worked and studied as never before. Using the barber kit his father had given him some years before, he got a job at a shop near the school and supplemented his income by helping out as a coach for the school's track teams. Taking the advice of his Boston patrons, Pollard did not compete on the high school teams. In the spring, he took and passed his language examination and then waited for word from Brown. One morning in late May 1915, Pollard recalled, "I received a letter with Dean Randall's name on the envelope. My hands were shaking when I opened it. 'You have been admitted to Brown with all requirements satisfied' " was all it said. "It was," Pollard said, "the ten happiest words I'd ever read in my life."[33]

Brown, 1915

4

The year 1915 was not an encouraging one for African Americans. Woodrow Wilson, the first southern-born president since the Civil War, was in the process of implementing his executive order segregating Negro federal employees in their work places. The wartime migration of southern blacks to northern cities created competition for jobs. American marines invaded the black Republic of Haiti in order to restore internal order, killing several hundred Haitians in the process. In Cuba, Jack Johnson lost the heavyweight championship to Jess Willard as a result of a controversial knockout. The movie director D. W. Griffith released his blatantly racist film *The Birth of a Nation*, sparking black protests across the country. In Alabama, Colonel William J. Simmons revived the Ku Klux Klan, touching off numerous incidents of racial violence. Late in the year, the esteemed civil rights leader Booker T. Washington died, leaving a vacuum in the movement that would be difficult to fill.[1]

During the summer of 1915, Pollard had little time to consider these momentous and troubling events. He was well aware that Brown did not accept married students and that his father-in-law, Joseph Laing, would be unwilling to accept Ada and young Fritz in his home. Therefore, Pollard left his wife and infant son with friends in Springfield and went to Narragansett Pier to earn money for his room and tuition costs at Brown. In early July he boarded a train for the small Rhode Island town. Beginning in the late nineteenth century, Narragansett Pier had emerged as one of the most fashionable summer resorts in the nation. Rivaling, and some thought surpassing, the elegance and splendor of Newport which stood just across the bay, Narragansett Pier catered to some of the country's wealthiest citizens. It had several miles of white, sandy beaches sheltered from the chilled waters of the Atlantic Ocean, a fabulous casino, and all of the amenities a summer visitor might desire.[2]

Since the turn of the century, middle-class and elite African-American families had sent their sons to Narragansett Pier to work for the summer. Some worked on the many excursion boats that plied the waters between Providence, Newport, Block Island, and Narragansett. Others worked in restaurants, laundries, and other small establishments that served the needs of the summer residents. Beginning with the summer of 1914, Pollard had operated a small pressing and tailoring shop in the resort town which he modeled after his enterprise at Brown. Most of the young African-American summer employees attended such black colleges as Lincoln, Howard, and Hampton Institute. Pollard was an exception to the general rule in that he intended to enter a prestigious, primarily white university. Another exception was Paul Robeson, who had recently graduated from Somerville High School in New Jersey and had been accepted at Rutgers University. At six-foot-two and 210 pounds, Robeson was a prominent figure among the summer workers at Narragansett Pier, and he and Pollard became immediate friends. In their free hours, they played baseball together, and at a small club organized by the summer employees, Pollard often played the piano while Robeson sang, to the delight of the audience. Robeson later recalled that at Narragansett, "I made many friendships which last until today. From among these student workers came many of the leading Negro professionals whom I meet around the country today." The same was true for Pollard. The small coterie of student workers who toiled at Narragansett Pier each summer became a network for upwardly mobile African-American youth of that era. The contacts and connections that they made were valuable stepping stones to prominence in the black community, as they would be for Robeson and Pollard.[3]

In mid-September, Pollard returned to Providence to begin his academic and athletic career at Brown University. Founded in 1764, Brown was a mid-sized, Baptist-affiliated university with an enrollment of about a thousand undergraduates in 1915. According to Pollard's classmate Watson Smith, "Brown was not a 'great university' but a small, respectable New England college, with a tradition of fairly high but not top rank scholarship, a strong religious heritage, and mostly a middle-class student body." He recalled that "there was Chapel every week-day morning at nine o'clock where attendance was taken and absences reported to the dean. Services were non-sectarian but there was always a prayer, a hymn, and then usually a short talk, often by the president, Dr. Faunce." College regulations for freshmen were strict and a bit intimidating; the university handbook for 1915–16 indicates that freshmen could not smoke on campus, carry a cane, or wear a straw hat until Memorial Day. All freshmen had to wear a brown skullcap with a white button on all occasions within the city limits, excepting Sundays, until Decoration Day.[4]

Campus life was definitely class-structured and a bit stuffy by today's standards. Wardwell Leonard, who roomed at the same dormitory as Pollard, remembered that "students dressed in coats and ties at all times." Both Leonard and Smith emphasized that the twenty or more fraternities on campus were important and dominated student life. These fraternities had a hierarchical structure, with those catering to men from such preparatory schools as Worcester Academy and Moses Brown considered to be among the elite campus organizations. Leonard, who attended Providence's Classical High School, maintained that the social structure at Brown was not stifling, but "you felt it." He recalled that "studies at Brown were not that difficult," and that he took an extra course each semester without difficulty. Neither Leonard nor Smith remembered that athletes at Brown were accorded many special privileges. Smith maintained that the athletes were "regarded with respect but not with reverence."[5]

This was the social and academic environment which Pollard confronted. In 1915, across the nation, fewer than two thousand African Americans attended black colleges and fewer than fifty were enrolled in predominantly white institutions. Pollard was one of only two African-American students on campus. Brown, like most of the other schools that would later form the Ivy League, had admitted a small number of black students since the latter part of the nineteenth century, with the first admitted in 1877. Some, such as Brown's John Hope, who became president of Morehouse College, and Harvard's William E. B. Du Bois, a founding member of the National Association for the Advancement of Colored People, had earned academic honors, but many African-American students were admitted because of their athletic potential. As Harvard President Charles W. Eliot noted in 1907, most black students won recognition "on account of their remarkable athletic merit." He reassured southern alumni "that while Harvard would do its duty by the Negro, should his numbers swell to such a point 'as to impede the progress of the College,' limitations would be imposed." Although there were periodic disputes concerning the rights of African-American students at the future Ivy League schools, students and alumni were often less concerned about their presence on campus than they were about Jews or other minorities, because the number of blacks was always small.[6]

The first black to participate in football at Brown was Edward Stewart, who played in the mid-1890s. A few years before Pollard had arrived on campus, Herbert Ayler, an outstanding African-American lineman, died of injuries apparently received from playing football. Pollard's black classmate in 1915 was Rudolph Fisher, later a medical doctor and an important writer during the Harlem Renaissance. Pollard and Fisher became two of the most prominent members of the Class of 1919. In 1916, Jay Mayo "Ink" Williams, a five-foot-ten, 170-pound end from Monmouth, Illinois entered Brown and would go on to become one the school's outstanding football players, followed by a successful business career. Alumni who remember the Brown campus at the time maintain that there was little prejudice against the African-American students. Wardwell Leonard recalled that there was "not one single inch of trouble. Not one single bit. Ink Williams either. I don't recall, this is honest now, one single slur along the line that would show racism on the part of anybody on the campus."[7]

Some of the subtleties of racism no doubt eluded the white students. Pollard was barred from membership in the fraternities, and if he read the campus humor magazine, *The Brunonian*, he saw an occasional racist cartoon that depicted deeply entrenched racial stereotypes. Because he chose to live on campus, Pollard was virtually forced to room alone because Fisher commuted from his Providence home—and no white student was willing to reside with a black man. Campus rooms were rented on the basis of double occupancy, so Pollard owed the university $71 after the first semester, an amount that may have been absorbed by some grateful alumnus after the football season.[8]

There was no doubt that Pollard became a popular man on campus, especially after he displayed his talents on the gridiron. As Wardwell Leonard put it, Pollard "was a likeable fellow. Even if you had distaste for the Negro element, you could't help like him."[9] He had, of course, run a campus pressing shop in 1914, which had made him known to some of the undergraduates. Years later, numerous stories circulated that Pollard was the best-dressed man on campus because he "borrowed" clothes left at the pressing shop. It was said—and Pollard never denied the stories—that he used the borrowed suits to attend parties and dances in the predominantly black Fox Point section of the city.

Pollard's second chance at Brown began in disappointment. University officials barred him from football practice while they wrestled with the question of his eligibility. There was now no question about his proficiency in Spanish, but his sojourns to Dartmouth, Harvard, and Bates caused concern for Brown administrators, who were becoming more sensitive to eligibility requirements under the code of conduct set down by the newly formed National Collegiate Athletic Association. Pollard watched from the stands as Brown opened its football season with a 33–0 rout of Rhode Island State College, a school that traditionally served as cannon fodder to inaugurate the fall campaign. Two days later, Pollard was allowed to join the football team. On a warm Monday afternoon, he walked down to Marston Field House at Andrews Field to draw his equipment and begin practice. As he entered the locker room, Pollard remembered, a few players were changing into their practice uniforms. When he approached, the room gradually became very quiet. The near silence was broken by a low voice with a soft southern drawl. "Christ, a nigger." Another player said: "That's Fritz Pollard." The southerner quickly shot back: "I don't care what he calls himself, he's still nigger to me."[10]

Pollard heard, but he did not break stride. He had known various forms of racial prejudice and discrimination since he had been a boy, in the schools, on the beaches, and especially in athletics, but the words hurt. Many years later Pollard recalled that "the remark by that southern boy—his name was Butner, John Butner—stung me like a bee. Sometimes I can still hear that one voice cutting through the silence of the locker room." Pollard pointed out that "back in those days the black, at best, was accepted grudgingly at most colleges. As long as he minded his own business, which meant staying out of the white man's way, he was all right. But when the black man tried to become a joiner, when he tried to sign up for the college newspaper, the band, or an athletic team, then, in the eyes of the white students, he was passing himself off as an equal. And college men of the 1915 period, many of them men of good intentions, just were not ready to accept a black as an equal." Pollard did not expect Brown to be any different. His family had prepared him to face such situations, but still the remark stung.[11]

Pollard proceeded to the training room where Charlie Huggins, Brown's athletic trainer and swimming coach, was in charge of equipment. According to Pollard, Huggins, who made it his business to know everything about each athlete on campus, greeted him with a pleasant, "you're Pollard of Chicago, aren't you?" Pollard was pleased that his reputation had preceded him and cheerfully told Huggins to give him the best equipment he had. Huggins pushed across the counter an odd assortment of football gear that included a large pair of extensively patched canvas pants, a threadbare jersey at least two sizes too big, a pair of what the players of that day called religious socks, very holey, and a pair of tattered shoes. Sensing Pollard's disappointment, Huggins explained that "we've got more than fifty men out for the team and you're the last to report." In an obvious understatement, Pollard remarked that "some of the stuff looks a little big."[12]

Putting on his tattered and oversized uniform, Pollard remembered hurrying out to the field, where the other players had paired off and were tossing footballs back and forth. When no one lobbed a pass in his direction or invited him to join in, Pollard picked up a football and started playing catch with himself. Among those watching Pollard was Coach Edward N. Robinson, a big bear of a man who had graduated from Brown in 1896 after an illustrious football career. Alternating between fullback and end, the six-foot-two, 210-pound Robinson had scored 104 points for Brown in that rough-and-tumble era. Robbie had been a tough athlete. When his nose was broken in the 1903 Harvard game, he called for time, ran behind the stands, set his nose himself, and threw himself back into action. Because Brown had only a modest athletic budget, Robinson was a part-time professional coach who tended to his Boston law practice during the off-season. Some former players and alumni maintain that Robbie, despite his size and rough appearance, was too soft with the players and was not an outstanding coach. Robinson, however, had good credentials as an offensive coach, along with the good sense to hire competent people to help him with the defensive part of the game. When he left Brown after the 1925 season, his record was 140–82–12, and in 1955 he became one of the first coaches inducted into the National Collegiate Football Hall of Fame.[13]

Robinson blew the whistle to signal the start of practice and the squad formed a circle around him and his two assistants, William E. Sprackling, a former three-time All-America quarterback at Brown, and Arthur "Buck" Whittemore, a tough and profane line coach who was a better-than-average player at Brown around the turn of the century. Pollard positioned himself directly in front of Robinson, anxious to be seen and itching to make up for the three weeks lost due to eligibility problems. When Robbie read out the lineups for the varsity and the scrub teams, Pollard's name was not mentioned. Many years later Pollard chuckled when he recalled that first encounter with the famous Coach Robinson. "I'm afraid I was a bit naive that day. On the basis of my ability and reputation, I honestly expected to start for the varsity in that scrimmage. So when Robbie read off the varsity line-up and my name wasn't called, I was momentarily disappointed. But then I figured, shucks, I'll start for the second team, the scrubs, and I'll run those varsity players silly. Then Robbie read off the starting line-up for the scrubs—and again I wasn't mentioned." Pollard recalled being stunned and disappointed. He wondered whether Robinson knew he was even there. Fifty-five years later he related that "now I think I understand. I was a newcomer, I was black, and Robbie was just playing it cautious."[14]

One who agreed with Pollard's assessment of the situation was Irving Fraser, a varsity fullback in 1915. Fraser later recalled that "the squad had lived together, practiced together, and played together for nearly a month by the time Fritz showed up. At this point, any newcomer to this tightly knit squad would have been considered an intruder. When that new face happened to be black, well, there was even more resentment toward him. That's the way things were back in 1915." Charlie Huggins, Jr., son of the Brown trainer and substitute quarterback in 1915, remembered being equally annoyed with Pollard that first day. "He had sort of a breezy approach," Huggins recalled. "Almost cocky, like when he walked up to my dad and asked for the best equipment in the house. Oh, there was nothing really wrong with Pollard's attitude. He was well spoken. And polite. I honestly don't think that I would have been turned off at his breezy style if Pollard had been white. But he was a black man, and I guess I was surprised by his assurance as much as anything else. I didn't expect it of a man of his race."[15]

After the two squads had paired off for the start of the scrimmage, Robinson summoned Pollard and instructed him to go to the far end of the field and practice his punting by himself until he was called. Pollard took a ball and headed for the far corner of the field that served as a baseball diamond in the spring. A bit dejected, he remembered booming punts and racing after them, hoping the coach or some of the players were watching. But no one was watching him then, or for the next hour. He could hear the sound of the whistle, the thump of bodies hitting against each other, and the cheers of the substitutes strung out along the sidelines, but he did not hear what he was anticipating—a call from the coach. Pollard recalled that "the thing I most remember about that first day out for the team was the humiliation. In my mind I could run faster, block harder, and punt longer than any man on the squad. Yet, I was sent off by myself practicing a part of my game that didn't need practicing."[16]

Pollard later recalled that while he was practicing his punting an incident occurred which added insult to injury. A young boy, perhaps nine or ten, jumped the wooden fence that circled Andrews Field and stood watching him. "I must have been quite a sight," Pollard remembered, "with the patched canvas pants down almost to my ankles and the baggy jersey." After about ten minutes of just standing there, never saying a word, the boy spoke up. "Hey, mister, are you a football player?" he asked. "Sure, I'm a good football player," Pollard told him a bit defensively. "Then why aren't you over there where all the real football players are?" the youngster asked, pointing to the scrimmage that was the center of attraction at Andrews Field that day. "There I was, Fritz Pollard, maybe the best darn halfback ever to come out of Chicago and I'm dressed like a circus clown and holding a debate with some little kid about whether or not I'm a football player. I think of that incident now and I can laugh. That day, though, things didn't seem so funny."[17]

Late in the afternoon, Pollard finally got the long-awaited summons from Coach Robinson. He covered the distance from his isolated position in a sprint. "I'm ready, coach," he recalled saying, starting toward the varsity squad; but Robinson motioned toward the scrub team which had the ball at midfield. Young Charlie Huggins, the second-team quarterback that day, gave Pollard a nod and told him he was calling his signal for a run around right end. Pollard, at five-foot-eight, 165 pounds, lined up at left halfback. He took the pass from center, swept swiftly to his right, found no opening, and then cut back sharply against the defensive flow and raced through the varsity for twenty-five yards before being thrown to the ground. With a smile on his face, Pollard remembered jumping up and clapping his hands. Just then Robinson blew the whistle and ordered the men to hit the showers. He turned to Pollard and told him to retrieve the football he had been punting at the far end of the field.[18]

When Pollard reached the locker room, still a bit dejected, he could hear the other players in the showers, singing, laughing, and fooling around. Taking off his oversized uniform, Pollard headed for the shower room, but as soon as he walked in, the horseplay stopped, the singing ceased, and the players started filing out. In a few seconds, he had the shower room all to himself. Pollard's day of humiliation did not end there. An open trolley picked up the players after practice each night and took them back to the campus, about two miles away. When Pollard boarded the trolley and slipped into a seat near the front, some of the players in the surrounding seats moved back. Others jumped off, preferring to hike back to campus rather than ride with a black man. Pollard remembered that he gazed straight ahead, his face burning and his eyes moist. He was grateful for the protection the darkness brought.[19]

The conditions Pollard faced during his first day of practice at Brown were mirrored elsewhere. At about the same time in New Brunswick, New Jersey, Paul Robeson encountered an even more hostile reception from his white teammates the first time he practiced with the Rutgers team. As Robeson later recalled, the players "set about making sure I wouldn't get on their team." On the first day of scrimmage, "one boy slugged me in the face and smashed my nose, just smashed it," he said. "And then when I was down, flat on my back, another boy got me with his knee, just came over and fell on me. He managed to dislocate my right shoulder. Well, that night," Robeson remembered, "I was a very, very sorry boy. Broken nose, shoulder thrown out, and plenty of other cuts and bruises. I didn't know whether I could take any more." After ten days in bed, Robeson returned to the practice field in a fury and inflicted some pain on his white teammates before he gained their acceptance. One might assume that the experiences of Pollard and Robeson, two of the few recorded commentaries of African-Americans who tried out for predominantly white northern college teams in 1915, were fairly typical, although black players perhaps faced less humiliation and physical abuse at such colleges as Dartmouth, Northwestern, and Amherst, which had longer traditions of accepting blacks on their teams. Evidence also suggests that the relative acceptance of African American athletes at predominantly white colleges was declining as a result of increased racial tensions in the World War I era.[20]

Pollard's second day of practice was an improvement over his first. On the way out to the field, he recalled that Clair Purdy, a freshman quarterback, sidled up to him to assure Pollard that the players would eventually accept him. "Frankly, Fritz," he said, "we just never expected to see a nigger coming out for practice yesterday." Purdy confided in Pollard that he had troubles of his own. A former standout player at Dean Academy in Massachusetts, Purdy had been relegated to Brown's second and third teams. He was convinced that the reason for this was his Roman Catholic faith, which put him in a minority at the mainly Protestant school. Purdy told Pollard that "they don't want any Catholics and niggers on this team," and he assured Pollard that "if we ever get in there together, nobody's going to carry the ball but you and me." Pollard remembered being somewhat amused by the freshman quarterback's comments. During the practice session, Pollard played on the scrub team again and broke for several long gains, but most of the players continued to snub him.[21]

The day of trial for Pollard came the following afternoon on what was known as "Bloody Wednesday." Each week, Coach Robinson held a no-holds-barred scrimmage game designed to determine which men deserved positions on the first team. It was the only real opportunity that the scrubs had to demonstrate their ability and perhaps earn a position on the starting eleven. With the scrubs fighting tooth and nail to move up in the world, and with members of the first team fighting equally as hard to protect their elevated positions in life, it was hardly surprising that the day of these scrimmages was known as Bloody Wednesday. Student interest in the games was usually high, especially at the beginning of the season, because Brown, like most of the more prominent schools, padded its schedule with easy opponents at the start of the fall campaign. Almost six hundred students, three times the usual number, took the trolley or made the two-mile trek to Andrews Field. Betting among the students, not an uncommon occurrence at these scrimmages, was especially brisk, with the scrubs proving to be the sentimental favorites.[22]

Charlie Huggins, Jr., remembered that "Many students showed up that day out of curiosity. Most of them, maybe all of them, had never seen a black man playing football. Unfortunately, Fritz was a curiosity piece." According to a number of witnesses, the scrimmage turned into a personal duel between Pollard and John Butner, the Atlanta end, whose carefree, slashing style of play had earned him a starting position the previous year. Early in the game, Pollard swept wide around right end, where Butner attempted a head-high flying tackle on him. Had he not seen Butner coming, Pollard recalled, his collegiate career might have ended right then and there. But Pollard saw Butner out of the corner of his eye, stopped on a dime, and went down so low that for a moment he was balancing himself on the knuckles of his right hand as Butner flew over his head. As the teams lined up for the next play, Pollard remembered Butner yelling across the line of scrimmage, "send that black son-of-a-bitch around my end again." Scrub quarterback Tom Conroy obliged. This time Pollard gave a head fake to the outside and then cut between end and tackle, leaving Butner flat-footed and clutching air.[23]

As muffled cheering went up from the students along the sidelines, Pollard saw Butner jumping up and down and screaming, "Try me again, try me again. This time I'll kill the nigger." Caught up in the drama of the moment, Conroy again sent Pollard around his own right end. On this play, Pollard's initial fake was to the inside before a sharp cut to his left got him to the sideline and into the clear. Butner had missed his man again. Later in the year on the train ride to Pasadena for the Tournament of Roses game, Butner confided in Fritz that after that third run, he went up to Coach

Robinson and said, "Say, we better let that nigger join us." In Butner's view, that was when Pollard made the team.[24]

The details of the Bloody Wednesday confrontation between Pollard and Butner, as well as many other particulars about his years at Brown, were supplied by Pollard many years later. At the time, he was a successful businessman who had experience as a newspaper columnist and knew the importance of drama and individual confrontation in any story. His account highlighted the fact that he, a northern-born African American, had triumphed over a southern-born segregationist. Other witnesses essentially confirmed Pollard's story but did not give as much emphasis to Pollard's clash with Butner. In 1970, when Pollard gave his most detailed account of the incident, he had renewed friendships with many of his 1915 teammates; he also related the story to a white interviewer. It is probable that Pollard had confronted more general resistance to his presence on the Brown gridiron from his future teammates than he was willing to concede in 1970. Butner, who never denied his early antagonism toward Pollard as some of the former players did, may have symbolized the ingrained racism Pollard had confronted at Brown, to which he increasingly drew attention in general terms during his declining years.[25]

On Friday, his spirits boosted by a successful week at practice, Pollard reported to Marston Field House to draw his game uniform for Saturday's clash against Trinity College. Incredibly, he did not find his name on the varsity roster pinned to the bulletin board. The trainer came by and told him that there was still some question about his eligibility, and Robbie had decided to hold him out for another week or so. Pollard said nothing. He later recalled that "I walked over behind some lockers, sat down on a bench, buried my head in my hands, and cried like a baby." On the long, lonely walk back to campus, Pollard decided to pack his bags the next day and return to Chicago. "At that point," he recalled, "it was becoming clear to me that I never should have left Chicago in the first place."[26]

Later that afternoon, Coach Whittemore arrived at Pollard's dormitory room and convinced him to stick it out. Although he never said so, Pollard undoubtedly told the coach he was planning to leave school. Whittemore told Pollard that a scrub team was going to play a practice game at Worcester Academy on Monday, and that he would see to it that Pollard got a chance to display his talent. If he made good, then Whittemore would intercede with Robbie and Athletic Director Frederick W. "Doc" Marvel in an effort to restore Pollard's eligibility. Pollard did better than good against the Worcester prep school. While the Brown scrubs struggled to a 6–0 victory over Worcester, the *Brown Daily Herald* reported that "Pollard for Brown played a great game. It was almost impossible for the Worcester man with the ball to get by him, and his consistent gains were a feature of the game." The following day Pollard was practicing with the varsity and eligible to play football at Brown.[27]

The next Saturday, Brown traveled to western Massachusetts to play Amherst College. A small college with a rich football tradition, Amherst was a cut above the weaker schools Brown usually played to open its season. That early October day in Amherst would be the low point of the Brown season. As Pollard watched from the bench, the Brown team, which considerably outweighed its opponent, repeatedly lost the ball on fumbles and failed to penetrate the Amherst goal line. In the third period, Amherst scored a touchdown and took a 7–0 lead. Frustrated by the numerous fumbles and lack of consistent offense, Robinson made a number of substitutions in the third period. The *Brown Daily Herald* reported that "this did not improve the situation, however, except in the case of Pollard, who played a great game and made several spectacular runs," including a sixty-yard kickoff return. The game ended with Amherst registering a 7–0 upset over Brown.[28]

After the game, Purdy, who had played just a few minutes in the final period, was angry and upset about his limited playing time. He remained convinced that the Brown team and coaching staff were discriminating against him because of his religion. Purdy suggested to Pollard that they stay behind after the team left and spend a couple of days in the nearby city of Springfield. Pollard was all for the idea because it would provide an opportunity to visit his wife and son. During their stay in Springfield, Purdy renewed his pledge that if he and Fritz ever got into a game together "nobody's going to carry the ball but you and me." The following Wednesday they returned to Providence, received a mild reprimand from the coaching staff, and were once again relegated to the second team.[29]

That Saturday Brown faced a weak Williams College team at Andrews Field. During the early part of the first period, the Brown regulars played raggedly, failing to move the ball effectively against the smaller Williams team. Robinson had seen enough. He inserted a group of substitutes, including both Purdy and Pollard. Purdy, whom Charlie Huggins, Jr., later described as the greatest quarterback in America from the shoulders down, gave Pollard a wink and, according to Pollard, said, "Fritz, God bless you, but you better run the ball like hell. I'm going to give you a chance." Pollard recalled that every time Brown got the ball within striking distance of Williams's goal line, "Purdy would give me the ball. And he'd say 'get on my behind,' and I followed Purdy, and I scored the touchdowns during the first half." The *Brown Daily Herald* reported that Pollard "dove through the Williams line like a catapult and found little trouble in gaining whenever he tried. He scored three of the five touchdowns for Brown and made another which was not allowed" due to a penalty. Brown romped over Williams 33–0, and Pollard and Purdy had secured positions in the starting lineup.[30]

The first big game of the season was against the powerful Syracuse Orangemen, who had suffered a single loss to Princeton. More than eight thousand fans jammed Andrews Field to watch the hardfought contest. Syracuse jumped off to an early 6–0 lead before Brown threatened to win the contest after a third-period fumble recovery deep in Orangemen territory. Pollard skirted the end for two substantial gains before "Brown's hopes for victory were smothered when he fumbled and a husky Syracusian fell on the ball." Despite the fumble, the student newspaper praised Pollard's effort, saying that again and again he "brought the stands to their feet with a wonderful exhibition of speed and agility." Pollard was crestfallen, however, as the Orangemen left Providence with a 6–0 victory over the Brown Bruins. The following week Coach Robinson disclosed that he suspected that someone had betrayed his team's signals to Syracuse before the game. Robinson surmounted the incident by closing Brown's practice sessions to all spectators, "whether college men or not," for the remainder of the season.[31]

While Brown attempted to regroup after its disappointing loss to Syracuse, Pollard faced something of a crisis of his own which might have affected his future on the Brown team. It centered around Wallace Wade, Brown's starting left guard and future college coaching great at Vanderbilt, Alabama, and Duke. More specifically, it involved Wade's father, who had traveled to Providence from Tennessee and threatened to take his son out of school if Pollard was allowed to remain on the Brown team. Pollard later recalled that he did not "know exactly what must have happened because Wally never opened his mouth, never talked very much." The dispute was somehow resolved because both Pollard and Wade remained on the squad and in later years became "the best of friends." Apparently, either young Wade refused to honor his father's threat or Coach Robinson convinced the elder Wade to withdraw it. Robinson never contacted Pollard about the matter. With the crises of late October behind it, Brown proceeded to thrash a weak Vermont team by a score of 46–0. The *Brown Daily Herald* noted that "Pollard was again the star of the Brown team." Trouncing the Green Mountain Men was one thing, but now Pollard and the Brown eleven had to face, on successive weekends away from home, two teams that most people believed represented the top football schools in the nation, Yale and Harvard.[32]

On the morning of November 6, 1915, a confident Brown team boarded a train in Providence for the ninety-mile trip to New Haven for the Yale game. The Brown campus and alumni maintained considerable interest in the contest because the Providence eleven had a reasonable chance to defeat the Mighty Blue of Yale. Three hundred and fifty Brown students took a later train to New Haven in order to witness the contest in the newly constructed Yale Bowl. The optimism of the Brown team and its supporters was based in part upon the poor performance of the Yale team in 1915. Racked by injuries and the loss of several top players due to academic ineligibility, Yale was struggling with a record of three wins and three losses. The school was still considered among the elite in college football, however. Since the beginning of intercollegiate play in the 1870s, Yale and Harvard, and to a lesser degree Princeton and the University of Pennsylvania, had been regarded as the dominant forces in the game.[33]

Brown's position in college football was that of a distinctly second-rate power, dominating weaker foes but unable to compete with the elite teams. Overall, Brown had a combined record of only four victories in sixty games against the Big Four teams, with one victory over Yale and none against Harvard since Brown began intercollegiate play in 1878. The 1915 Bruin team showed considerable promise but was also struggling with a record of three wins, two losses, and a tie as it entered the Yale contest. Brown supporters were encouraged by the emergence of a potent running attack in recent games, an attack anchored around the left halfback, Fritz Pollard.[34]

On the day of the game in New Haven, a small group of African-American Yale students went to the gym on Elm Street, where the Brown team was dressing, to catch a glimpse of Pollard. Among them was William M. Ashby, a student in the School of Religion, who had read articles in the New York *Tribune* about the Brown team and a "burly Negro" halfback named Pollard. Ashby recalled that he and his colleagues expected to see a fellow about six-foot-two and weighing 210 pounds. When they saw Pollard, they were afraid that the large Yale line "would murder this little man." The group proceeded to the Yale Bowl and decided to sit on the Brown side to give Pollard as much support as possible and to avoid the racial animosity from the Yale stands, where they knew they would "be baited with the foulest and vilest epithets."[35]

Before the game, Pollard was instructed to enter the field by a separate gate in order to avoid an ugly incident or possible injury at the hands of some unruly Yale fans. As Pollard recalled, "I ran out on the field through another gate and they didn't know what had happened. The team ran out there first and I ran out after them just before the game started. The whistle blew 10 or 15 seconds after I got there." When the game began, Yale received the kickoff and mounted an impressive drive deep into Brown territory, which was halted on downs at the Brown six-yard line. It turned out to be the high point of the Yale offensive attack for the afternoon.[36]

For William Ashby, the greatest thrill of the day was watching Pollard return Yale punts in explosive bursts for gains of ten and twenty yards. According to the Yale student, Pollard mastered the art of returning kicks to a degree "seldom ever equalled and never surpassed by any other halfback." He played deep and, like a center fielder catching a short fly, received the ball on the dead run as he burst by would-be Yale tacklers. Each time Pollard returned a punt, Ashby recalled, the Yale stands arose and screamed, "Catch that nigger. Kill that nigger." Safe in the Brown stands, Ashby could not contain himself as he jumped up and hollered "Run, nigger, run. Go, Fritz, go." On one of Pollard's runbacks, two frustrated Yale players, Jim Sheldon and Bob Bingham, attempted to maim the Brown halfback in a pincer created by their simultaneous flying tackles near the Yale sideline. As Ashby recalled, Pollard accelerated, eluded the pincers, and as he approached the sideline "jumped off the field and landed straight up on the Yale bench." Meanwhile, the two Yale players collided and moments later were carried off the field.[37]

During the course of the afternoon, Pollard provided most of the Brown offense, breaking for several long runs from scrimmage in addition to his spectacular punt returns. He also lofted several long punts which kept Yale deep in its own territory. The game was decided in the third period when Brown captain Harold "Buzz" Andrews booted a field goal from the twenty-two-yard line to give Brown a 3–0 lead, which it maintained to the end. The African-American New York *Age* boasted that "Pollard gained more ground than any other Brown player. His end run of thirty yards featured the third period, while his catching of punts and his cleaver fast runs back held Brown safe after its lead of three points had been secured." Brown had defeated mighty Yale for only the second time in their twenty-three meetings since 1880, and Pollard had emerged as a budding star in college football.[38]

After the game, Jim Sheldon, who was from Atlanta, burst into the Brown locker room and demanded to see the Bruin halfback. As Pollard emerged from the dressing cage, according to Ashby, the large Yale lineman approached Fritz, thrust out his hand, and said, "You're a nigger, but you're the best goddamn football player I ever saw." For the 350 Brown students and numerous alumni who had accompanied the team to New Haven, the day was one of joyous triumph. When the Brown eleven returned to Providence, they were greeted by a large crowd of Brown partisans, some of whom had heard accounts of the game relayed by telegraph and broadcast by megaphone to the fans outside the Providence *Journal* Building. That night, ecstatic students marched in triumph through the newly constructed trolley tunnel that connected downtown Providence with the Brown campus on the heights above. By the next week, Pollard had become a national sports figure in the black press and to a lesser degree in the white dailies.[39]

Harvard, like Yale, did not deign to play Brown in Providence. All twenty-one football games between the two schools had been played at Harvard, with the most recent matches contested at venerable Harvard Stadium, which seated more than twenty-five-thousand fans. As far as football was concerned, Harvard did not take Brown seriously, and with good reason; the Crimson had defeated the Bruins twenty straight times, with the exception of one scoreless tie in 1914. For the past several years under Coach Percy Haughton, Harvard had sent nearly half of its starting varsity lineup to the Yale-Princeton game on the day of the Brown contest to scout the New Haven team in anticipation of the all-important Yale-Harvard game a week later. In 1915, Haughton, the fullback Eddie Mahan, a three-time Walter Camp All-America at the end of the season, and several other Harvard regulars were in Princeton on the day of the Brown game. Despite the absence of the varsity starters, Harvard still fielded a formidable team. Of the twenty-four players listed on the pre-game roster, Harvard had twenty-one men from prominent New England preparatory schools; about half had played football at Exeter, Andover, or Groton, which virtually served as farm teams for Harvard in that era. Brown, by contrast, fielded a team divided between prep school men and high school graduates, who usually had less experience. Nevertheless, the Brown players were optimistic as they boarded a train for Boston on the morning of November 13.[40]

With both teams playing old-fashioned, straight-ahead football, Brown controlled the ball for most of the day. Bruin backs gained a total of 208 yards on line rushes to only 97 for Harvard. Only nine forward passes were thrown, with Brown completing two and Harvard one. But when the final whistle blew, Harvard had recorded a 16–7 victory over Brown, primarily because of three critical lost fumbles. After Harvard took an early 3–0 lead, Pollard fumbled the ball late in the first period on his own eight-yard line, where it was recovered by a Harvard lineman. A short time later Harvard increased its advantage to 9–0. The period ended on Pollard's thrilling thirty-yard run to the Harvard seven-yard line.[41]

After Harvard held Brown on downs near the Crimson goal line, Harvard punted out of danger. Brown gained control of the ball and was driving smartly toward the Harvard goal line in the second period when disaster struck again. Clair Purdy was tackled at the Crimson forty-yard line after an eight-yard gain when he fumbled the ball. A Harvard back retrieved it and ran it back fifty-five yards for Harvard's second touchdown and a 16–0 lead. The *Brown Daily Herald* reported that "even Pollard was unable to stop the fleet fullback." At the beginning of the fourth period, Brown threatened to score as Purdy, Pollard, and Buzz Andrews moved the ball to the Harvard one-yard line on a succession of short runs. Then Pollard smashed into the line, hit a stone wall, and fumbled, with Harvard recovering once again. Later in the period Brown scored on a forward pass to narrow the margin to 16–7, where it stood at the end of the game.[42]

Although Pollard was the game's leading ground-gainer with feature runs of thirty and twenty-two yards, the Harvard contest was a bitter disappointment for him and Purdy, who between them accounted for the three crucial fumbles. In later years, Pollard never discussed the game much. More than a decade later, Frank A. Young, a prominent African-American sportswriter and then a close friend of Pollard's, wrote a column in the Chicago *Defender* that touched on the 1915 Harvard-Brown game and the larger problems black athletes faced when they competed against whites. Whether Young's information was from Pollard or from other sources, he felt that too many well-meaning blacks tell young athletes that "the race is at stake today and whatever you do has a direct bearing on the race" in games against white teams. According to Young, such advice "works havoc with the athlete." He cited the case of the 1915 Harvard game, when "those 'yours for the race folks' in and around New York and Providence had got to Pollard with that same old gag. They had the young man thinking," Young asserted, "that 17,000,000 of our folks in this country would die if Fritz made a mistake." Young then gave an exaggerated account of the game in which he had Pollard fumbling four times at the Harvard goal line.[43]

Brown's final game was a Thanksgiving Day contest against the famous Carlisle Indian School, which until 1915 had been guided by the innovative collegiate coach Glenn S. "Pop" Warner. Carlisle was an unusual "college" because it barely offered its graduates the equivalent of a high school education. The Indians played most of their games on the road, and many of the players were in their mid-twenties before they completed their period of extended "college" eligibility. Under Coach Warner, Carlisle had played a rigorous sched-ule that sometimes included as many as fifteen games in one season. The Indians had fielded good teams—especially during the era of Jim Thorpe—were entertaining, and the fans loved to watch them play.[44]

By 1915, however, Carlisle, coached by Victor Kelly, was on the decline as a football power due in part to a federal investigation stemming from charges of professionalism levied against Thorpe after the 1912 Olympic games. It would be Carlisle's last game in Providence, and the Pennsylvania school would close in 1918. Nevertheless, the largest crowd ever to watch a game at Andrews Field turned out on a wet and raw Thanksgiving Day in 1915 to see the Indians. Featuring a lineup that included such colorful names as Downwind and Lookaround, Carlisle was clearly outmatched by the Bruin eleven that day. Even their star halfback Pete Calac, whom Pollard would later encounter many times in the professional game, had a difficult time on the wet turf. Reminding some fans of a miniature version of Thorpe, who played in Providence in 1912, Pollard simply ran wild that Thanksgiving morning. The *Brown Daily Herald* stated that "Pollard, his fumbling fault conspicuously absent, realized the expectations of his many admirers, making any number of beautiful broken field runs, which brought the stands to their feet again and again." In all, Pollard scored three touchdowns in Brown's 39–3 thrashing of the Carlisle Indians. He could look back with some satisfaction on a football season that included many ups and downs but ended with such a spectacular performance.[45]

The Tournament of Roses

5

Brown's victory over Carlisle was the final game of the regular 1915 season, but Bruin players were already aware that they would play a postseason game in California over the Christmas recess. Two weeks before Thanksgiving, L. H. Turner, president of the board of directors of the Pasadena Tournament of Roses Committee, had visited Providence and invited Brown to play a football game on New Year's Day in Pasadena. The Brown athletic director, Frederick W. "Doc" Marvel, recalled that the invitation was "something of a bolt from the blue." As well it should have been—Brown's season record at the time stood at four wins, two losses, and a tie. After due consideration by the athletic staff and university administration, President William Faunce agreed to accept the offer. The proposal was put to the players, who voted for it overwhelmingly; only Wally Wade registered a negative vote. Wade, who was working his way through Brown with a job as a college representative for a local laundry, had another job for the Christmas recess to help him meet second-semester expenses. Upon hearing of his financial problems, the Providence *Journal* hired him to write a column on the team's venture in the West, and Wade agreed to make the trip. It would be the first of several Tournament of Roses trips for Wade, who later coached Alabama and Duke to Rose Bowl victories.[1]

On November 17, more than a week before the Carlisle game, the *Brown Daily Herald* reported that Faunce had agreed to the trip, and that Brown would oppose the University of Washington. In an apparent effort to underscore the solid academic tradition at Brown, the reporter mentioned twice that because of the Christmas recess the players would lose only two days from their "college duties," and added that it "will be of great educational value to the men who are fortunate enough to be included on the team." Years later Pollard did not remember where he was at the time he heard the news, but he did recall his reaction. "Oh, just like a kid," he said, "my head got big and I was the happiest guy in the world."[2]

Brown's invitation to play a postseason game in Pasadena came about as a matter of luck and happenstance. The Tournament of Roses celebration was the outgrowth of the Valley Hunt Club of Pasadena's tradition of riding to the hounds on New Year's Day. It became a custom for members to write their friends in the frozen East, advising them of the balmy climate in Pasadena as evidenced by the early January fox hunt. Around 1890, Charles Holder, a zoologist at Throop College of Technology, now California Institute of Technology, suggested that the townspeople bring roses and other flowers to display as a way of celebrating the ripening of the California fruit crop. Soon a parade was organized, with carts, saddle horses, and bicycles adorned with roses as the main attraction. In the afternoon, a sports program was held that included races of various kinds and an old Spanish game called "tourney at the rings" in which horsemen riding at full speed attempted to spear with wooden lances wreaths of roses hung from posts.[3]

In 1901, the Tournament of Roses Association, having taken over direction of the winter event which had become a major Southern California tourist attraction, organized an East-West football game as part of the afternoon festivities. On the afternoon of January 1, 1902, Fielding Yost's first point-a-minute University of Michigan team took the field to oppose the West Coast's Stanford University Indians. More than a thousand paying spectators viewed the game at Tournament Park. The event was a financial success but an embarrassment for Pacific Coast football. The powerful Wolverine team thrashed Stanford by a score of 49–0 in a game terminated before the final whistle because the Indians were unable to continue due to injuries. After the 1902 debacle, tournament officials discontinued the East-West football contest in favor of a variety of sporting events including chariot races, which proved popular until spectator interest began to wane around 1912.[4]

In the meantime, most West Coast colleges had abandoned

eastern-style football after the 1905 football crisis and had adopted a rugby-type game. When that game did not generate much spectator interest, many far-western schools, particularly those in the Pacific Northwest, reverted to the eastern brand of football by 1913. At a dinner sponsored by the Pasadena Chamber of Commerce in the fall of 1915, Ralph Glaze, a former Dartmouth College football captain and then coach at the University of Southern California, suggested that the Tournament of Roses Association renew the East-West football contest as part of its festival. When advised of the suggestion, the committee was receptive to the idea. Brown alumnus A. Manton Chace, who was present at the dinner, proceeded to propagandize the selection committee on the merits of Brown University and its football tradition. Chace later recalled that he was somewhat dismayed at first because "this august body had never heard of Brown University." He was soon aided by fellow alumnus Ralph Elrod, who joined in the campaign to promote Brown. Syracuse was the committee's first choice of an eastern team, but the New York school rejected the invitation primarily because it had already scheduled a three-game western swing toward the end of the season. Given the fact that Cornell, Michigan, Notre Dame, and Pittsburgh were all enjoying undefeated seasons, Chace and Elrod must have been extremely persuasive, because in mid-November the committee authorized an invitation to Brown.[5]

After the Carlisle game, Coach Edwin N. Robinson began practice immediately in preparation for the big game, which would be against Washington State instead of the University of Washington as first reported. Because of the frigid late-fall weather in Providence, practice had to be held indoors, with only an occasional workout at Andrews Field or Lincoln Field on the main campus. The only available indoor facility was in downtown Providence at the Armory of Mounted Commands—a site that presented problems of a different kind. As the quarterback Charlie Huggins, Jr., recalled, the team practiced "in the dirt where the horses were. In the horse manure to be perfectly frank. We ran and dove in that thing and we tackled and everything and you got it in your mouth and your ears and eyes and everything else." The team practiced hard, but more than a few players were overconfident, believing that their brand of eastern football was vastly superior to that played on the

West Coast. Washington State had a record of 6–0, racking up a total of 145 points to its opponent's twelve, but the Cougars had not played any big-name teams.[6]

The idea of an eastern team traveling three thousand miles to play one football game in California attracted widespread attention in 1915. The New York *Times* gave full coverage to the preparations for the trip (including the use of a special steel Pullman car) and the journey itself. As the Great War in Europe continued into a second winter and President Wilson struggled to maintain American neutrality, coverage of Brown's transcontinental football journey must have provided a pleasant diversion for many Americans. Athletic Director Marvel recalled that "we were immediately deluged with time-tables and propaganda from all of the railroad companies . . . as well as from most of the hotels and scenic areas between here and there, and there was so much fan-fare that it was difficult to get down to the serious consideration that the trip invitation entailed." Brown officials prepared for the trip as though it were a trek through a vast wilderness, as indeed some thought it was. Extra insurance was taken out for each member of the party, and enough bottled Rhode Island water was taken aboard to last the entire trip. Finally, on December 22, hundreds of students, excused from their 9:20 A.M. recitations, snake-danced down to Providence's Union Station to give the party of twenty-six, twenty-one of them players, a rousing send-off. Amid the songs and cheers, team captain Buzz Andrews gave a short speech in which he promised to bring home "a good long slice of Washington bacon."[7]

For Pollard, the trip to California was a double adventure. He would be traveling in close quarters with most of the players who had initially resented his presence on the team, and on a Pullman car at that. Pollard recalled, with some exaggeration, that "in those days the black man didn't ride in Pullman cars. It simply wasn't done." During the trip, he would have numerous confrontations with the black sleeping-car porters, who were among the elite in the African-American working class of the day. There were also a number of incidents along the way in which dining-car waiters refused to serve Pollard. He later recalled that he would either tell the waiter "to go to hell" and wait for his teammates to come to his rescue, or his teammates would rise up as a group and demand that Fritz be served. Sometimes he was served and sometimes he was not. But in general the players traveled in a relaxed atmosphere, and as Pollard later admitted, most of the earlier tension with his teammates had vanished. After the Brown Pullman was attached to the rear of a Chicago express at Worcester, Massachusetts, and headed west, "the players had the porter turn up the heat and nearly everyone stripped down to BVDs," which became their traveling costume most of the way. To occupy time, the players broke out packs of cards and played interminable games of red dog. As far as Rhode Island newspaper readers who followed the progress of the trip knew, however, the Brown men behaved like gentlemen—and studious ones at that. "Both morning and afternoon," Wally Wade reported in his column for the Providence *Journal*, "the boys spent considerable time plugging away on their books, not one member of the squad having forgotten he is a student first and a football player second."[8]

As the train made its way west, Coach Robinson and Doc Marvel were informed that Jimmy Prosser, a substitute halfback who had been included on the trip primarily because he was one of the heavier backs on the team, had some years earlier tried out with the Detroit Tigers baseball team and thus might be considered a "professional." With the recent flap over Jim Thorpe's alleged professionalism fresh in their minds, Robinson and Marvel took no chances and had Prosser left off at his hometown of Cleveland before proceeding to Chicago. While Pollard never mentioned the incident in later years, he no doubt felt a little anxious because he had not only played football for pay in Chicago, but apparently had fought in several professional boxing matches before making his way to Brown. He later told Jay Barry, referring to a boxing match which Pollard fought in Coaldale, Pennsylvania, in 1923 while playing football in the Coal Region, that he could not tell everything he had done in athletics before going to Brown because "they" might take away his medals too. The reference was to Thorpe, who was stripped of his Olympic medals after the 1912 games for having played professional baseball.[9]

In Chicago, Doc Marvel had made arrangements for the Brown team to hold a workout at the Northwestern University field house. Pollard was delighted to be in Evanston and so close to his family and boyhood friends again. He recalled that "this made me feel good because I attended Lane Tech High School in Chicago, and had run in several indoor track meets at this famous gym." At the field house, the Brown team was disappointed to learn that its equipment trunks had not arrived with the train. Northwestern officials generously opened their equipment room to the Brown players, who trotted onto the field wearing uniforms of various colors, red, blue, pink, orange, and green. "Fritz Pollard," according to Marvel, "had gone most of the group one better and had an outfit that had every color in the rainbow. He won the prize that afternoon." It is possible that Pollard's choice of this bizarre attire was his way of trying to fit in by playing the clown, a role that whites of the era commonly assigned to African Americans. In the evening, when Brown's Chicago alumni held a dinner for the team at the University Club with Elmer Stevens, who had been instrumental in recruiting Pollard for Brown, in charge of arrangements, Pollard declined to attend the function. He spent the evening in Rogers Park, where his family and friends held a banquet in his honor. Faced with a conflict of interest and loyalty, Pollard chose to be with his family and members Chicago's African-American community.[10]

Early the following day the Brown Pullman was switched to the Santa Fe line, and the team headed for Albuquerque. At a watering stop in Empire, Kansas, correspondent Wade reported that the squad engaged in an impromptu snowball fight on the station platform and that many spectators were caught in the crossfire. They took it good-naturedly, Wade wrote, because they knew "the rah-rahs from Brown" were on the train. With the exception of seeing two Sioux Indians, the rest of the journey to New Mexico was uneventful. Arriving in Albuquerque on Christmas morning, the team held a workout at the University of New Mexico field, a workout that had to be curtailed because the players were affected by altitude sickness. At the end of the practice session, however, the exuberant Pollard suggested to Purdy that they jog over to the base of a nearby mountain, a distance Fritz estimated to be a half mile. Coach Sprackling vetoed the idea, pointing out that the thin air was deceiving and the distance was probably more like fifteen miles. That evening the squad was treated to a New England Christmas dinner at a local country club and exchanged presents they had bought in Chicago. Early the following morning they embarked on the final leg of the journey to Pasadena and the Tournament of Roses.[11]

Southern California appeared to be all that it had been touted when Brown's train arrived in Los Angeles at 5 A.M. on December 27. The air was warm, and the sun was already shining brightly as the team headed for its accommodations at the Hotel Raymond in Pasadena. The proprietor, Walter Raymond, an 1873 Harvard graduate, went all-out to welcome his eastern guests. Decked out in a Harvard football uniform complete with headgear, which he had ordered specially from Harvard, Raymond was on the steps of his hotel to greet the Brown team. The trees surrounding the establishment were decorated with miniature footballs marked with the letter *B*, and brown and white streamers were everywhere. All were welcome except for Pollard. When Fritz attempted to register at the desk, a clerk informed him that he could not be accommodated. The players put up a fuss, and then Coach Sprackling intervened and told Pollard "don't say anything," everything would be taken care of. After that, Pollard recalled that he really "didn't know what happened," however a short time later he had a single room overlooking a sunny Pasadena boulevard.[12]

After breakfast the skies clouded over, it began to rain, and according to Doc Marvel, "we never saw the sun again while we were in California." The following day it turned cold, and Marvel recalled that the supposedly hearty New Englanders "almost froze to death" in their poorly insulated hotel rooms. It even snowed one day in the nearby mountains, and a car coming down from the hills with its back seat filled with snow was a curiosity on the Pasadena streets. Undeterred by the weather, the Brown squad began practice sessions appropriately enough at the Horace Mann School, named after the famed educator who was an 1819 Brown graduate. In general, they enjoyed themselves despite the unusual Southern California rain and cold. Photographs of the team visiting a Southern California tourist attraction show the diminutive Pollard, who had a reputation as a fancy dresser, attired in a three-piece suit and what appears to be an expensive overcoat. Pollard recalled that the Brown party was "entertained very lavishly and were taken to outstanding places in Pasadena, and also to all the movie studios and met several of the outstanding movie stars of that era." He also remembered that the hotel had a side elevator which "the fellows used to go out, stay over their time and sneak . . . up to their rooms so that the coaches waiting on the main floor to catch them, didn't know they were out." Apparently the team did not take the Washington State Cougars as seriously as it might have.[13]

The Washington State team had arrived in Southern California more than a week earlier. The Cougars were coached by William H. "Lone Star" Dietz, a Sioux who was one of the most colorful and able coaches in the early history of the game. While in his mid-twenties, Dietz had played tackle on the famous Carlisle Indian teams of 1909–11, which featured Thorpe as running back in the latter year. From 1912 to 1914, Dietz was assistant coach under Pop Warner at Carlisle and taught design at the School of Applied Art in Philadelphia in the off-season. An intelligent, multitalented young man who was a bit of a dandy, Dietz had "a flair for the stage, movies, art, fancy clothes, thoroughbred dogs, Indian lore, music, and writing, as well as football." He caused a sensation on the Pullman, Washington, campus in 1915 when he appeared at his first practice session "wearing a silk hat, Prince Albert cutaway, yellow gloves, and spats and jauntily swinging a Malacca cane." He was a keen student of the game as a result of his tutelage under Warner, however, and quickly taught the Carlisle system to the tough pioneer boys at the Washington school. After winning only two games in 1914, the Cougars, in Dietz's first season, had gone undefeated in six games during 1915.[14]

During its stay in the Los Angeles area, Washington State held its practice sessions on the movie set of the film *Tom Brown of Harvard*. The players worked as extras in the low-budget film with a football theme, and Coach Dietz had a principal role. Dick Hanley, a star halfback on the 1915 team, recalled that "for two weeks before the game we were busy all day filming the football scenes. We thus combined our movie work with training for the game." He added that the players made about $100 apiece for their movie work and "bet it all on ourselves to beat Brown." Meanwhile, the Brown players continued to enjoy guided tours of the major Southern California tourist attractions. Two days before the game, they visited an ostrich farm, where the players gorged themselves on unripened oranges; by kickoff time, many had diarrhea.[15]

Most sportswriters, in deference to the alleged superiority of eastern football, made Brown a heavy favorite in the contest. Coach Dietz, "who regard optimism as the arch enemy of good football," feigned agreement when he told the press that "Brown will simply wipe the dirt with us." Damon Runyon, who was covering the game for the Universal News Service, was one of the few reporters who disagreed. "I don't agree that Brown will win," he wrote. "Washington State is faster and acts like it wants to play football and is not here just for the trip. I think they mean business and are going to win."[16]

The Brown team's holiday attitude and its haphazard preparation for the game were not unusual for the eastern entrant in the early years of the Rose Bowl. Lou Little, an outstanding coach at Columbia and tackle for the University of Pennsylvania in the 1917 Tournament of Roses game which Penn lost to Oregon, recalled that in 1917 "the Rose Bowl game was in its infancy. Too much emphasis was not placed on the importance of the contest. As a player, I can say that Penn didn't view the game with great seriousness. We enjoyed the trip, had a wonderful time attending social activities and the result was we were not mentally and physically ready for a hard game of football." The western representative, however, took the game very seriously. The Oregon fullback Hollis Huntington, who also played in the 1917 contest, remembered that the East-West clash was "the most important of our lives. Remember, the West Coast was not recognized in football at that time." As the Brown players assembled to watch the Tournament of Roses parade on the cold and wet New Year's morning in 1916, they were a relaxed and overconfident group.[17]

According to the Pasadena *Evening News*, the parade, which began at 10:30 A.M. in a light drizzle (the first rainy New Year's Day in Pasadena in more than twenty-five years), was a huge success. Floats decked with thousands of roses made their way through the Pasadena streets and delighted spectators. The newspaper reported that "the rain only served to freshen the flowers which blossomed as though in a natural garden. Not daunted by the weather, dainty girls were clad in chiffons and satins, while from the beaches were girls in bathing costume." Doc Marvel received the dubious honor of judging the floats. He was later told that he was selected as judge because in the past there had been an unusual amount of bitterness on the part of those who did not win. Because he and the Brown party were leaving town early the next morning, it was one way "to avoid any extended bantering here." Then and there Marvel made up his mind "that it might be just as well if I never did return to Pasadena again." As kickoff time approached, the drizzle turned into a downpour that soaked the Tournament Park field. Pollard later recalled that the bathing beauties, who appeared at the park in their "black bloomers, stockings and swimming tops . . . were the only ones dressed for the weather."[18]

Only about four thousand spectators, huddled under umbrellas, were present when the opening whistle blew, but the number increased steadily as word circulated that an exciting football game was underway. Various estimates of the total crowd range between seven and fifteen thousand, with the former figure likely being closer to the actual attendance. Pollard recalled that ticket prices ranged from 50 cents to more than $4 for the best seats. In all, the tournament committee lost around $11,000, primarily because of the $5,000 guarantee it tendered to both schools. Within minutes of the opening kickoff, the players' uniforms were caked with mud, as was Lone Star Dietz's splendid white satin suit and top hat. Brown guard Edgar "Spike" Staff recalled that within three minutes Dietz "looked like a mud statue." By the end of the first quarter, the field had been churned into a quagmire, with large puddles of water forming on the low spots of the uneven turf. Few noticed or cared at the time that when Pollard took his position at left halfback, he became the first African-American athlete to play in what soon would be known as the Rose Bowl game.[19]

Despite the miserable conditions, Brown got off to a quick start and dominated play during most of the first half. Following an exchange of punts after the opening kickoff, Purdy intercepted one of the Cougar's few passes of the afternoon on his own thirty-eight-yard line and returned it across midfield. Pollard then dashed for fifteen yards around right end in one of his few long runs of the game. Using straight-ahead plays out of its double-wing formation, Brown advanced the ball to the Washington State four-yard line before being stopped on downs by the big Cougar line. In the second period, Brown initiated another scoring drive through a "line-smashing campaign" directed by quarterback Purdy. Aided by a Cougar pass interference penalty, the Bruins advanced to the Washington State twenty-one-yard line with a first and ten. Line bucks by Pollard and Andrews and a seven-yard pass from Purdy to Andrews gave Brown a first down at the Cougar ten-yard line. Brown's hopes were dashed, however, when Washington State intercepted a Purdy pass at the ten-yard line and punted out of danger as the first half ended in a scoreless tie.[20]

During the first half, the Brown ends Josh Weeks and John Butner sustained injuries, leaving six-foot-two, 230-pound tackle Mark Farnum as the apparent bulwark in the Bruin line. Stories circulated for years among Brown alumni that a Bruin fan, hoping to help the team, went to Coach Dietz at the half and indicated that Farnum was the weak link in the Bruin defense. Whether or not the account is true, Dietz directed his second-half offensive attack against Farnum and the right side of the Brown defense with devastating results. Washington State racked up 202 yards rushing in the second half against only seventeen for Brown. The Cougars literally pushed the Bruins all over the field as they took a 14–0 lead into the final minutes of the game. After the game, the large but immobile Farnum was so battered by the Washington State assault that Charlie Huggins had to cut off his bloody, mud-caked canvas uniform with a pair of scissors.[21]

By the third period the usually fleet and agile Pollard had been neutralized by the mud-soaked playing field and a stiffening Cougar defense. While praising the Washington State defense, Pollard later explained that "we'd all left our rain cleats back in Providence. Who'd need them in sunny California we'd figured. The shorter dry-weather cleats allowed me to move faster and got me going sooner, but Lord, they'd be an anchor in the mud." Five minutes into the third period, Pollard was tackled face down in the middle of what Coach Sprackling described as a four-inch-deep mud puddle, with Cougar players falling on top of him. "And were those Washington guys slow getting up," Sprackling remembered. "Honestly, with Fritz bound to be out of breath and panting, I thought he would drown."[22]

After the referee untangled the players, Pollard was taken out of the game and returned to the bench, choking and gasping. Throughout the third period, he repeatedly jumped off the bench and implored Coach Robinson to put him back in the game. Robbie refused, explaining that Pollard could not improve much on what substitute Irving Fraser was doing unless Pollard had rain cleats. Years later Pollard recounted that he met Walt Disney while playing professional football in California. Disney was at the game, "and the sight of me jumping up and down from the bench had never left his mind. Years later he used the scene in a Mickey Mouse cartoon. It's the one in which Mickey's team plays these big lions, and Mickey keeps popping up from the bench and says, 'Put me in, please, Coach, put me in.' "[23]

Late in the fourth period after Washington State scored its second touchdown, a sympathetic locker-room attendant brought Pollard a pair of rain cleats. Pollard remembered that "they were way too big, but I strapped them on any which way. I knew we couldn't change the outcome, but I wanted to show them what might have happened if things had been different." On the last play of the game, Pollard got loose for a nine-yard run to the Cougar thirty-six yard line as the final whistle signaled a 14–0 Washington State victory. Pollard had gained only forty-seven yards rushing for the day, the lowest total of his collegiate career. Like the rest of the Bruin players, Pollard was disappointed but recalled that "the crowd loved the action and the publicity we generated convinced the promoters there was money to be made in an annual East-West game."[24]

Over the years, members of the Brown eleven, including Pollard, were generally gracious about their defeat, giving ample praise to Washington State's superior effort. Most believed, however, that Brown would have won the game had the field been dry. Pollard later claimed that "had it not rained, our open brand of football would have enabled us to have won this game, and as it was, we played a beautiful defensive game." On another occasion he remarked, "Now believe me, this is no excuse — but I had no idea California could have such weather. I left my shoes with cleats at college in Providence. I couldn't accelerate. Washington State outweighed us 13 pounds to a man. Their line was very rough." A few of the Brown players believed that the superior play of the heavier Washington State team was in part attributable to the lack of eligibility requirements in the Pacific Northwest. Charlie Huggins, Jr., maintained that at that time some of the Washington State team attended college only during the football season and played for five to eight years. According to Huggins, who did not make the trip, some Brown players told him that they were opposing Washington State players who were old enough to be their fathers. Be that as it may, the triumphant Cougar team returned to Pullman, where they were greeted by the mayor and a group of businessmen decked out in full Sioux regalia and riding ponies. They greeted Coach Dietz with the yell, " 'Lonestar, Lonestar, Yip Yip Yu; How we love you, Oh You Sioux!' Two of the business men led 'Brown's goat,' suitably labeled."[25]

After a postgame party attended by both teams, the Brown contingent boarded a train early the next day for San Francisco and a one-night diversion before making the long journey east. The players filled the two five-gallon bottles, which had earlier contained Rhode Island drinking water, with California wine and settled in for the first leg of the transcontinental trip. The team suffered a final indignity when it was discovered that some California well-wisher had sent along a crate of partially ripened oranges for the players, many of whom who still suffered from diarrhea. Back in the East, the New York *Times* gave the game limited coverage, burying the story on a back page along with the weather report and the shipping news. The *Times* maintained that the weather and luck were mainly responsible for the Washington State victory, and that the game was not "a true test of football skill." In San Francisco, Pollard was once again barred from the team hotel, and this time the protests of the players and coaches were to no avail. Substitute backs Irving Fraser and Jimmy Murphy escorted Pollard to a black section of the city, where Fritz managed to get a room. He rejoined the group early the next morning, visibly shaken. He had seen several knife fights, he reported, and had put a bureau up against his door in order to get a few hours' sleep.[26]

The trip eastward which began the following day was largely uneventful, at least for a group of college men, and the Brown players did not seem overly depressed by their defeat. Because the players had grumbled about the food on the way out, Doc Marvel gave each player $21 (for twenty-one meals) and the privilege of arranging their own meals rather than eat in the train dining car as they had done en route to California. Most of the men foraged from the free lunch counters at saloons along the way, and reportedly Jimmy Murphy got home with $17 left over from his food money. Wally Wade almost missed the train at a stop somewhere on the prairie when he attempted to show his northern teammates how to catch a rabbit. Spike Staff actually did miss the train at one station, but beat the team back when railroad authorities permitted him to ride a fast mail train into Providence. On January 8, the team train arrived at Union Station, where a fair-sized crowd was on hand. A Providence *Journal* reporter interviewed several of the players before they made their way up College Hill. "All of them," he wrote, "did not hesitate to say it was a 'corking' trip from start to finish." There was no mention of the missing slice of Washington bacon.[27]

During the spring semester, Pollard concentrated his energy on indoor and outdoor track and his studies—in that order. Despite the limitations of his technical education, Pollard clearly had the ability to do the classroom work at Brown, however he simply was not a conscientious student. Pollard often missed classes and took frequent trips to Springfield to visit his wife and son. In later years, Pollard would sometimes complain that he did not receive the private tutoring and other academic benefits available to athletes who were members of fraternities. In fact, however, Pollard simply did not apply himself to his studies. He seemed to be rebelling against the strict discipline, particularly academic, which had been imposed upon him by his family back in Chicago. It was also his view, which he often stated in later years, that star athletes contribute much to a university and should be taken care of by college officials. During his first year at Brown, Pollard recorded eight Ds and two Es (failures) in his course work, which must have barely kept him in school and eligible for intercollegiate athletics. Yet, he was ambitious in terms of future goals. Pollard told a Providence *Journal* reporter the following fall that after four years at Brown he intended to enter medical school at either Harvard or Columbia. Given his dismal academic performance, one would have to consider Pollard either extremely naive or self-confident.[28]

On the track, Pollard had a more productive winter and spring. He set the New England Amateur Athletic Association indoor record in the sixty-yard low hurdles, with a sprint of 8.4 seconds. Outdoors, he ran the 220-yard high hurdles in twenty-five seconds flat. At the end of the spring term, Pollard returned alone to Chicago (it is not clear when he told his parents about his wife and baby) to visit his family and friends. After arriving in downtown Chicago, he was unable to find a taxi driver who would drive him, an African American, to the North Side of the city. Pollard may have become a budding college football star, but he was not immune from the prejudice and discrimination that affected his race.[29]

AN ALL-AMERICA SEASON

6

During most of June 1916, Pollard remained in Chicago at his family's house in Rogers Park. In his free time, he assisted his brother Luther in his venture into the moving picture business. A year earlier, Luther had become one of the first African Americans to operate a movie company when he became a partner in and director of the Ebony Film Company, a firm that was primarily white-owned and that produced comedies with all-black casts in downtown Chicago and at a studio near Oshkosh, Wisconsin. The company had a repertory group of forty black actors, many of them members of the George M. Lewis Stock Company. Among them were Sam Robinson, cousin of the vaudeville star Bill "Bojangles" Robinson, and the youngest Pollard brother, Frank. Pollard was a talent scout and casting agent for Ebony and gained a useful introduction into an industry that would provide part of his livelihood in future years.[1]

Between 1915 and 1922, Ebony produced a total of sixteen two-reel comedies, and in 1918 showed a net profit of nearly $1.5 million. A concerted attack against Ebony's films by the Chicago *Defender* helped to force the company's closing in 1922, however. The *Defender*, which objected to the blatant racial stereotypes depicted in Ebony films, maintained that film patrons should not be "subjected to the humiliating experience of seeing things which lower the Race in the estimation of its own people as well as in the eyes of whatever members of the 'other' Race who may happen to be in attendance."[2]

In July, Pollard left Chicago and reopened his tailor shop at Narragansett Pier, enjoying the cool Atlantic breezes and renewing acquaintances with members of the youthful black elite who flocked to the southern Rhode Island resort to find summer employment and have fun. It is not clear whether Ada and Fritz, Jr., accompanied Pollard to Narragansett or stayed with friends in either Providence or Springfield. The couple spent much time apart while Fritz was in college, and the relationship would become strained, at least by the early 1920s. Fritz seldom mentioned Ada in later interviews, and had the reputation of enjoying the company of other women and a fast-paced night life.[3]

Pollard was also reunited with Paul Robeson, who had completed his freshman year at Rutgers and was again working at Narragansett. He recalled seeing Robeson on the baseball field. According to Pollard, Robeson came up to him wearing a black sweater with a big red R on it. Pollard remembered asking, "What's that thing stand for?" The huge New Jersey lineman cooly replied, "Rutgers." Pollard supposedly shot back that "we play some *little old* team like that." Robeson, later an All-America end, did not reply, but Pollard would remember the 1916 Brown-Rutgers game as the bloodiest and most "murderous game" in which he ever played. It is not clear whether the story of meeting Robeson on the baseball field is true or apocryphal (it seems certain Pollard would have known that Robeson played for Rutgers by mid-1916), but it does reveal something about Pollard. He was self-assured, at least on the surface, and a bit of a showoff. Robeson remembered Pollard as a flamboyant character who was always ready with a wisecrack and was usually the center of attention. Underneath this veneer of bravado, it is likely that Pollard was still plagued by the insecurities of an undersized athlete trying to live up to the standards his brothers had set for him. He returned to Narragansett for several summers not just to make money, but because he, like Robeson, represented a kind of elite at the summer resort because of their successes in white society, a feat most young African Americans of the time admired. Pollard was active in the social life at Narragansett and was generally remembered as being the life of the parties in the black workers' colony. Those who remembered him at such social events recalled that he was a sharp dresser, drank quite a bit, and was popular with women.[4]

In early September, Pollard closed his shop at Narragansett and returned to Providence to begin football practice. Preseason practice was held at a farm near New Bedford, Massachusetts, owned by J. A. "Daff" Gammons, a former Brown football star and head coach. The Brown team had lost three starters from the 1915 squad but had added a half-dozen promising freshmen. Among them was Jay Mayo "Ink" Williams, who did not play much in 1916 due to injuries and academic difficulties, but went on to become one of Brown's greatest ends and an outstanding professional player. It is possible that Williams had played professional football in Hammond, Indiana, before coming to Brown, and that he and Pollard had met in Chicago. He, Rudolph Fisher, and Pollard were the only three black students at Brown, and Williams and Pollard became close friends, both on and off the field. Williams had a room on Meeting Street near the campus, but spent most of his time at Pollard's Hope College room, which also served as a pressing shop. By the end of the season, Williams was a junior partner in the business. He, like Pollard, was reputed to have "borrowed" suits turned in at the pressing shop to attend dances and social functions in the Providence black community.[5]

As preseason practice ended, most observers agreed that the Brown team was much improved over 1915 because of three weeks of additional practice preceding the Tournament of Roses game and the infusion of freshmen talent. Pollard was also a more confident player and more comfortable with his surroundings on campus and in the Providence community. Occasionally his self-assuredness caused him to step across the unspoken color line which existed in Providence at the time. According to Fritz Pollard, Jr., Providence was a prejudiced city in 1916, as it was in 1933 when he was a freshman at Brown. He remembered that the downtown business district was strictly segregated as late as the 1930s. One incident illustrates the more subtle racial discrimination that the elder Pollard faced in 1916. Clair Purdy and his girlfriend would sometimes pick up Pollard and speed around town in Purdy's fire-engine-red Stutz Bearcat. After several of these jaunts, President Faunce called Pollard into his office and "delicately suggested to him that he tour the town in a less sensational fashion."[6]

Pollard, however, was not above playing on the white community for financial support. Like most African-American athletes of his era, he viewed athletics as one of the few available avenues to establishing a reputation and making a comfortable living. He was frustrated by the amateur code which mandated that college athletes should play for no pay. Coach Bill Sprackling, who held a full-time job at the Collier Wire Company in Providence, later recalled that numerous stories circulated that Pollard would attempt to solicit funds from downtown businessmen who were enthusiastic about Brown football. Just before a Saturday game, the stories went, Pollard would explain that he was financially strapped, and that if he did not get his bills paid he would not be able to play in the upcoming game. The former Brown assistant coach maintained that Pollard "was quite successful in this." Although there is no solid evidence to support Sprackling's account, it is consistent with Pollard's business dealings in later years. His son recalled him as an "operator," who always had several financial deals going to support himself and his family.[7]

Brown opened its 1916 football season on September 30 with a game against Rhode Island State at Andrews Field. The Rhode Island Rams were clearly overmatched, but made a stronger showing than in previous years. Brown rolled up three touchdowns by the early part of the third period and went on to an 18–0 victory. That Brown missed three extra points in the game was not unusual for a team of that era. In 1916, points after touchdown either had to be kicked from placement or drop-kicked from a position perpendicular to the point where the ball crossed the goal line for the touchdown. In many cases, the kicker was forced to attempt the conversion from an acute angle. The alternative for the scoring team was to punt the ball out of its end zone to the kicker, who then attempted a kick in the face of the on-charging defensive team. Thus, the success of a conversion after touchdown most often depended on where the ball crossed the goal line on the scoring play.[8]

Pollard had an outstanding game against Rhode Island, but like most of the regulars sat out the fourth quarter. The *Brown Daily Herald* designated Pollard and halfback Jimmy Jemail, who scored two touchdowns, the stars of the game. The highlight of the game for Brown was the outstanding play of about a half-dozen freshmen who played most of the second half. The play of fullback Walter de Vitalis, who scored one touchdown, and Dunc Annan, a future professional player who replaced Purdy at quarterback in the fourth period, indicated that Brown had more depth than in 1915.[9]

During the first few weeks of the fall campaign, Pollard faced a greater challenge at the Brown practice scrimmages than he did from the Bruins' lackluster opponents. In the second game against Trinity, which the *Brown Daily Herald* characterized as "more of the nature of a practice game for Brown," the Bruins racked up twenty-eight second-period points on the way to a 42–0 whitewash of the Connecticut school. Pollard did not start the game and was used only sparingly in the second and third quarters. The student reporter noted, however, that in the final period "Pollard, in the short time he played, showed a delighted audience that he had lost none of his old 'wrigglesomeness,' scoring practically unaided, except by Purdy, the only touchdown of the period."[10]

On the practice field, however, Pollard carried more than his share of the workload. The Brown scrimmages were very spirited because of the keen competition for starting positions on the varsity team. Wardwell Leonard, who held one of the first-down markers at the scrimmages, recalled that Pollard occasionally became angry because the scrub team usually keyed on him. Because the huddle was not used in 1916, the quarterback called out the play at the line of scrimmage and, of course, the second team knew the play and who would be carrying the ball. During one practice scrimmage, Leonard recalled that the quarterback called for Pollard to carry the ball twice in succession, and that he was stopped for no gain each time. Then, the quarterback called Pollard's play again, Leonard said, "I heard Pollard swear, I was right down on the sidelines. That's the last I saw of him before he was over the line. He was that fast. He broke through the line before I could raise my head from the stake. He just got mad on the third call."[11]

In contrast to the rugged midweek practice scrimmage, Brown's third straight home contest against Amherst College was a cakewalk. The Bruins overwhelmed the Lord Jeffs by a score of 69–0 in one of the most lopsided contests ever held at Andrews Field. The *Brown Daily Herald* reported that "the first three times that Pollard was given the ball he went over for touchdowns on runs of from 18 to 32 yards." After one period Brown led 27–0. When Brown had piled up a commanding 34–0 lead by the end of the third period, Coach Robinson replaced most of his regulars, including Pollard. The substitutes proceeded to score thirty-five unanswered fourth-quarter points to demoralize Amherst.[12]

The following week Pollard became embroiled in a political controversy involving the 1916 presidential race between Woodrow Wilson and Charles Evans Hughes. Stories appeared in several Providence newspapers that Pollard had been engaged by Brown's Wilson Club as a member of its speaking staff. He flatly denied the report and maintained firmly that he supported Hughes. Although the source of the stories is unknown, it is clear that the rumor was both politically and racially motivated. Hughes, who was scheduled to speak in Providence the following week, was an 1882 Brown graduate and the overwhelming presidential favorite among the normally Republican student body. The rumor associating Pollard (and black voters) with Wilson was undoubtedly intended to discredit the president by linking him with the unpopular African-American minority. There was some irony in this because African Americans, when they voted, normally voted Republican. President Wilson had won a surprising number of black votes in 1912, but after his inauguration was particularly unpopular because of his 1913 order to segregate federal offices in Washington, D.C., and his endorsement of *The Birth of a Nation*. Beyond this, the Pollards had been staunch Republicans since the time of Reconstruction. After Pollard's published denial, the incident was soon forgotten, but it did indicate that he was becoming a prominent figure in Providence, albeit in this case in a negative context.[13]

Although the important presidential campaign, which many believed would determine America's future policy with regard to the Great War, was heating up and would reach its climax in early November, Pollard and his teammates were more concerned about their upcoming game with Williams College. The team traveled to Williamstown on October 21 to oppose the small Massachusetts school. In a game played in the rain on a muddy field, the Bruins came away with their fourth straight shutout, 20–0, by scoring three second-half touchdowns. The Williams squad was decidedly stronger than Brown's first three opponents, and the game was closer than the final score indicated. Although the *Brown Daily Herald* reported that Pollard played a brilliant game, breaking away for several long runs leading to Brown touchdowns in the second half, he also made two crucial fumbles in the first half that ended Bruin scoring drives. In the past, Coach Robinson had been critical of Pollard's tendency to fumble, attributing it to Fritz's flamboyant style of running, particularly on punt returns.[14]

Pollard certainly was a flashy runner who took many dangerous chances on the field in an effort to break away for long gains. He received punts while running at full speed and was noted for his hurdling somersaults over the line, when he would sometimes land on his feet and dart off into the clear. Pollard was a fundamentally sound football player in all aspects of the game, however. Fred Huggins, who later coached at Providence College, remembered working out with him in the fall of 1917 when both of them were ineligible to play at Brown. He recalled that Fritz knew more about how to block, tackle, and play defense than any of the Brown coaches at the time. Huggins remarked that Pollard was "the best blocker Brown ever had. He was the best tackler-defensive tackler and he weighed 155 pounds."[15]

Most people, however, remember Pollard's blinding speed. Fred's brother, Charlie, who generally played second- or third-team quarterback in 1915–16, recollected handing off to Pollard many times in practice. "He used to say to me, 'now Charlie, never, never, put that ball in my stomach. You just hold it out there, I will take it.' And when he came by me," Huggins recalled, "it was like a cyclone and it was like somebody had hit me and took it out of my hand. The fastest man to cross the line that I had ever seen to that day." Huggins added that Pollard could go through the smallest hole. He ran low to the ground and "went through nothing—you couldn't see where he went through—he could just smell it." Brown had only two running plays for Pollard. He either went between guard and tackle on a quick-opener or off tackle with the option of veering around the end. Pollard's speed, cutting ability, and sheer athletic ability usually took care of the rest.[16]

Despite his small stature, Pollard was remarkably rugged. The Brown football program listed him at five feet seven and 145 pounds. Over the years, he won many bets from people who underestimated his weight by as much as twenty-five pounds; his actual playing weight at Brown was around 165 pounds. Charlie Huggins, Jr., explained that Pollard "was very muscular, tremendously muscular. Legs on him like they had put on plaster and his back was lumps of muscle." One of his problems, Fritz told Huggins, was that "he was inclined to get muscle bound." Both Fred and Charlie Huggins agreed that they learned more about football from Pollard than anyone they had ever known.[17]

Wally Wade, who played two years with Pollard at Brown and later became one of the nation's premier football coaches, maintained that Pollard was "a great runner. He ran with considerable drive, force, and then he changed directions very well." Wade was particularly impressed by Pollard's cross-step dodge, which many modern coaches have confused with the contemporary stutter-step. The former Alabama and Duke coach explained, however, that in the cross-step dodge Fritz was always moving forward, would fake to either the inside or outside, and then cross one foot over the other. It was effective, according to Wade, "because when he crossed, that gave him a lot of force and with that kick he'd knock that tackle off." Wade attempted to teach Pollard's cross-step dodge during his early coaching career, but found that it was too difficult for his young players to master and settled on the side-way dodge which is still popular. Pollard's former teammate concluded that Fritz "was one of the good runners that I've known in all my football experience. Grange and all those fellows. I've studied Grange. Seen Grange play. He was a great runner. Fritz could go up with any of them."[18]

Pollard and his teammates would face their first real test of the season when they opposed Rutgers at Andrews Field on October 28. The day before the game Pollard was confined to bed with a cold, but likely attended the mass football rally on the eve of the game. Brown alumnus Charlie Sisson exhorted the students by proclaiming that "Brown is up against a team that Yale and Princeton are afraid to play. The Rutgers game starts a sort of an ascending ratio that ends with Harvard. . . . Charles E. Hughes may make one touchdown next week," Sisson told the students referring to the national election, "but Brown is going to break Rutgers' record for holding and make three tomorrow." Sisson turned out to be an accurate prognosticator as far as the football game was concerned, although he misread the outcome of the presidential contest.[19]

Rutgers, under Coach Foster Sanford, was reputed to be the roughest team in the East, and the Saturday game did nothing to tarnish that reputation. The 1916 Rutgers team was well known for its multiple-kick formation, in which two players held the ball on field-goal attempts in an effort to increase the kicker's accuracy, but its main strength was in its big and strong line. Paul Robeson played tackle and linebacker in 1916, and Al "Budge" Garrett and Bob "Nasty" Nash were at guards, all three of whom would be Pollard's teammates in the professional ranks during the early 1920s. Rutgers pushed Brown all over the field in the first half and in the process sent several Bruin players to the hospital, including Josh Weeks with a concussion. Rutgers only managed to score one field goal, however, and took a 3–0 halftime lead into the clubhouse.[20]

Pollard later reflected that "it was a rough game. We normally didn't play that way. But they were rough. They had this Nasty Nash out there. And some damn little Indian, Budge Garrett. Oh, gee. Rutgers, to me, was the roughest school in the country at that time." Pollard also might have mentioned that it was his defensive play that kept the game close after two periods. The *Brown Daily Herald* reported that Fritz's defense was brilliant, as "time and again Pollard stopped the Rutgers backs after they had plowed through the line."[21]

Late in the third period, Brown got on the scoreboard as a result of Rutgers's fumble on its own one-yard line. Pollard plunged over the goal line, and Brown led 7–3. A short time later Pollard raced forty yards for a touchdown on the criss-cross play, which was a reverse, run from an unbalanced line with a tackle pulling. Pollard later recalled with satisfaction that before the play he "went back and told Purdy to call that criss-cross play. We hadn't used it. I said 'Robeson's playing back there and, hell, he can't cross those big feet fast enough to catch me.'" Brown added a final touchdown in the quarter on a fifty-six-yard run by Andy Hillhouse and came away with a hard-fought 21–3 victory. The *Brown Daily Herald* concluded that "the game was certainly a test of strength of the Brown and White, as it is doubtful if a harder playing team will be met this season than Rutgers was in the first half."[22]

During the following week, many of the Brown regulars were too battered to even practice. Pollard played sparingly in the Bloody Wednesday game but managed to score one touchdown. The team was regrouping for its next two big objectives, victories over Yale and Harvard. In the meantime, Brown had a "set-up" game against the Vermont Mountaineers at Andrews Field on Saturday. Coach Robinson substituted liberally as Brown rolled up a 42–0 victory over the undermanned Vermonters, with Pollard making two touch-downs. After six games, Brown was undefeated, scoring 211 points to its opponents' three. The New York *World* commented that "in the past few years some of the larger universities have regarded their game with Brown as a practice contest. Anybody who plays Brown this season is going to get plenty of practice defending their own goal line." With the presidential election over and the local favorite, Hughes, narrowly defeated, most of the attention on the Brown campus was directed toward Yale and Harvard. Pollard was primed to play two of the most spectacular games in his long gridiron career and to establish himself as a Brown legend and one of the premier players in the first half century of American football.[23]

The 1916 Yale team was far stronger than the one Brown had defeated in New Haven the previous year. Under the new coach, a former Yale All-America, Thomas "Tad" Jones, the Eli juggernaut was undefeated in six games while allowing only two touchdowns. Before the season, Jones had told his players, "Gentlemen, you are now going out to play football. Never in your life will you do anything so important." Jones enticed football demigod Walter Camp to return to the practice field as unofficial backfield coach and employed the Yale football legend William W. "Pudge" Heffelfinger, a three-time All-America, as line coach. Striving to mold one of Yale's finest teams, Jones was the first coach to use action photographs taken during games to instruct his charges. The Mighty Blue was determined to win the Big Three competition among Yale, Harvard, and Princeton and end the season undefeated with consecutive victories over Brown, Princeton, and Harvard. Yale would accomplish the first objective for the first time since 1909, but fail to attain an unblemished record, primarily because of a superb performance by Pollard.[24]

More than a thousand Brown partisans, including some five hundred students, were among the throng of twenty-five thousand that awaited the 2 P.M. kickoff at Yale Bowl on November 11. It was the first year that Brown and Yale players wore numerals on their backs, causing displeasure among some Yale football purists. The diminutive Pollard, number eight, could hear strains of "Bye, Bye, Blackbird" coming from the Yale stands as he lined up for the opening kickoff. At the time, and for many years thereafter, Pollard said little about the racial abuse he received in these college games.

Late in his life, however, when he was retired and most of the participants were dead, he complained bitterly that he had been "niggerized" at Yale and Harvard. Unlike thirty years later when Jackie Robinson broke the color barrier in baseball, Pollard received no encouragement from newspapers, either black or white, to hold his tongue and fists and make his statement on the field. He simply did it. To have made an issue of racism at the time would have raised the specter of Jack Johnson. Undoubtedly, Robinson faced more pressure than Pollard because of the army of reporters that followed his every move, but he also had millions of supporters and admirers in black America and white. Pollard's struggle against racism was in relative obscurity. Both men, however, had the skill and courage to turn a hostile environment to their advantage.[25]

Using a strong defensive game anchored around a solid line led by Captain Clinton "Cupid" Black and the booming punts and versatile offensive play of Harry LaGore, Yale kept the ball in Brown territory throughout most of the first half. Midway through the first period, Eli halfback LaGore, who had been suspended from the 1915 team for playing semipro baseball, swept right end for twenty-two yards before Pollard pulled him down on the Brown thirty-yard line and prevented a touchdown. A short time later, after Brown had held the Elis on downs, Andy Hillhouse's punt was blocked in the Brown end zone where Pollard scooped up the ball and returned it to the Brown thirteen-yard line for a first down, thwarting another Yale tally. As the half ended, Pollard intercepted a LaGore pass on the Brown five-yard line. Despite Pollard's defensive heroics and a successful goal-line stand by the Brown line, Yale's relentless attack resulted in two made field goals for a 6–0 halftime lead. During the first half, Brown had run only twenty-five offensive plays for a total of forty yards gained, with Pollard carrying only three times for twenty-eight yards. It was not an auspicious start.[26]

Brown received the second-half kickoff on its own twenty-yard line and moved the ball steadily down field with a series of short rushes, including two five-yard sprints by Pollard. With the ball on the Yale thirty-nine-yard line, Pollard suddenly broke outside and darted and weaved until he was tackled on the Yale five. After the Eli line held and LaGore had punted out of his own end zone, Brown began a new drive from the Yale thirty-five. After several short rushes, Pollard made a spectacular catch of a pass from Hillhouse and raced to the Yale three, where Cupid Black brought him down. This time Brown was not denied, as Purdy dove into the end zone from two feet away; after de Vitalis made the point, the Bruins led 7–6. The period ended with Yale controlling the ball deep in its own territory and Brown clinging to its slim lead.[27]

On the second play of the final quarter, Yale's LaGore boomed a punt from the Eli ten-yard line to the Brown forty. Pollard received the ball there, and as the New York *Times* reported, "dexterously threw off the Yale ends, started toward the right, drawing the entire pack of the Yale tacklers in that direction, then using a puzzling side step, switched to the left, where he outstripped every Yale pursuer in a desperate sprint for the Yale goal line, sailing across with the second touchdown for the visitors. This heartbreaking performance nailed the lid down on Yale's hopes, and the Elis were never dangerous afterwards." The *Yale Alumni Weekly* reported that "the ovation to Wilson at Madison Square Garden was nothing to the handclapping Pollard got as he ambled circumspectly back to his position after their goal."[28]

Pollard was not finished. Hoping to reverse the momentum of the game by forcing a Brown offensive mistake in its own territory, Yale elected to kick off to Brown after Pollard's touchdown. The strategy was unsuccessful. After an exchange of punts following the kickoff, Brown started on a thirteen-play scoring drive that featured two outstanding long gains by Pollard. With only a few minutes left in the game and Brown leading 21–6, Coach Robinson substituted for Pollard after he had run another Yale kickoff back for thirty-one yards. Brown rooters and many Yale partisans gave Pollard a sustained ovation.[29]

Many years later, Tad Jones maintained that he was personally responsible for the Yale loss because at halftime he had urged the Yale regulars to let up and save themselves for the upcoming games with Princeton and Harvard. Former Yale tackle Mac Baldridge reminded Jones that "a fellow by the name of Fritz Pollard had a lot to do with what you call our letdown that afternoon." According to Baldridge, Jones shuddered and said, "Please don't mention Pollard. I can still see him racing across the goal line. I wouldn't be surprised if he wasn't just about the best ball carrier any of us ever saw." Walter Camp also came away from the game convinced that Pollard was "one of the greatest runners I have ever seen."[30]

The pro-Yale New York *Times* conceded that Pollard, "a lithe, dusky, six foot half back, displayed the cleverest all around back field success attained on Yale field this season." It was not uncommon for white reporters to imagine that Pollard was six-feet tall or taller because they could not comprehend how a small African-American athlete could outshine larger white men. In Providence, the *Journal* called Pollard "the bronze Mahan" (a reference to 1915 Harvard All-America halfback Eddie Mahan) and "a greyhound with Mercury speed, a veritable human torpedo on line smashing and the greatest broken field runner in the East." The New York *Evening Sun* went so far as to compare Pollard's open-field ability with that of Jim Thorpe, maintaining that Fritz made up in "agility what he lacked in physique." In the African-American press, Pollard's athletic achievement had social and political meaning. The New York *Age* addressed his success on the editorial page, commenting that "Mr. Pollard is doing a very great deal to help solve the race problem."[31]

The Brown team returned at 10:30 P.M. to a wild celebration in Providence. After the students snake-danced triumphantly through the city, the largest bonfire in the school's history was ignited at Lincoln Field. "The Bear has made his kill," President Faunce noted at the rally, but everyone knew that mighty John Harvard loomed ahead. It became clear that Brown was in the running for the mythical national football championship when George Daley, the New York *World* sporting editor and well-known football expert who wrote under the name "Herbert," arrived on campus Tuesday and pronounced the squad sound.[32]

The Harvard coaching staff was apparently not as impressed by the Brown team. Reginald Brown, Percy Haughton's assistant and chief strategist, noted that "the material on the Yale team was considerably superior to that of Brown and with a little different handling should have had no difficulty defeating the eleven from Providence. The Brown team is an ordinary one, not a well rounded out machine and consists of a halfback, a line defense, and an offensive formation." Reports from Cambridge indicated, however, that Harvard's coaching staff had spent most of the week devising methods to contain Pollard. A Boston newspaper confirmed that in midweek scrimmages the Harvard scrub team operated with a left halfback whose face was blackened "to bear out the resemblance to Pollard, who is one of those natural star-colored athletes."[33]

The day before the game Coach Haughton announced that he, Assistant Coach Brown, and more than a half-dozen first-string players would scout the Yale-Princeton game rather than attend the Brown-Harvard clash. Harvard, which had a 7–1 record with an inexplicable 7–3 loss to a superb Tufts team, was looking forward to The Game against Yale and a possible Big Three championship. The Crimson had piled up 184 points during the season to the opposition's seven, and its second and third teams had performed admirably in most games. Brown fans greeted the news with mixed emotions; it was an advantage for their squad to play against some of Harvard's second-team athletes, but an insult to Brown's aspiring football program. Knowledgeable football observers recognized, however, that Harvard teams always had ample depth, and that the second- and third-string players usually performed just a notch below the regulars.[34]

Assistant Coach Leo Leary led the Crimson against the visiting Bruins before an estimated crowd of thirty-two thousand at Harvard Stadium on November 18. Brown mobilized its offense early and threatened the Harvard goal line with regularity during the first ten minutes of play. After Harvard held Brown twice within ten yards of the Crimson goal line, Pollard virtually took over the game and made it his own. Receiving a punt on his own thirty-seven, he sprinted twenty-five yards to the Harvard thirty-eight. Two plays later Pollard circled right end and dodged his way to the Crimson four before he was dragged down. He then made a "terrific lunge" through right guard for the score, and de Vitalis's goal from a bad angle made it 7–0 for Brown.[35]

As the period ended, Pollard made the first of two touchdown-saving tackles. With only seconds remaining in the quarter and Brown in possession of the ball around midfield, Purdy fumbled in his own backfield. A Harvard lineman picked up the ball and seemed to have clear sailing to the Brown end zone before Pollard appeared out of nowhere and tackled him on the Brown forty. During most of the next period, Brown continued to control the ball, but the Harvard defense stiffened and neither team seriously threatened to score. Suddenly, with two minutes left in the half, Harvard's offense came alive. Crimson halfback Rufe Bond tore off twenty yards to the Harvard forty-yard line. Then lining up quickly, Harvard used the hidden-ball play to spring Bond into the open with two blockers in front of him. Pollard was all that stood between Harvard and the tying touchdown. As a Providence *Journal* reporter described the action, Pollard moved forward on his toes and "judged the flight of the runners to the fraction of a second. As they neared him the interferers launched themselves through the air to ward off, but on the same instant Pollard side-stepped and he hurled himself full tilt at Bond's legs." The result was that "both runner and tackler went down with terrible force" on the Brown twenty-four-yard line. Two plays later the half ran out while Harvard was setting up for a field-goal attempt, and Brown clung to a precarious seven-point lead.[36]

As in New Haven a week earlier, Pollard broke the game open in the second half. After an exchange of punts, Brown lined up on the Harvard forty-six-yard line with a third down and four to go. Taking a hand-off from Purdy, Pollard shot off-right tackle and out-sprinted three Crimson defenders to the goal line. The New York *Times* reported that after Pollard's dash "it became only a question of the size of the score," as Brown took a 14–0 lead. A short time later, Harvard tried to take care of the Pollard problem once and for all. After a Crimson drive stalled, Henry Minot punted to Pollard on the Brown thirteen. He returned the ball nine yards before heading for the Harvard sideline. At that point, Fred Huggins re-called, "Fritz went out of bounds and these three fellows [Harvard players] came after him right up to the side of the stadium," which was fifteen yards from the sideline. "But, Fritz came out with this big smile on his face and teeth and eyes showing. As I remember two of the Harvard men got hurt and had to go out of the game." Harvard was penalized fifteen yards for roughing, and Pollard re-mained in the game.[37]

In the final period, Pollard delivered a final blow to the proud Crimson eleven and helped secure Brown's first victory over Harvard in twenty-four tries. With five minutes remaining in the game and Brown in possession on the Harvard forty-five, Hillhouse passed to Pollard in the right flat. After juggling the ball precariously for several seconds, Pollard grabbed the aerial, eluded three Crimson tacklers, and sprinted to the Harvard three-yard line before he was downed. Three plays later, Purdy dove into the end zone and de Vitalis added the point for a 21–0 Brown lead. When a substitute replaced Pollard after the touchdown, the more than eight thousand Brown fans gave Fritz a standing ovation. A few minutes later, the final whistle sounded to signify a 21–0 Brown victory, making the Bruins the only team, except for Princeton, to have defeated both Yale and Harvard in the same season.[38]

The New York *Times* summarized the game by stating that "from a spectacular point of view, the game was all Pollard." The writer maintained that as a result of the victory, Brown "will have an excellent claim to the college championship, and Pollard, its star dusky little halfback should be unanimous choice for a position on the mythical All American eleven." Rejecting Harvard's alibi that its substitutes had played against Brown, the *Times* pointed out that "it is doubtful, even, if all the Harvard regulars could have defeated Brown today." Conceding that Harvard's star halfback Eddie Casey might have scored one touchdown and that Captain Harrie Dadmun and the regular Crimson ends might have prevented one Brown score, the reporter maintained that "none of the first string players could have stopped the dusky streak in his sensational runs." The *Times* account concluded by stating that "considering the fact that there has been little to choose all season between Harvard's first and second string, with the exception of Casey, Dadmun, and the ends, Brown is entitled to full credit for a decisive victory over a representative Haughton eleven."[39]

Returning to Providence, the Brown team was treated to the greatest football rally in the school's history. After a parade through downtown and an enormous bonfire at Lincoln Field, several campus notables addressed the crowd. President Faunce, whose remarks underscored the ingrained racism of the period, noted that the victories over Yale and Harvard meant "that Brown football has reached its manhood and can take care of itself. If a man wants to get paid for playing football Brown University is no place for him. There is no bigger white man on the team than Fred Pollard." After the president finished, Brown alumnus Corky Dyer coaxed Pollard into saying a few words. "I know I'd rather face Harvard, Yale and Princeton together than face this crowd," Fritz began. "I can only say that we have a wonderful student body, faculty and coaches. I know that if the students give us the support next year which they gave us this year that we shall beat Harvard by a score of 61–0 instead of 21–0." Professor Courtney Langdon concluded the evening by saying that "the finest thing about the season when you come to think of it is the wonderful modesty of Pollard."[40]

During the next week, the Brown eleven held light workouts in preparation for its final game, but most of the football interest still centered on the Harvard game. In an editorial, the *Harvard Crimson* criticized the decision to use substitutes against Brown, calling it an affront to good sportsmanship and fair play. The *Crimson* maintained that "the increasing tendency of college athletics is more and more toward the calculating efficient ideal of modern business, and away from a recreative standard of true sport for sport's sake." In fact, as the historian Ronald A. Smith has shown, Harvard had abandoned the amateur ethic some years before. The following day, the Harvard graduate football manager, Fred Moore, defended the coaches' decision, pointing out that Brown had been informed that the substitutes would be used and "made no particular objection." He stated that the game would have been changed to an earlier date, well in advance of the Yale game, had the coaching staff known before the season that Brown would have such a powerful team.[41]

Almost forgotten amid the joy and controversy surrounding the victory over Harvard was Brown's final game with Colgate. Coach Robinson later recalled that the team was photographed to death the week before the Thanksgiving Day game, and numerous newspaper accounts called Brown the coming national champions. Many of the players later stated that the team was overconfident going into the Colgate game. Pollard did not recall the overconfidence but did point out that "back in those days, beating Harvard or beating Yale seemed monumental in the football world. It didn't make any difference what other teams you defeated. If you could defeat Harvard and Yale, you were it." He did recollect that in New Haven some of the Yale players had warned the Brown team to watch "that Colgate team because they have one of the greatest teams in the country." The Yale players conceded that they had been lucky to beat Colgate by a score of 7–3.[42]

The night before the Colgate game Brown students spread hay on Andrews Field to protect it from frost. During the early-morning hours, however, a hard, cold rain began that continued throughout Thanksgiving Day. As the 11:30 A.M. kickoff approached, a record crowd estimated at nine thousand, shivering and huddled under umbrellas, watched the teams line up on the field of mud and hay. Colgate put a powerful eleven on the field, featuring three future 1916 All-America selections: Belford West and Clarence "Steamer"

Horning at tackles and Oscar "Oc" Anderson at quarterback. The Red Raiders boasted a 6–1 record with an impressive 15–3 victory over Bob Zuppke's Illinois team. From the outset, the game was no contest. Colgate's offensive line opened gaping holes in the Brown defense which its backs exploited to the fullest. The Red Raider defense double-teamed Pollard and, with some aid from the soggy turf, held him in check. Horning and West were bulwarks at the defensive tackle positions. Colgate pushed over a touchdown in each period and came away with an impressive 28–0 victory.[43]

The score might have been much worse had it not been for Pollard's superb defensive play. "Even though Colgate did crush out all of Pollard's chances to gallop his way to glory," the New York *Times* reported, "they could not get him out of the way on the defense." The *Times* correspondent paid tribute to a part of Pollard's game that previously only football experts seemed to appreciate. "He was the one man in the Brown team who was able to tumble the overwhelming Colgate rush. Playing on the secondary defense, Pollard rushed in headlong and often dumped the Colgate runners after they had successfully shaken off the other Brown tacklers. Colgate's warriors tried in vain to box him up as they did the others, but the elusive negro outguessed them and wriggled his way through to spill romping opposition."[44]

Some Brown partisans maintained that the Bruin defeat was the result of a combination of the team's overconfidence and the muddy playing conditions, but few had anything but praise for the Colgate eleven. Fred and Charlie Huggins, who witnessed the game, later speculated that Pollard might have scored on a dry field, but conceded that Colgate would have scored six or seven touchdowns without Pollard's exceptional defensive play. They readily admitted that Colgate was the superior team and would have won regardless of the field conditions. The *Brown Daily Herald* summarized the thoughts of many Brown fans, "There are no post-mortem and no alibis; we were beaten fairly, squarely, and well by a football team par excellence." The paper maintained, however, that "this final defeat does not take away from us the glory won earlier in the season." Pollard remembered Colgate as "just another one of those Rutgers teams that came down there. They were rough, rough as all outdoors. The only difference between Rutgers and Colgate was that Colgate just didn't fall apart. . . . They just bowled us over."[45]

After the devastating defeat by Colgate, Brown's claim to the mythical national championship vanished, with most experts awarding the title to either Pittsburgh or Army. There was much speculation on the Brown campus, however, that Pollard would be named an All-America halfback. Pollard recalled that many students tried to relieve him of concern that he might be excluded from Walter Camp's mythical team because of racial prejudice. Although Pollard later maintained that he did not give the honor much thought at the time (which is doubtful), he would have had good cause for concern in 1916. In the two years before America's entrance into World War I, racial tension in the country was increasing dramatically. Eighty blacks had been lynched in 1915, a twentieth-century high; the Ku Klux Klan was being revived in many states; and a Virginia-born president and Democratic-controlled Congress seemed intent on reversing the modest gains made by African Americans in the years since Reconstruction.[46]

Pollard's supporters, and probably Fritz himself, were relieved when the New York *Times* named its All-Eastern football team in early December. The *Times* devoted six paragraphs to Pollard, chronicling his spectacular season and calling him "easily the greatest half back of the year," in naming him to the prestigious team. Two weeks later, Walter Camp, the dean of American football coaches, made his selections. Camp's All-America teams traditionally reflected an eastern bias because the former Yale head coach seldom viewed games outside of that region, and usually included a good number of Yale men. His 1916 team proved to be no exception. Pollard was named on the first team as the left halfback and called "the most elusive back of the year or of any year." It certainly benefitted Pollard that Camp had attended Brown's final three games against Yale, Harvard, and Colgate. Camp commented that "no one who did not see the Colgate-Brown game appreciates the wonderful work Pollard did in that game in stopping man after man who broke through the Brown defense. . . . He was never down and is hard and resilient as an india-rubber ball; but often his offensive work, on account of its very brilliancy, obscured his really sterling defense." Pollard became the second African American named to the Walter Camp first-team All-America squad, and the first to be selected at a backfield position.[47]

Pollard first heard the news while he was delivering clothes around campus and had stopped off at Rockefeller Hall, which served as the student union building. As Pollard recalled, "the fellows said hello Mr. All-American." He went back to his room, checked the newspaper, and sure enough, it was all true. "Boy, everybody went crazy and so did I," Pollard remembered. "I thought I was the luckiest guy in the world." In Pollard's native city, the Chicago *Herald*, a white daily, printed an editorial noting that Pollard had joined William H. Lewis of Harvard as one of only two blacks on Camp's first team. "They have proved that color is not an insuperable handicap to honor on the field of sport," the paper continued optimistically. "The demonstration is altogether encouraging." In a more cautious vein, the writer pointed out that "the larger public may take a wholesome satisfaction in the fact that a clean football player, an intelligent amateur, has succeeded an unsavory pugilist as the foremost athlete of his race." The specter of Jack Johnson, who had recently lost his heavyweight title to Jess Willard in Havana, continued to haunt aspiring African-American athletes. For Pollard, however, the future seemed bright. He was enrolled in one of the nation's most prestigious schools and, barring injury or some other misfortune, could look forward to two more All-America seasons and perhaps football immortality.[48]

A young and dashing Fritz Pollard at the time he entered Brown University in 1915. (Brown University Archives)

Pollard at Brown's Andrews Field during the 1916 campaign. (Brown University Archives)

Fritz Pollard in a Brown University track uniform. (Brown University Archives)

The 1915 Brown team before the trip to Pasadena. Mark Farnum is a right tackle, and the future coaching great Wally Wade is at right guard. (Brown University Archives)

Pollard racing for a long gain in the memorable 1916 Harvard game. The hay piled up along the sideline was often used to cover the field before games to prevent the gridiron from freezing. (Brown University Archives)

The 1921 Akron Pro team, the reigning world champions of professional football. Pollard is at the extreme left, Paul Robeson is sixth from the left, and owners Art Ranney and Frank Nied are on the extreme right. (Pro Football Hall of Fame/NFL Photos)

Pollard and the shivering members of the Providence Steam Roller NFL team before the "Red Grange" game at Boston's Braves Field on December 9, 1925. The Steam Roller defeated the Chicago Bears 9–6, marking the Bears' first defeat since Grange joined the team on Thanksgiving Day 1925. (Brown University Archives)

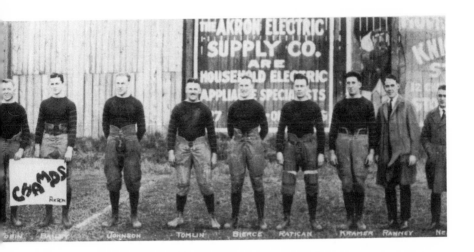

ORIN   BAILEY   JOHNSON   TOMLIN   BIERCE   RATICAN   KRAMER   RANNEY   NE

General Studios 109 Stuart St. Boston.

Fritz and Fritz, Jr., in front of Brown University's historic Van Wickle Gates. Pollard first saw the gates in 1912, a sight that helped convince him to attend Brown. (Pearce Johnson)

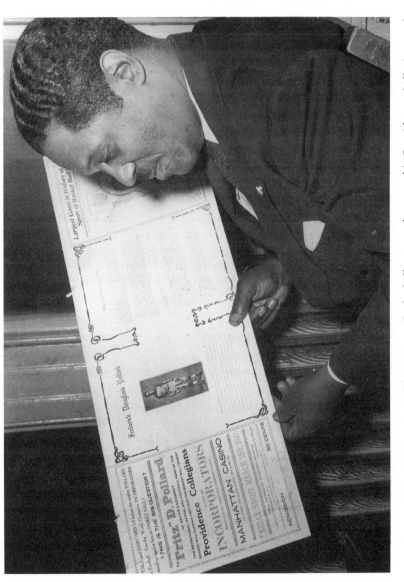

Pollard and memorabilia on a World War I-era basketball contest between his Providence Collegians and Will Anthony Madden's Incorporators. The game was never played. (Brown University Archives)

With Vice-President Richard Nixon during the late 1950s. (Fritz Pollard, Jr.)

Pollard greeting Governor Nelson Rockefeller at a Touchdown Club of New York Touchdown Club banquet. (Fritz Pollard, Jr.)

The former West Point All-America Halfback Elmer Oliphant congratulates Fritz upon his selection as a member of the Touchdown Club as Jimmy Jemail, Pollard's former teammate, looks on. (Brown University Archives)

Fritz Pollard—still going strong in his mid-eighties. (Brown University Archives)

WAR AND TRANSITION

7

Being named to Walter Camp's All-America team changed Pollard's life dramatically in both the long and short term. Reflecting on the honor more than fifty years later, Pollard said, "having been placed on the All American team by Walter Camp helped me all through my life. Having been the first Negro backfield man to have been given the honor. It helped me in business because people trusted me and I had to live within that trust. It gave me recognition wherever I went and cleared the way for me many times when otherwise I would have been very much embarrassed."[1]

The immediate effects of his selection were quite overwhelming for the twenty-two-year-old sophomore. As Pollard recalled, "I began receiving invitations to make speeches from all over the country. I first talked with President Faunce for his advice." Pollard related that some of his admirers wanted to present him with a car, Faunce "advised against it. That set the pattern for me, and I only accepted invitations to speak where my advisors felt it best." Nevertheless, during the Christmas recess and well into the second semester, Pollard remembered speaking "in Chicago, Philadelphia, Pittsburgh, Washington D.C. and Baltimore and many other places especially New York where the NAACP held a very large reception for me as did the other places." Despite his recollection of relying on the advice of Faunce and others, Pollard was clearly determined to cash in on his newly gained status in both white and black America.[2]

His widespread fame in the African-American community seems a bit surprising because the major black newspapers had given scant coverage to his gridiron heroics of the past two years. The larger black newspapers of the day such as the New York *Age*, Pittsburgh *Courier*, Baltimore *Afro-American*, and the Chicago *Defender* were weeklies with rudimentary sports pages. In most cases, the one page devoted to sports was divided between athletic news and theatrical events. The papers were dated for a Saturday but were usually on the streets two or three days earlier, which meant that football news was almost a week old. None of black weeklies of the prewar period could afford full-time reporters to cover college football games; they occasionally reprinted or rewrote week-old accounts from white dailies about games involving white colleges in which blacks participated. The only sustained coverage of football in the African-American weeklies was devoted to games played by black colleges, and this was often sporadic. In 1915–16, for example, the New York *Age* contained week-old reports on only four games in which Pollard played. Pollard's celebrity status in the black community was the result of a channeling network among middle-class and elite blacks, readers of the white dailies, who filtered news of Pollard's exploits to other African-American citizens through the black churches and other social organizations.[3]

On the Brown campus, Pollard was also a celebrity, but he was careful to share credit for his good fortune with his teammates and the university. As Pollard later explained, "I felt very highly honored and only wanted to keep my feet on the ground because I felt that our whole team had played a very important part in my having received this great honor and I did not want to do anything which might reflect on Brown University or any of the players." While Pollard was genuinely grateful to his teammates and school, he also knew that the racial code of the day demanded that he, a young black man, be properly modest and humble in accepting this honor. Yet, he would have a difficult time keeping his feet on the ground. His brash, assertive personality took over. He later admitted that "I was young and foolish and crazy. I was Fritz Pollard, All-America, and my head was getting a little bit big then."[4]

One day in mid-January 1917, President Faunce summoned Pollard to his office and introduced him to a dignified looking gentleman whom Faunce identified as John D. Rockefeller, Jr. Faunce asked whether Fritz knew who Mr. Rockefeller was, and Pollard replied that he did not. Rockefeller, an 1897 Brown graduate and former manager of the school's football team, asked Pollard a number of questions, and then he was excused. The next day Faunce visited Pollard's Hope College room and explained that Rockefeller thought Fritz's room was too cramped, with all the pressing equipment and the clothes hanging everywhere. Rockefeller, the president explained, had made arrangements for Pollard to have another separate room for his living quarters and new pressing equipment, all at Rockefeller's expense. Evidence suggests that Rockefeller later had the files destroyed which related to his subsidy of Pollard; at the time, Pollard recalled Faunce telling him that "from now on you won't have any financial worries."[5]

Apparently Faunce saw no inconsistency with the arrangement despite his earlier statement at the Harvard football rally that "if a man wants to get paid for playing football Brown University is no place for him." Rockefeller's visit to campus came within a week of a National Collegiate Athletic Association meeting at which the University of Chicago football coach and athletic director A. Alonzo Stagg introduced a resolution calling for a survey of intercollegiate athletics "with particular reference to their moral influence." Stagg maintained that "a college was responsible for the actions of its athletes, and that when they practice the dishonesty that is known to be the case in many instances, the fault is that of the college." Certainly Pollard had no qualms about Rockefeller's generosity; he purchased the latest pressing equipment in downtown Providence, selected a second, more spacious room in Hope College for his living quarters, and forwarded the bills to Faunce's office.[6]

During the spring semester, Pollard engaged in a large number of campus and off-campus activities which consumed a good deal of his time. In the winter, for example, he cultivated his lifelong interest in music by playing the slide trombone in both the Brown Band and Orchestra. Late in March, Pollard performed in a musical number in a popular student-produced theatrical farce along with Ink Williams, who did a clog dance with quarterback Jimmy Murphy. The inclusion of the two African-American students indicated that they were being accorded a greater degree of acceptance by the white student body. Pollard was also a member of the varsity indoor and outdoor track teams, and quickly established himself as one of the premier hurdlers and sprinters in New England. Beyond this, he played in the student-organized interclass basketball league. Brown did not field an intercollegiate basketball team in the prewar era because of the opposition of Athletic Director Marvel, who maintained that the Brown gymnasium was too small. The interclass games were spirited, however, and according to reports in the *Brown Daily Herald*, Pollard was a quick, agile guard whose dribbling and playmaking abilities were valued in an era of ball control and low-scoring games.[7]

In the late winter, Pollard planned to capitalize on his fame and basketball skills by bringing a team called the Providence Collegians to New York City for a game against Will Anthony Madden's Incorporators. Madden, a black athletic promoter and sportswriter for the New York *Age*, coached the Incorporators, who were touted as "the colored world champions" for 1914–16. Pollard and Paul Robeson had played a few games that winter for St. Christopher's, a New York African-American club team that Madden also coached. The game, scheduled for early March at the Manhattan Casino, was given heavy publicity in the New York *Age*, the *Crisis*, and other African-American publications. The *Age* noted that Pollard would captain the Collegians, most of whom were Brown undergraduates recruited from the class teams, and quoted Pollard as saying that "in them he has a combination that he is confident will take the measure of Madden's world-beating machine."[8]

Basketball was a game of growing importance in the black community by World War I and received considerable coverage in the African-American press. In New York, about a half-dozen premier teams were sponsored by social, cultural, and athletic clubs. While some of these teams played under sanction of the Amateur Athletic Union (AAU) and were ostensibly amateur, there was evidence by 1917 that professionalism was a growing problem for the New York clubs. By the early 1920s, many clubs sponsored professional teams. Although it is not known what financial arrangements Madden offered to entice Pollard to bring his Providence Collegians to New York, it is clear that the Incorporators were, in fact, a professional team. The game was aggressively publicized, with Madden calling it "the biggest basketball game in the history of the sport." Then, for reasons not explained in the New York black press, the contest was cancelled. It is likely that Brown's President Faunce heard about the impending game and advised Pollard against such a venture that might jeopardize his and his teammates' amateur standing.[9]

A month later, however, Pollard did make his New York City

sporting debut at an indoor track meet sponsored by the Smart Set
Athletic Club. Smart Set was one of several African-American athletic
clubs in the city such as St Christopher's, Alpha Physical Culture,
and the Salem Crescent, which fielded teams in a number of sports.
The meet, held on April 13 at the 13th Regiment Armory in Brooklyn, included a number of white contestants from the college ranks
and various other New York athletic clubs. Howard P. Drew, the
famed black sprinter and member of the 1912 U.S. Olympic team,
was a featured performer at the competition. While Drew, who had
aspirations of competing in the 1920 Olympic games, was beaten in
the hundred-yard dash by less than a foot, Pollard beat two premier
hurdlers, including the reigning national champion, in the sixty-five-
yard low hurdles. According to the New York *Age*, Pollard "surprised
even his many local admirers by defeating such cracks as Jack Eiler
and Arthur Engels" with a time of eight seconds flat. Pollard undoubtedly took special pride in his New York triumph because, as
he told his son many years later, "if you can't make it in New York,
you can't make it anyplace."[10]

By the time of the Smart Set meet, the United States had been
at war with Germany for more than a week. America's entrance
into the worldwide conflict would change the lives of many Americans, including Pollard. On April 2, President Wilson called the
nation to arms and would lead it into what he called "the most
terrible and disastrous of wars, civilization itself seeming to be in
the balance." The president told the country, "the right is more
precious than peace, and we shall fight for the things which we have
always carried nearest our hearts,—for democracy," and to "make
the world itself at last free." The response to Wilson's summons
was particularly enthusiastic on the nation's college campuses. Even
before the congressional declaration of war on April 6, many Brown
students had been drilling on the college green, and some had joined
an artillery unit of the Rhode Island National Guard. At Brown and
other colleges, a few students had already dropped out of school
and joined the Allied war effort even before America entered the
Great War.[11]

For many African Americans the war presented a dilemma. With
the majority of blacks relegated to second-class citizenship, support
for the Allied cause varied in the black community both before and
after America's declaration of war. Some black urban newspapers

such as the Washington *Bee*, the Iowa *Bystander*, and the Chicago *Defender* opposed American intervention and the participation of black soldiers if war came. The *Messenger*, a radical labor publication edited by A. Philip Randolph and Chandler Owen, suggested that flag-waving leaders in the African-American community should "volunteer to go to France, if they are so eager to make the world safe for democracy. We would rather fight to make Georgia safe for the Negro." The majority of black leaders, however, and particularly those associated with the NAACP and the National Urban League, supported American intervention and African-American participation in the war effort. W. E. B. Du Bois, editor of the NAACP's publication, the *Crisis*, played a leading role in mobilizing black support for the war. Once it became clear that African Americans would be drafted, most of the black press accepted Du Bois's point of view in order to give black men as much support as possible.[12]

Although Pollard never stated his views on the war at the time or in later interviews, it is likely that he endorsed the Urban League and NAACP position. His brother Leslie, who had died in a tragic accident in early 1915, was an early member of the New York Urban League; another brother, Hughes, was serving with French forces on the Western Front. Being married with a family to support, Pollard was in no immediate danger of being drafted and had reason not to volunteer for service as many of his classmates and teammates did in the spring and summer of 1917. It is unclear whether his future career as a college athlete was a consideration in his decision to remain in school. It was already evident, however, that the war would disrupt college athletics, as several major track meets were cancelled in the spring due to the mobilization effort.[13]

By the time American mobilization had begun, Pollard had problems of a different kind. In early May, Dean Otis Randall declared Pollard ineligible to compete in intercollegiate track meets. The *Brown Daily Herald* explained that "Pollard is at present ineligible on account of unexcused absences." Having spent a good part of the spring semester making personal and athletic appearances in a number eastern cities, combined with occasional trips to Springfield to visit his family and the time devoted to athletic and musical activities, Pollard simply had missed too many classes. While he admitted that the All-America honor went to his head and made him "crazy," one wonders if he did not interpret the Rockefeller subsidy and Faunce's role in it as a signal from university officials that he could do much as he pleased.[14]

By mid-May, Pollard's eligibility was restored in time to compete in the New England track-and-field championships. After the meet, the New York *Evening Mail* reported that "in the select circle of hurdlers a new candidate was enrolled at dusk Saturday. Fred Pollard gained admittance after he had captured New England titular honors in both the high and low hurdle events. The sensational Brown University football player defeated a fair field over the 120-yard and 220-yard fences, finishing the first named in 16⅗ seconds and the other in 26 seconds." After his hurdles victories, Pollard returned to broad jump twenty-one feet, four inches to take third in that event. The *Mail* article pointed out that because of wartime conditions only eight of the seventeen colleges enrolled had participated in the meet, with "most of the leading athletes . . . doing business with Uncle Sam — the serious kind." The reporter did single out Pollard as "one of the best athletes turned out by the so-called small colleges in a decade." Pollard's triumph was short-lived, however, because when semester grades were posted, he had only managed to pass two of five courses. That record combined with his lackluster academic performance in his first three semesters put his athletic eligibility in serious doubt for the forthcoming football season.[15]

After a brief trip to Chicago and another summer running his tailor shop at Narragansett Pier, Pollard returned to Providence in mid-September, eagerly awaiting the beginning of football practice. Because of the war and the fact that a number of players had spent the summer working on farms as part of the mobilization effort, practice did not begin until late September, only six days before the traditional first game against Rhode Island State. The *Brown Daily Herald* reported that "there is much uncertainty at present whether Pollard, all-American halfback, will be eligible this year." On the day of the game, the student paper noted that both Pollard and Andy Hillhouse would be lost for the season because of academic difficulties. Due to the large number of former players in military service, only one varsity starter, end Josh Weeks, remained on the Bruin squad from the previous season. Pollard had maintained only slightly above a D average and had failed several courses in four semesters, which dropped him below the minimum required at Brown for participation in intercollegiate athletics.[16]

While some of the larger eastern schools such as Harvard and Yale discontinued varsity football for the season, Brown would play a full ten-game schedule, including two games against military teams. The school's enrollment was down by about 325 students, while Harvard and Yale each lost about two thousand. Throughout the semester, Pollard attended classes sporadically, ran his pressing shop, and devoted much of his time to his first love, football. During the week, he divided his time between working out with the Brown team and serving as a backfield coach for the Providence Steam Roller, a professional team coached that season by 1915 Brown football captain Edgar "Spike" Staff. In viewing the Brown season from the sidelines, Pollard no doubt took some satisfaction in the fact that Ink Williams emerged as a star on the inexperienced team which posted a surprisingly good 8–2 record. Pollard remained an apathetic student, however, failing two courses out of five for a D average. Why he was unwilling to devote enough time to his studies and improving his academic standing is unclear, but the result was that Pollard faced another semester of athletic ineligibility.[17]

In early February just before the second semester began, Pollard announced that he was dropping out of school to enter military service. Perhaps dejected about his academic shortcomings or inspired by the government's mounting appeal for patriotic commitment to the war effort, he had accepted an appointment as physical director of the army's Young Men's Christian Association (YMCA) unit at Camp Meade, Maryland. The *Brown Daily Herald* explained that "this action is part of the Government's plan to place popular college athletes as physical directors of the Y.M.C.A. classes at the different army camps." While the *Herald* statement was correct, Pollard's appointment was undoubtedly influenced by the War Department's growing concern about rising racial tensions both on and off military bases since the start of mobilization. Pollard, the heavyweight boxer Sam Langford, the former Dartmouth football star Matthew Bullock, and a few other prominent African-American athletes were recruited to help soothe racial unrest at the military camps and mollify black leaders who complained about unfair and discriminatory practices in the armed forces.[18]

The cause of the tension between white and black Americans was white racism. Since the beginning of the war, racial conflict had intensified, due, in part, to the massive migration of southern blacks to northern urban areas and—after America's entrance into the war—to the mobilization and training of African-American servicemen. In early summer 1917, a major race riot erupted in East St. Louis, Illinois, triggered by labor disputes between local whites and southern migrant black workers. Illinois National Guardsmen stood by as angry whites killed or wounded more than a hundred African Americans and destroyed a large portion of the black section of the city. Eight whites were killed in the rioting that lasted for several weeks. Black Americans were shocked and angered; in late July, five thousand African Americans marched in a silent parade in New York City, with another twenty thousand standing silently along the route, to protest the brutality and injustice in East St. Louis.[19]

A month after the conflict in East St. Louis, violence broke out in Houston involving the Third Battalion of the 24th Infantry Regiment, a black regular army unit. After the arrival of the black soldiers in the south Texas city, the enforcement of Jim Crow laws had been tightened and a number of racial incidents followed. On the night of August 23, according to the official army account, more than one hundred soldiers of the Third Battalion mutinied and attacked the city. In the ensuing riot, two soldiers and seventeen white men were killed, including five policemen. After a cursory investigation and a long court-martial proceeding, twenty-nine black soldiers were sentenced to death, although only thirteen were actually executed, and fifty-three others were sentenced to life imprisonment. Black leaders once again protested against what they believed was a miscarriage of justice, this time involving African-American soldiers.[20]

In response to the protests and to head off efforts by German propagandists to exploit the racial unrest, Secretary of War Newton D. Baker appointed Emmett J. Scott, Booker T. Washington's former secretary, as a special assistant for Negro affairs in October 1917. Scott's official responsibility was to serve as "confidential advisor in matters affecting the interests of 10,000,000 Negroes of the United States and the part they are playing with the present war." Although Scott would later be accused with some justification of cooperating too closely with the War Department and whitewashing a number of serious racial charges brought against the military services, his appointment signified that the government was alert to a serious and growing morale problem among black servicemen and civilians.

It was under these circumstances that Pollard was appointed by the army as YMCA physical director at Camp Meade.[21]

The Maryland camp served as one of seven training facilities for the Negro 92nd Division, which was scattered around the country. Due to the racial unrest and the army's reluctance to station any more black troops in the Deep South, the 92nd was not brought together until it reached France, and even then never reached full strength. When Pollard arrived at Camp Meade, the black 368th Infantry and 351st Field Artillery, with a compliment of a hundred black officers as well as white officers in the higher ranks, were training. In later interviews, Pollard seldom had occasion to mentioned his military service or his experiences at Camp Meade. He was clearly proud of his service during World War I, however, because he nearly always listed his wartime record in brief published summaries of his career. It was something in which to take pride, because as Gerald W. Patton has noted, "black military men enjoyed high esteem in the black community; they were seen as an elite whose deeds and sacrifices were a key to improving the status of the whole race."[22]

Although he was not an officer, Pollard's status at Camp Meade was on a par with the hundred black officers who had been commissioned at Fort Des Moines, Iowa, and assigned to the 92nd Division. Early in the mobilization, a majority of civil rights leaders reluctantly agreed to the establishment of a separate facility, Fort Des Moines, for the training of African-American officers. In the segregated army of World War I, the life of a black officer was difficult as he confronted racism and discrimination at nearly every turn. The army had decided even before the opening of the officers' training camp in Iowa that few blacks would be commissioned, none should rise above the rank of captain, and that they should "be washed out as quickly as they could be charged with incompetence."[23]

At Camp Meade, for example, Howard H. Long, a newly commissioned black lieutenant, would later charge that higher-ranking white officers deliberately encouraged friction between the college-educated black lieutenants trained at Fort Des Moines and the black officers with regular army backgrounds and less schooling. According to Long, the regimental commander promoted the discord, which resulted in some black officers snooping on others and reporting misconduct, in order to dismiss as many African-American officers as possible, which he did. The problems at Camp Meade were not exceptional, and numerous cases of discrimination were reported to Scott or the black press. Many of the racial incidents were hushed up, however, because leaders such as Scott and Du Bois urged black citizens to "close ranks," put their grievances aside, and march shoulder to shoulder with their fellow white citizens in the name of the war effort. As one embittered African-American officer of the 92nd charged after the war, high-ranking white officers saw to it that "the 'ignorant' Regulars and the 'passive' Hampton Institute men got the highest commissions to insure that the black division would fail."[24]

Although life was arduous for black officers at Camp Meade and at other cantonments of the 92nd Division, evidence suggests that Pollard survived the ordeal better than many of his contemporaries, and to some extent prospered in the environment. In a later interview related to other matters, he noted that he made a number of good friends among white officers during the war. Late in the spring of 1918, moreover, Jay Williams was assigned to Camp Meade, and after a training course was commissioned as a first lieutenant. By that time, the army had closed the black officer school at Fort Des Moines, reduced the minimum age for African-American officers from twenty-five to twenty-one, and designated that the few future black officer candidates destined to serve as replacements would attend regular training camps, which included Camp Meade. It seems likely that Pollard used his influence with high-ranking white officers to secure Williams's assignment to the Maryland camp and expedited his entrance into the officer training program. Pollard's apparent leverage with the white officers at Camp Meade might have been due to his celebrity status as an All-America athlete or his relatively nonthreatening position as YMCA physical director, but he also had more experience in dealing with the white establishment than many of his contemporaries. He had grown up in a white neighborhood, been schooled by his family on how to survive and prosper in the white world, and had confronted and surmounted racial barriers at an elite white university. It is probable that Pollard carved out a niche for himself within the power structure at Camp Meade.[25]

During the summer of 1918 after most of the 92nd Division

had embarked for Europe, Pollard was reassigned as a physical director in the war department's new Student Army Training Corps (SATC) program, designed to train commissioned and noncommissioned officers on college campuses. As a result of pressure from African-American leaders including Emmett J. Scott, the army established units at a few black colleges. Pollard was assigned to the SATC detachment at Lincoln University. Given the fact that his brother Leslie had been a football coach at Lincoln, there is reason to suspect that Pollard used his influence both within the army and in the black community to secure the appointment. In October, while units of the 92nd and 93rd Negro Divisions fought against the German army on the Western Front, Pollard was transferred to the Lincoln University campus in Oxford, Pennsylvania, about forty miles southwest of Philadelphia. There, he assumed duties as athletic director of the Lincoln SATC unit, which included the position of head football coach.[26]

Lincoln University was one of the oldest black colleges in the nation. It was founded in 1854 as Ashmun Institute by John Miller Dickey, a white Presbyterian minister, and renamed Lincoln University in 1866. The school was small (usually about 300 students, but down to 140 in the war year of 1918) and originally designed to train religious leaders for Liberia and America. By 1918, Lincoln was under fire from more radical African-American leaders and some of its own alumni for being the only black college that refused to hire black faculty members or appoint African Americans to its board of trustees. In a scathing letter to the college dean in 1916, Reverend Francis J. Grimke, a Lincoln graduate and prominent civil rights leader, wondered "how colored people with any self-respect can continue to feel kindly towards an institution that takes that attitude towards their race."[27]

From an educational standpoint, Lincoln was one of the more progressive black colleges, offering a curriculum that emphasized liberal arts rather than the technical training at most other black colleges. Pollard was probably not much concerned about these matters in the fall of 1918. With the birth of his second child, Gwendolyn, in Boston earlier that year, he was preoccupied with supporting his family on his meager army pay, completing his wartime service, furthering his education, and making his way in the world.[28]

After he had settled Ada and the children in New York City with friends in the early fall, Pollard moved to Philadelphia, where he enrolled as a part-time student at the University of Pennsylvania with the hope of rectifying his academic deficiencies and, after the war, entering the university's Dental School. He was a busy man during that last autumn of the Great War. After attending classes at Penn in the morning, Pollard took a noon train to Oxford, where he assumed the duties of athletic director and head football coach. Compared with major white universities, Lincoln's athletic program was primitive. Both before and for a few years after the war, Lincoln students retained a considerable amount of control over intercollegiate athletics. A manager, elected by the student body, oversaw the expenditure of funds appropriated for intercollegiate sports, which amounted to $2–3,000. The football captain, also elected by the students, was a powerful force on the squad, often serving as an assistant coach, as he did for Pollard in 1918. Many white universities, such as Brown, earlier had a similar arrangement for intercollegiate teams, but by the turn of the century had opted for university control of athletic teams and the hiring of a largely professional coaching staff. Pollard was content with the Lincoln system in 1918 because of his heavy schedule and the fact that he had no intention of becoming a full-time football coach, but it would later lead him into a serious conflict with Lincoln student leaders and alumni.[29]

Traditionally, Lincoln scheduled a small number of football games, with most of them viewed as warm-ups for The Game against Howard University, the equivalent of the Harvard-Yale rivalry for many black sports fans. For Lincoln Lion partisans, the success of the season depended on the outcome of that one game. In 1918, the Lions played five contests, two of them against army camp teams because of the wartime emergency and the fact that most black colleges without SATC units had discontinued football by 1918. Despite the fact that Lincoln had lost most of its 1917 team to the military draft, the Philadelphia *Tribune*, the city's leading African-American newspaper, reported that Coach Pollard, "the greatest halfback America has produced," after looking over his squad "expressed his belief that the greatest team in the country might be developed therefrom." The *Tribune* also praised the government's support of athletics, especially football, on campuses with military units, a policy which would contribute to a "take-off" period in college athletics and sports generally in the postwar era.[30]

Pollard's optimism concerning the 1918 season was typically boastful but well-founded because some of the best African-American athletes in the nation enrolled at the few black colleges with SATC units in order to play football, seek advancement, and garner prestige through their participation in the officer training programs. After a 6–0 victory in a practice game against the Langston Athletic Club of Chester, Pennsylvania, the *Tribune* compared the current Lincoln squad to the great Lion team of 1914, and praised Pollard, who, the writer claimed, was "inspired by the great work of his brother, Leslie Pollard, of Dartmouth fame." The game, like many played by black college teams at the time, was marred by what the *Tribune* described as "divers wranglings and riots in embryo." Small athletic budgets and meager gate receipts from the sparse crowds who attended the games prevented black schools from hiring professional referees with the ability to keep the games under control. Many of the games were officiated by men selected by the home team, or as the visitors might say "homers," which often led to disputed calls and trouble. The Langston-Lincoln contest, for example, was refereed solely by a Lieutenant Smith of the Lincoln SATC detachment. The partisan *Tribune* reporter assigned the blame for the rough play to the Langston team and remarked that "football is a game designed to bring out those sterner qualities so necessary in true manhood along with an emphasis on the ability to work in perfect harmony and that spirit of oneness and unity so essential in these wartimes and that it is not a prize fight."[31]

On the two weekends preceding the signing of the Armistice in France, Pollard's Lincoln eleven proceeded to score successive shutout victories over an all-black army team from Camp Dix, New Jersey, and the Hampton Institute SATC squad at its Virginia campus. Employing a double-wing formation and the open style of play he had learned at Brown, Pollard proved to be an innovative and successful coach. During the wartime emergency, he was fortunate to have superior athletes, including fullback James Law and halfback Samuel Parr, counted among Lincoln's all-time great players. As he did later in his coaching career, Fritz emphasized solid defensive play, and he scrimmaged with his team during practice sessions in order teach and demonstrate proper blocking and tackling techniques. It was no accident that Lincoln finished the 1918 season not only undefeated, but also unscored upon.[32]

A few days after the guns fell silent in Europe, the Lincoln SATC squad journeyed to New York City to oppose an all-black army team from Camp Upton. The New York *Age* reported that "never before in the history of football games held between soldier teams has so much genuine enthusiasm been stirred in the breasts of civilian supporters." Pollard's prominence and reputation in the African-American community as a football virtuoso was apparent as the article stated that "opinion on the whole seems to be about evenly divided concerning the merits of the players, but because of Fritz Pollard's connection with the Lincolns as coach, slight odds prevail on the latter team's side to pile up the winning score." And pile up the score they did, drubbing the previously undefeated Camp Upton Ponies by a margin of 41–0. The stage was set for the Thanksgiving Day showdown with Howard at its Washington, D.C. campus.[33]

In a driving rain before "a big crowd" of 2,500, Pollard's Lions easily defeated its southern rivals by a score of 13–0. Future black college All-America James Law was the star of the game, scoring one touchdown, gaining 115 yards, recovering three fumbles, and according to the Philadelphia *Tribune* account, he "was in on every tackle." The 1918 Lincoln-Howard clash marked the end of an era and the dawn of a new age in black college football. Future contests between the two schools, dubbed "the Classic," would draw five-figure crowds at least until the Great Depression dampened enthusiasm; the game became one of the premier social and athletic events in the black community. For the moment, however, Pollard was well pleased with his first campaign as a coach, finishing the season undefeated, with Lincoln's goal line uncrossed and a season-ending, decisive victory over archrival Howard.[34]

Soon after the Armistice, the Lincoln SATC detachment was disbanded, and Pollard, like many of his contemporaries, was quickly mustered out of the service. He retained his position as athletic director at Lincoln, which paid $50 a month, but had to supplement that income in order to support his family. He was still interested in attending Penn Dental School, but was also considering returning to Brown if the proper financial arrangements could be worked out. On one of his frequent visits to New York City to see his family,

Pollard went to the Rockefeller family office in an effort to arrange a meeting with John D. Rockefeller, Jr. Rockefeller's receptionist noted that Fritz requested the interview to discuss "his returning to Brown University," but in all likelihood Pollard also wanted Rockefeller's financial support. Rockefeller declined to see Pollard, and Fritz returned to Philadelphia a bit dejected. Philadelphia, however, was the home of some of the oldest and most socially prominent African-American families in the nation, and Pollard used his networking connections dating from his summers at Narragansett Pier and his celebrity status as an All-America halfback to secure additional employment. He was employed as a bond salesman at the Brown and Stevens Bank, one of the largest black financial institutions in the North. Edward C. Brown, president of the bank and a prominent Philadelphia businessman, was also an avid Lincoln football fan. Brown would initiate Pollard into the world of finance, where Fritz would earn great wealth followed by bankruptcy in the roller-coaster economic environment of the 1920s (chapter 10).[35]

During his spare time, Pollard organized an intercollegiate basketball team in order to earn additional money. Drawing on fellow students at Penn, college men he had known in the service, and a couple of students from Lincoln, Pollard put together an all-black team called the Inter-Collegiates, later Pollard's Collegiates. Although Pollard's team was not an intercollegiate club in the modern sense of the term, it was by the standards of the day. With college basketball in a primitive stage of development and only loosely supervised by the NCAA, which had been founded in 1910, officially sanctioned college squads regularly played amateur athletic club teams and even professional quintets. Pollard's team, although lacking an academic affiliation, would have been considered a college team simply because it featured student-athletes. The team was managed by Charles A. Lewis, a prominent Philadelphia physician and avid Lincoln sports booster. From the scanty reports in the Philadelphia *Tribune*, it appears that the Inter-Collegiates played mostly athletic club teams and only a few college teams. Given the unstable state of amateur basketball at the time, the loose supervision by the NCAA and AAU, and Pollard's views on the subject of amateur sport, it is almost certain that the team played for pay.[36]

For Pollard, like many other Americans both black and white, the war years were a period of great turbulence. He had squandered an opportunity to acquire a first-rate education and perhaps duplicate his All-America season at Brown University. Failing to maintain his eligibility at Brown and seeing that the war had eroded the quality of college athletics, as well as not knowing when the conflict would end, Pollard opted for national military service. Taking advantage of his athletic prominence, his gregarious personality, and the survival skills his family had taught him so well, Pollard emerged from the Great War with new prospects and opportunities. He was a successful college football coach and had secured additional employment to support his family. By early 1919, he was well on his way toward making up his academic deficiencies at the University of Pennsylvania, planned to enroll in the Penn Dental School the next fall, and was already looking forward to the possibility of continuing his intercollegiate athletic career with the Pennsylvania Quaker football team.

THE MAKING OF A PRO

8

During the winter and early spring of 1919, Pollard continued to coach and play guard for the Inter-Collegiates, but also spent some of his free time perfecting his skills as a hurdler. He joined the Meadowbrook Athletic Club in Philadelphia and competed in several important amateur track meets on the East Coast. In February, Pollard finished third in the seventy-yard high hurdles at the prestigious Millrose Games at Madison Square Garden in New York. He also won the second heat in the low-hurdles event before a controversial decision, which Pollard believed was racially motivated, put him fourth in a close four-way finish in the finals. A Boston track authority who watched Pollard perform in that city remarked that "Pollard is recognized as one of the fastest men in getting off the mark in the hurdles," adding that "it was this remarkable speed in getting away that made him such a success in football."[1]

Twenty-five years old and approaching the peak of his athletic potential, Pollard honed his skills and sought out sports competition whenever he found the opportunity. His daughter, Leslie, born in 1919 in New York City, remarked later that her father was a brilliant man but the only thing people "cared about was his sports ability." In that first year after the war Pollard also seemed preoccupied with finding an outlet to display his considerable athletic talent. He would be fortunate enough to benefit from a postwar surge of public interest in sports, a time commentators would later recall as the "golden age of American sport." By June 1919, newspapers carried detailed reports of the Inter-Allied Games—the "military olympics"—in Paris, which American athletes, including the black sprinter and broad-jumper Sol Butler, dominated. During the summer, many Americans, seeking relief from the rigors of war, were thrilled by accounts of the heavyweight title fight between Jess Willard and Jack Dempsey in Toledo and the home-run-slugging exploits of a young Boston Red Sox pitcher and outfielder named Babe Ruth. The sports craze that would accelerate in the 1920s was just beginning.[2]

The summer of 1919, the "Red Summer" as the writer and civil rights leader James Weldon Johnson called it, also ushered in the most sustained period of interracial violence in the nation's history. Beginning in June and continuing through the end of the year, more than twenty-five race riots, including a small one in Philadelphia, erupted around the country, with the largest and most destructive in Chicago. A miniature war broke out between black Chicagoans and white which lasted for nearly two weeks and resulted in thirty-eight deaths and 537 injuries; twenty-three blacks were killed and another 342 were wounded. Although the cause of the riots remained white racism and discrimination, African Americans had adopted a new, more aggressive posture in defense of their rights, an attitude fostered by the war and which contributed to the extensive strife. The riots and subsequent investigations failed to bring any immediate statutory relief for African-American citizens, but events did signal a significant change of outlook in the black community. As one student of the riots, Arthur I. Waskow, has observed, "there were few Americans, of whatever race or whatever persuasion as to racial policy, who could doubt that Negroes would from 1919 on be prepared to fight back against attack."[3]

It was in this atmosphere of anxiety and high racial tension that Pollard passed his qualifying examinations and began attending classes at the University of Pennsylvania Dental School in September. While he seldom spoke about the Red Summer in later years, Pollard, like most African Americans, was undoubtedly affected by the racial strife. He seemed to adopt a more militant racial outlook in the years immediately after the war. His most pressing concerns, however, were academics and football—not necessarily in that order. With a year of college athletic eligibility remaining and no rule preventing professional school students from participating in intercollegiate sports, Pollard tried out for the Penn football team. The Quakers had never had a black football player and, according to

Pollard, the players gave him the cold shoulder from the opening day of practice. He scrimmaged with the second team against the varsity for a couple of weeks before he decided to quit. "Here I was an All-American," Pollard remembered, "and these guys were looking for me to kiss their behinds to play football with them. Hell, I was doing them a favor by coming out for the team. After the kind of treatment I had received my first years at Brown, I decided it wasn't worth it and dropped my thoughts of playing football at U. Penn." While there is little reason to doubt the accuracy of Pollard's account, it was also true that Penn, like a number of colleges, required transferring athletes to sit out a year before becoming eligible for varsity play. The fact that he would not have been eligible for a varsity game until the fall of 1920 may have been a reason for Pollard's decision to quit the team.[4]

Pollard resumed his coaching duties at Lincoln in early October. The Philadelphia *Tribune* reported that the many new men on the squad "crowded about eager to see and hear the man who humbled Yale and Harvard; and they were overjoyed to learn that they were to come under his tutelage." Lincoln played an attenuated schedule in 1919, focusing its attention on the big game with archrival Howard. Pollard used the extra free time to work himself into shape at the Lincoln practice sessions and play in a couple of professional games for the Union Athletic Association of Phoenixville, Pennsylvania. After warm-up victories over local club teams, the Lincoln Lions traveled to Hampton, Virginia, where they defeated their southern rivals by a score of 14–6. The only other regular season game in addition to the Howard Thanksgiving Day clash, now being heavily promoted as "the Classic" and scheduled for the Baker Bowl in Philadelphia, was slated for the following week against Virginia Union in Baltimore. During the week before the Virginia Union game, Pollard was contacted by Ralph "Fat" Waldsmith, coach and co-owner of the Akron Indian professional football team, who sought Fritz's services for Akron's Sunday game against Massillon. He told Pollard to call the Akron official Frank Nied or "simply come out and play if I decided to." Pollard said, "I'll be there," and with that reply would begin an illustrious career in what would soon become the National Football League.[5]

After the Saturday game in Baltimore which Lincoln won 12–6, Pollard took an 8 P.M. express train to Cleveland and a slower train down to Akron. Arriving early Sunday morning, he had difficulty finding a cab that would take a black passenger. Finally, a cabbie who had heard he was coming drove him to Frank Nied's cigar store, where, according to Pollard's recollection, he received a chilly reception. Nied, who was apparently treasurer of the Akron team, simply said hello and motioned him downstairs where some of the players were hanging about. "They all seemed to know about me," Pollard recalled, "but never said hello or anything, even while dressing to go out on the field." He later learned that some of the southern-born college players on the Indians resented his appearance, which had been heavily touted in the local papers. As the players were leaving for the pregame practice, Pollard heard a voice calling, "Heh, Fritz, come here." It was his former Brown teammate Clair Purdy, who had joined the Akron team after a stint in the Army Aviation Corps. "I felt better when I saw and talked with him," Pollard remembered, "and knew he was the one who sent for me."[6]

Although he did not know it at the time, Pollard was a marked man before he even reached the Rubber City that Sunday morning. Not only were some of his own teammates not glad to see him, but the Saturday edition of the Akron *Beacon Journal* had also reported that "dire threats have come from the [Massillon] Tiger camp of just what they are going to do to the little colored chap." The paper pointed out that Pollard had proven that he could take care of himself in games against Yale and Harvard; readers were assured that "he will finish out the game and add enough strength to the Indian eleven to assure victory over the visitors." Pollard had stepped into the hotbed of professional football competition in which a few teams stopped at almost nothing to gain supremacy. Massillon, led by fullback Stan Cofall and quarterback Gus Dorais, and Canton with Jim Thorpe, competed with Akron and a few other powerful teams for what many considered to be the professional football championship of the world. It was largely because Akron had lost consecutive games to archrivals Massillon and Canton that Pollard had been summoned from the East to bolster the Indian attack.[7]

Massillon defeated Akron that day 13–6 before a crowd estimated at 8,500 at Goodrich Field, but Pollard emerged as one of the stars of the game, scoring the lone Indian touchdown. "In running back punts he was sensational," the *Beacon Journal* reported, "while from the backfield position he carried the ball many times for long gains. The threat to 'get Pollard' failed to materialize," the article noted. "True it is that Tigers galore would pile on him every down in which he carried the ball, but Fritz would always come up smiling." The reporter concluded that "had Pollard been given a cleared way in his end runs he would have likely turned the tide of victory." In the days that followed, Pollard became the center of attention for Akron football fans. "Is Pollard better than Jim Thorpe?" the *Beacon Journal* asked. "Can an interference be formed ahead of him? These and other questions have been circulated." Pollard was pleased with his first game in the informal Ohio League. He recalled that "for that game in 1919 I got $200.00 and my expenses. Later I said to myself, this isn't bad."[8]

With his appearance in the Massillon game, Pollard began a career that spanned eight seasons in big-time professional football. The game had begun in western Pennsylvania in the early 1890s, when athletic clubs began paying players. Most researchers credit William W. "Pudge" Heffelfinger as becoming the first pro when he received $500 to play for the Allegheny Athletic Association in 1892. Although a good number of college stars tried their hand at pro football in its first decades, it increasingly became identified as a working-class sport. Unlike baseball, the football season was too short and the gate receipts too meager to make pro football anything like a career occupation. Many players held full-time jobs in industry and played on Sunday for the joy of it and to supplement their incomes. The blue-collar orientation of the game seems significant in explaining the long-standing hostility or apathy toward the game by leading newspapers, university officials, and a large segment of the public.[9]

As with Civil War-era professional baseball, early professional football was chaotic. In his autobiography, George Halas remarked that "paid football was pretty much of a catch-as-catch-can affair. Teams appeared one week and disappeared the next." He might have added that there was a large amount of betting on the games, in addition to allegations of thrown games, dirty play, poor officiating, rowdyism by both players and spectators, players jumping contract from one team to another, and Sunday games. Many of these same practices had caused earlier criticism of pro baseball. The practice that received the most criticism in the press, as well as from college officials, was the custom of hiring intercollegiate players — or occasionally entire college teams — to play in the Sunday games. In the 1910s, Columbus Panhandle players insisted, for example, that Notre Dame's Knute Rockne, then an assistant coach at his alma mater, had played against them on six different Sundays for six different teams and under six different assumed names. Even with so much to criticize legitimately, it is likely that the principle underlying complaint of certain sportswriters, college administrators, and coaches against the pro game was that the cream of the nation's youth was being corrupted by unsavory, lower-class elements. Outside of the small cities where most of the games were played, much of the public was simply apathetic about pro football.[10]

Unlike their counterparts in baseball, pro football owners were slow to organize and begin to stamp out the alleged vices. Although some informal "leagues" were formed, players came and went too rapidly and teams appeared and disappeared too frequently to sustain any real movement toward more effective organization and reform. By late 1915, the center of pro football enthusiasm had shifted to eastern Ohio, where the Canton Bulldogs had signed Jim Thorpe, who became a major gate attraction and the most recognized name in the game. Thorpe's career is so entwined in legend that it is difficult to determine just how great a player he really was. Pollard, who played against most of the best players of the postwar era but only opposed Thorpe when the Canton star was in his early to mid-thirties, considered Jim the greatest player he had ever seen.[11]

After wartime problems in 1918 including transportation shortages and a severe influenza epidemic, the loosely organized Ohio League gained momentum in 1919, and with Thorpe once again as its centerpiece, teams were determined to sign the best available talent and put the professional game on the map.

When Pollard stepped on the field against Massillon on November 9, 1919, he became only the sixth African American to play professional football. Charles W. Follis, who had played halfback for the Shelby (Ohio) Athletic Club from 1902 to 1906, was the first known black to play pro ball. One of his teammates at Shelby was Branch Rickey, who was instrumental in integrating major-league baseball a half-century later. Follis was followed by Charles "Doc" Young, a halfback for Akron from 1906 to 1908 and again in 1911, and then Henry McDonald, a halfback for the Rochester Jeffersons from 1911 to 1917. Gideon "Charlie" Smith, a tackle for the Michigan Aggies, had played one game for Canton in 1915. The fifth black player was Robert "Rube" Marshall, a former two-time second-team All-America end from Minnesota in 1905 and 1906, who played at Rock Island in 1919 and 1920, and Duluth in 1925. Marshall was nearly forty when he opposed Pollard and the Akron Indians in the final game of the 1919 season.[12]

Although evidence is sketchy, it appears that life on the gridiron had been difficult for the black players who preceded Pollard. Henry McDonald recalled, for example, that in one game against Canton in 1917, the Bulldogs' Greasy Neale shoved him out of bounds, cocked his fists, and shouted, "black is black and white is white, and where I come from they don't mix." Jim Thorpe prevented a donnybrook, according to McDonald, when he jumped between the two players and said, "we're here to play football." McDonald related that "Thorpe's word was law on the field" and he never had any problem after that. Pollard was often coy in assessing the treatment of the few African Americans who played with or against him during his seasons in the pro game. He began one interview in the 1970s by saying, "I don't think we were targets or anything. There weren't any real bad situations." After rattling off a litany of abuses perpetrated against him by fans, opposing players, or townspeople, which included verbal insults, threats, stone-throwing incidents, dirty play, and discrimination in hotels and restaurants, Pollard modified his position. "Now that I think about it," he said, "maybe there was a little more prejudice than I first recalled."[13]

Pollard's first big challenge as the featured star of the Indians came the Saturday before the Classic, when Akron faced its traditional and bitter rival the Canton Bulldogs. As usual, there was heavy betting on the game, and Akron management predicted a crowd of more than ten thousand at Goodrich Field. During the week before the game, the Akron *Beacon Journal* heavily promoted the contest, emphasizing the expected duel between Pollard and Jim Thorpe. One typical headline read: "TWO GREATEST BACKFIELD MEN IN PROFESSIONAL FOOTBALL CLASH HERE SUNDAY AFTERNOON IN GRID CLASSIC." By the time of the Canton contest, Pollard later maintained that he had negotiated a new contract with the Akron owners calling for $500 per game, which would have made him one of the highest-paid players in the country. In a move that was not unusual for the

Ohio teams in important games, the Akron management had hired five college stars who were to be in the starting lineup playing under assumed names. The *Beacon Journal* noted that, with the exception of Pollard, the entire backfield would be replaced and that the imported collegians would be "well known to all Akron followers of the grid game."[14]

On the day of the game it rained and then it snowed, but the weather did not deter some seven thousand "football bugs" from jamming the sidelines and the bleachers. Despite the infusion of new talent, Akron was no match for the Bulldogs; Canton overpowered the Indians on the muddy field and came away with a 14–0 victory. The much-heralded match-up between Pollard and Thorpe never materialized, as Thorpe sat out the first three periods and only entered the contest in the final quarter at the urging of the crowd. According to the *Beacon Journal*, "the big chief" played cautious football and "did not extend himself." He did make one excellent open-field tackle on Pollard to prevent an Akron touchdown. The local newspaper, perhaps a bit partisan, declared Pollard the star of the game for his brilliant open-field punt returns in the mud and snow, noting that "it took from three to six Canton tacklers to get him." Undoubtedly, Pollard had not forgotten his mud cleats that afternoon. The reporter concluded that had Pollard "been given the protection afforded the Canton backfield men he would have run circles around the opposition."[15]

Akron had a 4–4 season record, with two games remaining on a western road swing that matched them against the Pine Village, Indiana, team on Thanksgiving Day and the Rock Island Independents the following Sunday. Pollard had to beg out of Pine Village game because of the Lincoln-Howard clash set for the same day, but promised to join the team for the final game against Rock Island. He hurried back to Oxford to help prepare the Lincoln team for its big game. Charles A. Lewis, an eminent physician and sponsor of Pollard's basketball team, originated the idea of making the annual game the focal point of a major social gathering for an emerging class of African-American professional men and women. This upper strata of black society was financially able to join in America's search for amusement in the postwar years but barred because of race from the usual outlets. Lewis, perhaps with encouragement from Pollard, hoped "to canalize the great currents of the National scene, where its Negro population was concerned, into the annual Lincoln-Howard game."[16]

Emmett J. Scott, who had become secretary-treasurer of Howard University after his wartime service, strongly endorsed the idea and expertly promoted the event in both the black and white press. The publicity contained a strong element of snob appeal, as the main emphasis was on the elegant dances, house parties, and other social events scheduled in Philadelphia both before and after the game. In contrast to the normal Thanksgiving Day crowd of two to three thousand, more than ten thousand fans attended the first Classic at the Baker Bowl. The Philadelphia *Tribune* devoted about half of its story on the game to accompanying social events, noting "the presence of thousands of fashionable and ultrafashionable visitors from Washington, Baltimore, New York, Atlantic City, and other neighboring cities." Maintaining the theme, the writer reported the final score by stating that "the best ye gods had to offer these pent up souls on this auspicious occasion was a scoreless tie."[17]

Pollard was disappointed about the outcome because his Lion team had dominated play throughout the game. What was worse, Lincoln ball carriers had penetrated the Howard ten-yard line five times and fumbled each time. If Pollard wondered what part his absences from practice contributed to the Lions' sloppy play, he never said. He had little time for postgame analysis because he had to leave the following day to rejoin the Akron team in Illinois. In a driving snowstorm, Rock Island defeated the Indians by a score of 17–0 in what the *Beacon Journal* described as a "listless attraction." In fact, Akron was forced to play its last two games on icy, snow-covered fields in order to collect its guarantee, which paid for the trip. Pollard had completed part of a season in pro football and liked what he saw. He made tentative arrangements to return to Akron for another campaign.[18]

When Pollard journeyed to Akron the following October to begin the 1920 season, he was surprised to learn that he would be playing for a new team in a new league. After a disappointing season, the Akron Indian team ceased, and Frank Nied and Art Ranney put together a new organization, the Akron Pros. They retained a number of their former players, but added a few talented new men including former Rutgers linemen Bob "Nasty" Nash, who had played for Massillon, and Al "Budge" Garrett as well as fullback Andy "Rip"

King, center Russ Bailey, and quarterback Harry Harris from West Virginia University. The new league was the American Professional Football Association (APFA), which had been organized the previous summer by a group of Ohio pro football owners under the guidance of Ralph Hay of the Canton Bulldogs. Two years later, at the suggestion of Chicago Bears owner George Halas, the APFA was renamed the National Football League. The primary purpose of the league was to bring greater organization and prestige to the game, to require members to honor their rivals' player contracts, and to avoid hiring collegians. For publicity reasons, Jim Thorpe was named president of the APFA. Despite the fanfare given the new league, the APFA was loosely organized. Few if any teams were pressed for their $100 membership fees, and records do not clearly state which franchises were official league members, although most sources list fourteen teams for the initial season.[19]

Akron got off to a fast start in the 1920 campaign, winning two nonleague contests and two against league opponents while scoring ninety-eight points to the opposition's zero. Pollard scored only three touchdowns in those games, but his spectacular romps on punt returns, pass receptions, and end runs made him the team's leading ground-gainer and star player. He remained, however, a marked man both on and off the field. "Nied and Ranney befriended me," Pollard recalled, "because I was a Negro and they were afraid *for* me." Even Akron fans had mixed feelings about Pollard. Some came to League Park to see his sensational runs while others turned out to abuse the diminutive halfback both verbally and possibly physically. "Akron was just like Mississippi in those days," Pollard explained. "A lot of Southerners came there after the war," and they were very prejudiced. To avoid potential trouble, Pollard dressed for home games at Nied's cigar store, was driven to the park just before game time, and sprinted on the field as the teams lined up for the kickoff.[20]

On the gridiron, Pollard was the target of especially rough play from opposing players. It is difficult to determine the extent to which the opposition was out to "get" Pollard because the early pro game was characterized by extremely rough and sometimes unethical play, but Pollard was keenly aware that some opponents singled him out for extra harsh treatment. "The white players were always trying to hurt me," he later recalled, "and I had to be able to protect myself if I was going to stay in the game." Pollard responded to the threat in a typically restrained but direct manner. When players roughed him up or called him foul names, he recalled, "I'd pay them no mind, but I would notice who the player was, and the first opportunity that presented itself I'd kick them right in the guts or hit my knee up against their knee, knocking it out of joint. And then I'd let them know, quietly, why I did it. This worked with the hotels and restaurants, also," he added. "It wasn't too long after that, when those places that didn't want me were begging me for my patronage because I was a star and a drawing card wherever I went." In the early 1970s, Pollard calmly reflected on how he dealt with the racial barriers he had faced during his early days in pro football. "My father had taught me that I was too big to be humiliated by prejudiced whites," he told a black sportswriter. "If I figured a hotel or restaurant didn't want me, I stayed away. I didn't go sniffing around hoping they'd accept me. I was never interested in socializing with whites. I was there to play football and make my money."[21]

By the 1920 season, Pollard was one of the best-paid players in the APFA, possibly second only to Thorpe. He was paid well because he was a spectacular player and thus a gate attraction, and also because of his race. As a small black player facing the then-giants of the gridiron, Pollard was a curiosity. Some fans came out to cheer him while others hurled racial insults at him and possibly hoped he would be maimed. They did turn out to see him, however, at Akron's League Park and other fields around the APFA.[22]

Pollard was also well paid because he began to assume duties as an Akron coach beginning late in the 1919 season. Although reliable sources indicate that he became the first black APFA-NFL head coach beginning in 1921, when he shared that position with the former Penn State halfback Elgie Tobin, Pollard maintained that he began coaching in Akron in 1919. The long-standing controversy over when Pollard became the first black coach in the soon-to-be NFL is understandable because the position of professional head coach was much different then than it is today. Pro teams placed less emphasis on who was head coach than did the colleges. According to pro football pioneer Pearce Johnson, coaches had a limited role. "The difference between then and now," Johnson stated, "is that the coach could not coach from the sidelines. Not at all. He had to sit in one place [on the bench]. So the captain really called the game." In addition, if a substitute entered the game and talked to the quarterback, the referee was supposed to call a penalty. Pollard maintained that in conjunction with Purdy, he introduced the more wide-open system of play they had learned at Brown to the Akron team beginning in 1919. "From that point on," he insisted, "I was really the head coach. Even though the record books don't give me credit, I coached Akron in 1919, 1920, and in 1921 when the league became the National Football League."[23]

The first showdown match of the initial APFA season in 1920 was the always exciting clash between Akron and Canton. Undefeated in four games, the Pros traveled to Canton in late October to meet the Bulldogs, who were undefeated in league play. Richard Lechner, an Akron resident at the time, recalled that "always, this game was a Titanic struggle between contrary styles; the small but magic Pollard arrayed against the lightning-fast Thorpe. Closing my eyes, I can see them now. As I said, a personal duel. Not passing, not the quarterback, but two running and tackling backs, beautiful to behold." Pollard remembered arriving in Canton late that Sunday morning because his Lincoln team had played and defeated Shaw University, 28–0, the previous day in Philadelphia's Baker Bowl. He immediately heard rumors that Thorpe had been going around town betting that "that nigger's scared to come and play." When Pollard entered the Courtland Hotel, Thorpe was standing in the lobby. As Pollard later recalled, "I saw him and said, 'Oh, hello there, black boy.' He turned around, looked at me, and replied, 'what do you mean by that?' I said, 'just what I said.' " Pollard later maintained, perhaps referring to his own Indian ancestry, that "Jim Thorpe was as black as I was."[24]

What Pollard meant by the remark remains unclear. It was common in that era, however, for white players to assert that opponents with darker skin had Negro blood. Babe Ruth, for example, who had a swarthy complexion, would sometimes become uncontrollably angry when the opposition called him a Negro or worse. It is clear that Pollard did not mean the remark as a compliment. The confrontation continued a few hours later at Lakeside Park before a crowd estimated at more than ten thousand. Akron took a 10–0 lead in the first half on a Charles Copley field goal and a fifty-yard touchdown run by tackle Pike Johnson on an intercepted pass. Early in the second half, Thorpe entered the game for the first time, and "the Canton squad put on a desperate offensive with both

Thorpe and Guyon making substantial gains through the line." The Canton drive failed to produce a score, however, as Thorpe's eighteen-yard field-goal attempt hit the cross bar and fell away. Pollard recalled that he was playing defensive quarterback and returning punts, and that Thorpe tried "to get me when we had the ball. But, I ran offside, twisted and squirmed, and kept out of his way."[25]

In the most memorable play of the game, the frustrated Thorpe ordered his punter to kick short to Pollard, while Jim and his former Carlisle teammate Joe Guyon sprinted downfield with the intent of knocking Pollard out of the game. According to the historian Harry A. March, "the Indians particularly hated Pollard and 'laid for him.'" The punt carried thirty yards past the line of scrimmage "and high enough that the Indians could cover it easily and be ready for the 'kill.' When Pollard caught the ball, Guyon did a flying tackle on the one side and Thorpe on the other. As the ball struck his ready hands, Pollard dropped face down on the ground, the Indians' heads collided like the impact of locomotives; both were unconscious and did not play any longer that half, while Pollard leaped to his feet and carried the ball back to the line of scrimmage." As with many early pro football tales, March embellished the story. He placed the incident early in the game when, in fact, Thorpe did not enter the contest until the second half. The game account also shows that neither Guyon nor Thorpe was replaced in the third or fourth periods. Pollard gave a similar account of the incident, placing it correctly in the second half, but he mistakenly had himself scoring a touchdown on the play. While the legend of the Thorpe-Pollard rivalry has been magnified over the years, there is little doubt that they were two of the talented, crowd-pleasing stars of the early APFA.[26]

Akron's 10–0 victory over Canton was one of the few league games widely reported upon by the national press and major African-American newspapers because it marked the first defeat for Thorpe's Bulldogs since 1917. A second showdown game was scheduled for Akron's League Park on Thanksgiving Day, where the once-defeated Bulldogs hoped to derail the Pros, who remained unbeaten, in their bid to become the mythical world champions of professional football. A collegiate tradition, Thanksgiving Day contests were then uncommon in professional football because a number of players, like Pollard, coached college or high school teams that had important games set for the day. But almost all of the players showed up in Akron, including Pollard, because of the importance of the professional game. Pollard placed his friend and former Rutgers All-America end Paul Robeson, whom Fritz had hired as his assistant during the season, in charge of the Lincoln Lions, who faced Howard that day in the Classic at the American League Park in Washington, D.C.[27]

In Akron, Pollard played a solid game on both offense and defense as the Pros made a first-quarter touchdown stand up for a 7–0 victory over Canton. The second consecutive victory over the Bulldogs gave the undefeated Akron team the inside track for the unofficial championship of the APFA. Before returning to Philadelphia, Pollard made a brief Saturday appearance in a pro all-star game played before a disappointing crowd of three thousand on a rain-soaked field in Pittsburgh.[28]

When Pollard learned of Lincoln's humiliating 42–0 defeat at the hands of Howard is not known, but he must have been amazed. Robeson, assisted by former Harvard baseball and football star William Clarence Matthews, coached Lincoln in Washington, but the Lions were apathetic and dispirited. Not long after the debacle Pollard became the target of much criticism. The Philadelphia *Tribune* charged that he had refused to allow the Lincoln team to travel to Virginia on the Thursday preceding the Saturday, November 6, game with Hampton Institute and had insisted that the Lions leave on Friday. The result was, according to the *Tribune*, that the Lincoln eleven had arrived in Hampton without Pollard and about "six hours before the game with a sleepy rest broken eleven." Although the team played well under the circumstances, the Lions lost 14–0, and the writer claimed that "this defeat broke the spirit of what had thus far seemed an invincible team." The *Tribune* further charged that Pollard had been absent from the team "over two-thirds of the time. Why Lincoln stood for such haphazardness," the writer concluded, "puzzled and still puzzles some of her many admirers."[29]

Pollard immediately defended himself in a public statement printed in the New York *Age* and other black papers. He declared that "I have no apologies to make for the showing of the Lincoln team. I have led them to victory and honorable athletic achievement during the previous two years." Pollard claimed that the football manager and members of the faculty interfered with him and "assumed authority over me and dictated my language and attitude toward the men on the field." He blamed the sleepless Hampton trip on university authorities who had insisted that the team travel to Virginia by boat. "As an indication of the lack of interest shown by the authorities at Lincoln," Pollard stated, "no football shoes were provided for the men. I myself bought and paid $200 out of my pocket for football shoes for my team. This money has never been repaid." Pollard maintained that Lincoln authorities understood that he could not support his family on his football salary, and that "they were satisfied to have me divide my time with professional teams." He concluded by saying that "the Lincoln faculty beat the Lincoln football team, not Howard."[30]

Pollard made a number of valid points in defense of his handling of the football team. Lincoln athletics were in a primitive stage of development in which students and faculty members largely controlled the program. Funding for the football team was minimal and primarily controlled by the student manager. Pollard's $50 a month salary indicates that his position was that of a part-time coach. He undoubtedly had permission of university officials to leave the team after Saturday games in 1919 and join the Akron squad for its Sunday contests. As his pay and coaching obligations increased at Akron in 1920, however, Pollard frequently left Oxford on Thursdays to perform his duties as an Akron coach. It is unclear whether or not Lincoln officials either knew about or condoned his increasing absences. The truth about the circumstances surrounding the disastrous Hampton trip is unclear. Pollard did make the trip to Virginia with the team, the *Tribune* story notwithstanding, but whether he or university officials insisted on the Friday boat trip cannot be determined. What is clear is that Lincoln needed a full-time professional coach by 1920, and that Pollard's commitment to professional football prevented him from filling that role.[31]

Shortly after the football controversy was aired publicly, Lincoln administrators and prominent alumni met in Jersey City and restructured the university's athletic program. As had happened several decades earlier at major white universities, the administration and alumni assumed a large measure of control over the football program from the once-powerful student manager and captain. A report on the conference stated that "it was agreed that the Lincoln-Howard game had now grown to proportions that merited more professional management than could be provided by students or members of the faculty." Lincoln alumnus Walter G. Alexander, the newly appointed graduate manager of athletics, appointed John Shelbourne, a recent star fullback at Dartmouth, as head coach and provided him with an assistant. Paul Robeson, who many expected to be the next head coach, may have turned down the job out of loyalty to Pollard.[32]

Although the New York *Age* article that carried Pollard's rebuttal stated that he received $10,000 annually for playing at Akron, the amount he actually made at the peak of his professional career is one of the intriguing questions that may never be answered accurately. He claimed in a number of later interviews that he was paid $1,500 per game for important contests with Akron, which put him ahead of the $1,000 he said Jim Thorpe earned. The modern researchers of the Professional Football Researchers Association estimate that the average pro salary for the era was $75-$150 a game, with star players receiving a little more. The highest documented per-game salary for 1920 is the $300 that the Chicago Cardinals paid star quarterback Paddy Driscoll. George Halas, who paid the salaries of the Decatur Staleys in 1920, maintained that his players averaged $125 per game and that Guy Chamberlin got the largest amount for the season, $1,650. From these figures, it appears that Pollard exaggerated his per-game salary. Given his superior play for the Akron team, his contribution as coach, and his enormous appeal as a gate attraction, however, there is little reason to doubt that Pollard was one of the highest-paid players in the APFA in 1920.[33]

While the Lincoln controversy continued to rage in the African-American community on the East Coast, Pollard returned to Ohio to finish out the pro campaign. He seemed little affected by the turmoil as he led Akron to a 14-0 victory over the Dayton Triangles in late November. During the third period of a scoreless game, Pollard scooped up Rip King's fumble at midfield and squirmed and twisted his way into the Triangle end zone. In the final quarter, he grabbed King's pass for a thirty-two-yard score that ensured the Akron victory. The following week in Buffalo Pollard stood out on both offense and defense in helping to secure a scoreless tie with the All-Americans. By virtue of the tie and an 8-0-2 overall record, the best in the APFA, Akron legitimately claimed to be the champions of professional football. With the title apparently secure, Akron planned to capitalize on its newly gained prominence with an exhibition tour of the West Coast to play professional teams there.[34]

Soon after the Buffalo game, while Pollard was preparing to play in a postseason game for the Union Athletic Association against Thorpe and the Canton Bulldogs in Philadelphia, he received a call from Halas, the coach and right end for the Decatur Staleys, who proposed a game between his team and Akron for December 12 at Cubs Park in Chicago. The Staleys, owned by a Decatur, Illinois, starch manufacturer, had one loss and one tie in twelve games, and had declared themselves professional champions of the West. Pollard had known Halas from their high school days in Chicago, and according to Fritz, he did Halas a favor by begging out of the Philadelphia exhibition contest and urging his reluctant teammates to schedule the game with Decatur. "We had won the world championship and the Akron team didn't want to go to Chicago," Pollard admitted. "But I said, 'I'm a Chicago boy. Let's go!' " Pollard's interest in the contest was no doubt heightened by the fact that he had not performed in Chicago since his semipro days in 1912. The Akron team and management agreed to the game, which would lead to a long-standing feud between Pollard and Halas.[35]

Twelve thousand Chicagoans, the largest crowd to see a professional game in the city, turned out in damp weather to see the eastern and western champions collide. The teams fought to a scoreless tie on the slippery turf, with Akron dominating the first half and the Staleys the second. In the later recollections of Halas and Pollard, the story of the game became clouded by the omission of significant facts, half-truths, and blatant embellishment. Halas mistakenly recalled in his autobiography that he intercepted a pass, broke into the clear, "and should have scored, but slipped." He failed to note that he broke league rules by hiring Paddy Driscoll of the Chicago Cardinals to play halfback for the Staleys that day. In his only mention of Pollard, Halas asserted correctly that he managed to tackle the Akron star on several occasions.[36]

Pollard's recollection of the game was no better. He mistakenly recalled making two touchdown runs which were nullified by "phantom" penalties called by a hometown referee. He undoubtedly exaggerated the importance of the game when he implied that the Akron-Decatur contest was the making of Halas, who would move the Staleys to Chicago the following year and became co-owner of the team, renamed the Chicago Bears, in 1922. "He used me to get recognized," Pollard said, and "then Halas refused to play Akron the next year unless Akron dropped me. And he refused to play Milwaukee the next year when I went up there." Pollard complained bitterly in a 1976 interview that "George Halas used me to get every goddam thing he could. Then after he used me and got power, he raised the prejudice barrier. If George Halas was still like he was then, he wouldn't have allowed a black player in Chicago because he was as prejudiced as hell." When confronted with Pollard's charges in the mid-1970s, Halas refuted them all: "He's a liar. At no time did the color of skin matter. All I cared about was the color of blood. If you had red blood, I was for you." When asked why there were no blacks in the NFL from 1934 until after World War II, Halas replied somewhat lamely that he did not know. "Probably the game didn't have the appeal to black players at the time." Halas concluded by saying that Pollard was "trying to involve me in something so he can have something to talk about. There is nothing to it. He was a fine football player. . . . But Jesus!"[37] Although he did not sign a black player during this period, Halas's Chicago team continued to play NFL teams that included black players through the 1933 season.

After the Chicago game, the Staleys proclaimed themselves world champions on the basis of the tie with Akron, and the title remained in dispute until former Columbus Panhandle manager Joe Carr was named president of the league in 1921 and rightly awarded a championship cup to Akron. At the time, the APFA awarded the title on the basis of a vote by league members at the winter meetings, with the best record and caliber of the opposition taken into consideration. On that basis, Akron was clearly best. The Pros went from Chicago to California, where they played a number of exhibition games with makeshift West Coast teams. According to Pollard, "it was the first time they ever had pro or semi-pro football in California." The trip was not entirely successful, however, as many of the scheduled games were cancelled, and Pollard and most of his teammates made their way back east with their pockets nearly empty. Somewhere along the way, he may have learned that he had been named to an all-pro team named by the Rock Island *Argus* sportswriter Bruce Copeland, who chose the players from his list of the "big eight" professional teams of Ohio and Illinois. All in all, despite his difficulties at Lincoln and the disappointing exhibition tour on the West Coast, Pollard had had a very successful football season.[38]

A FOOTBALL ODYSSEY

9

In early 1921, shortly after his return from the West Coast exhibition tour with the Akron Pros, Pollard moved with his wife and children to Cleveland. One can only speculate why Pollard left Philadelphia and what attracted him to the Ohio city. He had, of course, lost his job at Lincoln, but perhaps more important was the fact that his reputation had been damaged by the Lincoln football controversy. Despite his spirited rebuttal of charges made against him, articles in the Philadelphia *Tribune* continued to imply that Pollard was primarily responsible for the failure of the Lincoln football team. With his reputation under a cloud, it is possible that Pollard used his connections at Brown and Stevens, Philadelphia's largest black-owned bank, to make financial contacts in Cleveland. Brown and Stevens, moreover, was beginning to experience economic difficulties by 1921, and may have encouraged Pollard to seek new employment. As he would do several times during his career when he was publicly criticized, Pollard moved on to a new city and new opportunities.[1]

Cleveland was a logical choice for relocation because it was within easy commuting distance of Akron, where Pollard had agreed to play another season with the Pros. In 1921, the Associated Negro Press touted Cleveland as a "mecca for colored people." The nation's fifth-largest city, according to the dispatch, had forty thousand black residents, a 400 percent increase since 1900, and a liberal racial environment. "There are nearly 100 school teachers in the mixed public schools; there is an 'open door' policy in the theatres, restaurants and hotels; there is fellowship in civic and political progress, and there is a 'better understanding.' That latter is the secret of all."

Although the Associated Negro Press clearly exaggerated the degree of racial harmony in Cleveland, Fritz and Ada, who were expecting their fourth child, Eleanor, later in the year, no doubt welcomed the opportunity to set up a household closer to Akron. It is likely that Pollard was employed by either a black realty or banking firm in Cleveland, although no specific evidence documents that fact. The only record of his activities is that he coached a black basketball team, the Askin Specials, during the winter and spring, which would indicate that he had connections in Cleveland even before he arrived there in the winter of 1921.[2]

With his family settled and the birth of his third daughter, Pollard looked forward to his second APFA season in which Akron would defend its world championship. Although he maintained that he had assisted in coaching the Akron team beginning in 1919, the year 1921 is the first year that reliable sources list Pollard as head coach, along with Elgie Tobin. Akron got off to a strong start in the fall campaign, with 14–0 and 41–0 whitewashings of the Columbus Panhandles and the Cincinnati Celts before the home fans at League Park. The following Sunday at Normal Park in Chicago the Pros stunned Paddy Driscoll's Chicago Cardinals 23–0. Pollard must have taken special satisfaction in his performance before the fans in his native city. He was the outstanding player of the game, scoring two touchdowns, one on a line buck in which he "squirmed, twisted, sidestepped and broke away" on a fifty-yard jaunt.[3]

During the Chicago game, Paul Robeson made his professional football debut as a substitute tackle for the Pros and proved to be "a mountain of strength" as he broke up plays coming around his side of the line. Pollard had recruited the six-foot-two, 220-pound former Rutgers All-America end to replace Nasty Nash, who had moved on to the Buffalo All-Americans and who many, including Jim Thorpe, considered to be the best of the early NFL linemen. Robeson did not disappoint Akron fans; he had an outstanding season playing both tackle and end. A handsome and likable man who had won the coveted Phi Beta Kappa key at Rutgers, Robeson divided his time between attending classes at Columbia Law School in New York City and professional football engagements, mainly in the Midwest. Like Pollard, Robeson played because of his love of the game, the considerable money involved, and the status it represented in the African-American community. During the 1921 season, according to Pollard's account, he introduced Robeson to Florence Mills at the Cafe Zanzibar in the old Winter Garden Theater in New York, where she offered Robeson an opportunity to sing during the floor show, directly launching his musical career. By 1923, Robeson had abandoned his interest in the law and football and launched a spectacular career as a singer and actor.[4]

Led by Pollard and Robeson and featuring veteran stars from the 1920 championship team including Al Nesser, Pike Johnson, Russ Bailey, Charley Copley, and Rip King, Akron blitzed its way to a 7–0 record and blanked the opposition through early November. In Detroit where the Pros humbled the Panthers 20–0 on October 16, the Detroit *Free Press* commented that Pollard's sprinting receptions and runs on punt returns "would make Tris Speaker mad." The following week Akron defeated Canton 3–0 before a full house at the latter's Lakeside Park on quarterback Paul Sheeks's forty-yard dropkick. Playing for Canton that day was Pollard's former college roommate Ink Williams, whom Fritz had recruited to play for his friend Alva A. Young, owner of the Hammond Pros. In a move not that unusual at the time, Canton had signed Williams to play in just the one game because Hammond had an open date that day. Reflecting the racial climate of the time, the Canton *Daily News* could not resist pointing out that Pollard, Robeson, and Williams comprised "a trio of Ethiopians in action." Relatively easy wins over the Rochester Jeffersons and Columbus Panhandles left the Pros undefeated and kept intact a remarkable string of twelve consecutive league games without a defeat; no points had been scored against them dating back to November 14, 1920.[5]

Despite Akron's fast start, a number of Pros were badly injured by midseason as the team faced a stretch drive for another championship. Both Pollard—who led the league in scoring with forty-two points—and Robeson had game legs, and a number of other players had nagging injuries. Many years later when Pollard was asked to compare football in his time with the modern game, he noted that the biggest difference and most challenging aspect of the early game was that most players played the whole game. Teams only carried fifteen or sixteen players and, Pollard said, "if you didn't play 60 minutes you just might not have gotten paid." Akron used just thirteen players in its important clash with the undefeated Buffalo All-Americans on an icy field at Canisius College. The Buffalo game proved to be the turning point of the season for the Pros. With Pollard as well as the star Buffalo backs Elmer Oliphant and Oc Anderson, stymied by the ice and snow, the game ended in a scoreless tie. Although the Pros' unbeaten and unscored-upon streak remained intact, Akron suffered key injuries which seemed to affect its play the rest of the season. Both Pollard and Robeson reinjured their legs, and quarterback Paul Sheeks, an Indian from South Dakota University, was also injured. After ripping off seven touchdowns in the first six games, Pollard would fail to score for the rest of the season.[6]

The following week in Dayton the Triangles stunned the Pros 3–0, putting Akron's championship hopes in jeopardy. Robeson failed to start the game and played cautiously, the Dayton *Journal* reported, while "Pollard, the slippery colored boy, was on the side lines most of the time." Pollard imported Bunny Corcoran, an end, and Bruno Haas, a fullback, from the Cleveland Tigers to help bolster the Akron lineup for the upcoming pivotal home game against the Canton Bulldogs. With both Buffalo and the Chicago Staleys still undefeated, the Thanksgiving Day clash with Canton was a must-win situation for the Pros. Pollard and Robeson again played sparingly, and Sheeks watched from the sideline as the Bulldogs dominated the Pros 14–0, virtually eliminating Akron from the title chase. Despite statements in the Akron *Beacon Journal* that the players and management were not disheartened by the loss, Pollard came under criticism for his below-par play and for signing the two players from Cleveland who proved to be ineffective against the Bulldogs.[7]

When the results of the Thanksgiving Day games revealed that Buffalo had defeated the Staleys in Chicago, Akron still had a slim hope to repeat as champion. It needed to defeat Halas's team the next Sunday and somehow schedule and defeat Buffalo before the season ended. In early pro football, teams arranged their own games, and contending teams usually juggled schedules toward the end of the season to pit themselves against the league leaders. Pollard and the Pros were dismayed, however, when they learned that George Halas had cancelled the Staleys' tentatively scheduled game with Akron in order to get another crack at the league-leading Buffalo All-Americans. Halas's actions were businesslike when he cancelled the Akron game and scheduled a contest with Buffalo, however, because it was his team's only chance to win the championship.

Pollard, however, never forgave Halas for dashing whatever slim hopes Akron had to repeat as champions and attributed his actions to racial motives.[8]

In a desperate effort to stay in the championship race, Akron scheduled a rematch with Buffalo in New York on December 3, the day before the All-Americans were to face the Staleys in Chicago. Buffalo drubbed the Pros 14–0, but it proved to be a costly victory because the All-Americans were defeated by the well-rested Staleys the next day by a score of 10–7, which allowed Chicago to claim the championship. The Pros also moved on to Chicago on December 4, where they finished their season with a 7–0 victory over the Cardinals, giving them an 8–3–1 record and third place in the league.[9]

During the off-season, Pollard accepted an offer from two Chicago promoters, Joseph Plunkett and Ambrose McGuirk, to organize a team in Milwaukee which would join what by then was called the National Football League. Pollard had received criticism from Akron management and some of the players after the Pros went into a nosedive toward the end of the season. Playing injured and sparingly during the last third of the season, Pollard failed to match his usual spectacular performances. After the season, the Cleveland *Gazette* reported that "promoters of the team charge Pollard played indifferent football last fall, and have released him," adding that Robeson "was handed his release slip at the same time." Pollard's only recorded comment on the subject of his release was that he was well accepted as head coach by the players "until I got players from around Chicago and up North" — possibly a reference to Robeson, Sheeks, or the two Cleveland Tiger players. Pollard did not remain dejected for long about his release from Akron because he received an offer from his childhood friend, the famed golfer Charles "Chick" Evans, to help capitalize and to lead a black investment banking firm in Chicago. It is not clear whether the Milwaukee football proposition or Evans's offer came first, but it is likely that Pollard decided upon the move to Chicago first and then engineered the deal with Evans. He later recalled that his father retired from the barber business in 1922 and his brother Frank, who was expected to run the barbershop, had a good job in a laundry. "I didn't want him to lose it [the laundry job] so I had a summer and I took over the barbershop and ran the thing myself." It is probable that Pollard met Evans, a Rogers Park native, at the barbershop, where they discussed the establishment of the black investment firm to be called F. D. Pollard and Company. Pollard moved his family to nearby Evanston and commuted to Milwaukee in the fall as he helped organize a new NFL franchise to be nicknamed the Badgers.[10]

Pollard also may have welcomed the move to his native city because his marriage was unraveling. Apparently his relationship with Ada had been strained for several years. Sometime between 1918 and 1920, Pollard sent his young son to Rogers Park to be raised by his parents. It is unclear whether Ada approved of this decision, but young Fritz grew up in a separate household from his sisters. None of the children understood why their father made this decision, but it may have indicated an early breach in Fritz and Ada's relationship. Beyond this, the couple had been frequently separated since their wedding day and often lived in different cities.

In Milwaukee, Pollard shared head-coaching duties with Budge Garrett, a former teammate at Akron and adversary on the 1916 Rutgers team, while Joe Plunkett served as the team's general manager. During late September, the Badgers trained at St. John's Military Academy in Delafield, Wisconsin, a site familiar to Fritz from his high school days. Garrett and Pollard recruited a team comprised primarily of former eastern college stars, many from Rutgers. Pollard enlisted his former teammate Clair Purdy to play quarterback, the former Harvard All-America Dick King for a wingback, and Paul Robeson, who agreed to join the team as soon as he could transfer to Marquette University in Milwaukee to continue his law studies. Despite the abundance of former All-America players (seven would eventually play for the 1922 team), the Badgers got off to a slow start on the road. In the season opener, Pollard's first-period fumble led to a Paddy Driscoll field goal which stood up for a Chicago Cardinal 3–0 victory. The following week in Toledo, where Robeson joined the team, Milwaukee led the entire game until a Maroon touchdown with forty seconds to play tied the score at 12–12, the final result. Pollard scored a touchdown but also missed both extra points which if converted would have given the Badgers a more respectable start in the NFL.[11]

The Badgers were greeted warmly in Milwaukee, however, as more than six thousand fans turned out for the home-opener at Athletic Park against the Racine Legion Belles, who already had defeated Green Bay and barely lost to the Chicago Bears. Using an unbalanced line and "eastern formations," Milwaukee got off to a fast start, scoring two first-half touchdowns to take a 13–0 lead at intermission, Pollard making one on a short run. By the third period, it was clear that Pollard was the crowd's favorite and the game's dominant force. After he was taken out in the second half, the Racine *Journal-News* reported that "without Pollard the teams were more evenly divided and the Belles held them from going over." Pollard entered the game again at the start of the fourth quarter "upon the popular clamor" of the fans and proceeded to score a final touchdown, giving the Badgers a 20–0 victory. Robeson also played "a remarkable game," according to the Milwaukee *Journal*, which praised his ability "to stand in the midst of a crowd of secondary defensive players and pick passes out of the air."[12]

Despite the impressive home-opening victory, there is evidence that all was not right with the Milwaukee Badgers. The Milwaukee *Journal* reported that Badger linemen "frequently changed positions" and that "a certain amount of 'crabbing'" marred the team's play in the first half. The frequent movement of some of the Badger players was the result of defensive tackle John Alexander moving off the line of scrimmage and to the outside, making him the first outside linebacker in NFL history. Alexander had used the technique at Rutgers, but it had never been seen in the Midwest. The *Journal* attributed what it called "the disposition to superfluous conversation" to overanxiety to make a good showing, but there is reason to believe there was some dissension on the team. Possibly the Badgers had too many big-name players who had never played together and found it difficult to meld into a cohesive unit. Or perhaps some of the players resented the leadership of Budge Garrett, an Indian, and Fritz Pollard, an African American. One writer who later questioned Pollard about his problems in Milwaukee felt that "interference from some of the owners as to the team's operation, and resentment that a Black man was running the show, curtailed Fritz'[s] tenure in Milwaukee."[13]

The following two Sundays before the home fans the Badgers struggled to scoreless ties with Green Bay, called the Blues in 1922, and the Hammond Pros. When Pollard failed to start against Green Bay due to a leg injury, "a murmur of disappointment wizzed [*sic*] through the crowd" of 6,500 at Athletic Park. "But this was changed to roars of delight when the pygmy, colored star took his position

in the third period," reported the Milwaukee *Journal*. "The insertion
of Pollard completely changed the aspect of things" until the Blues
"got him" on an open-field run in the fourth period and knocked
him out of the game. The Blues seemed delighted to have come
away with a tie against the Badgers, whom the Green Bay *Press-
Gazette* referred to as the "moleskin celebrities." With Robeson,
Captain Jim Dufft, and himself injured, Pollard sent for his former
Akron teammate Charley Copley to bolster the Badger line. It was
to no avail, however, as Milwaukee could only manage a tie with
the hapless Hammond Pros. Entering the game for the first time in
the third quarter to a chorus of cheers, Pollard gained important
yardage but missed four field goals, two being blocked, to seal the
Badgers' fate.[14]

With key injuries and the team in apparent disarray, Joe Plunkett
announced the release of three players and the signing of three
others, including the former Syracuse All-America center Joe Alexander, for the upcoming home game with Rock Island. At the time,
Alexander was coach of Rochester, but the Jeffersons, who had
played recently in Racine, had no NFL games scheduled in the
immediate future. The Rock Island Independents took the field in
a driving rain for their pregame warm-up at Athletic Park before "a
pompous announcer" told the 1,500 faithful Badger fans that the
game had been cancelled. He was greeted with boos and hissing
from Milwaukee partisans and calls of "drag out those 'parlor babies'
and 'where are the big-time Badgers?' "[15]

The cancellation of the Rock Island game appears to have been
the cause of a major rift between manager Joe Plunkett and his
coaches, and possibly between Garrett and Pollard and some of
their players. It cannot be known for certain why Plunkett and
McGuirk cancelled the game, but it seems likely that they stood to
lose money with only 1,500 fans in attendance at $1.50–$2 each.
Of that, they would have had to pay their own players, pay rent to
Otto Borchert who owned the park, and possibly pay a share of
gate receipts or a guarantee to the Independents. It is also possible
that they had rain insurance to cover any losses in the event of a
rain-out. Naturally, the Milwaukee players wanted to play in order
to be paid; some may have blamed Garrett and Pollard for failing
to get management to go on with the game.[16]

Two weeks later when the Badgers opposed Jim Thorpe's Oorang Indians in their final home game, Plunkett and McGuirk assured Milwaukee fans that the game would be played "rain, snow, or shine." The hometown fans were forgiving of the Badger management and players, and some 7,500 turned out to see Thorpe and his entertaining Indian squad from Larue, Ohio. Milwaukee had signed a number of new players for the game including Alvin "Bo" McMillin, the former Centre College backfield star who had led the tiny Kentucky school to a victory over mighty Harvard the previous year. While the headlines focused on McMillin and Thorpe, who played the entire game, Robeson scored two touchdowns for a 13–0 Badger victory. Pollard, who started and played most of the game, received little notice as the Milwaukee *Journal* curtly noted that he "pulled off some neat runs."[17]

Despite the Badger victory, the feud between Milwaukee management and coaches Garrett and Pollard continued and apparently worsened with the importation of additional big-name players. Garrett resigned or was fired because he failed to appear in any of the remaining Badger games. Jimmy Conzelman, whose Rock Island team had completed its NFL schedule, was brought in as Milwaukee's head coach for the next game in Green Bay. The fact that Pollard and his good friend Copley, who were not reported injured, failed to play in the Badgers 13–0 loss to the Blues indicates that relations between Pollard and Milwaukee management were severely strained. Pollard had been fired as head coach, but he and Copley did play in Milwaukee's Thanksgiving Day defeat at Racine as Conzelman directed the team. Pollard apparently reconsidered his decision to quit the team because of his lucrative contract, which he later set at $1,500 a game for being player-coach. Milwaukee finished out the season in Canton with a humiliating 40–6 defeat at the hands of the undefeated and 1922 NFL champion Bulldogs. Canton fans demanded to know the whereabouts of Pollard and Robeson, who failed to appear for the game. The Canton *Daily News* explained that Pollard was laid up with several broken ribs, and Robeson "evidently got lost en route." It seems more likely that Pollard at least had come to a parting of the ways with his former friends McGuirk and Plunkett.[18]

A week later Pollard made his final football appearance of the season when he led a team called the Fritz Pollard All-Stars against a white all-star team coached by his former Badger teammate Dick

King. The event held at Schorling Park in Chicago was undoubtedly the first of its kind, featuring former white collegians against African-American stars, most of whom had played at predominantly white colleges. Pollard's All-Stars consisted of then-NFL players Robeson, John Shelbourne (Dartmouth-Hammond), Fred "Duke" Slater (Iowa-Rock Island), and Ink Williams. The team was augmented by members of the Lincoln Athletic Club eleven, organized by the Chicago *Defender* sportswriter Frank A. Young, which included the future NFL players Dick Hudson and Sol Butler, as well as Pollard's former Lane Tech teammate Virgil Bluett and Fritz's brother Frank. A small, shivering crowd braved subfreezing weather to watch Pollard connect with Robeson for a twenty-yard touchdown pass and a 6–0 win over the white all-stars. Despite the season-ending victory, what had begun as a promising season for Pollard had ended in disarray, and his future as a player and coach in the NFL was in doubt.[19]

During the summer of 1923, Pollard was contacted by Alva A. Young, owner of the Hammond Pros, who requested that Fritz play for his team in the fall. Hammond was one of several road teams in the NFL and played almost all of its games on foreign turf. Road teams usually played a small number of league games and had little realistic chance of winning the NFL title. Young, a medical doctor, was known as "the gambling sporting doctor" in Hammond because he not only owned the Pros but also sponsored horse racing and a group of boxers. According to his son, H. N. Young, Alva Young was "color blind" and signed a number of black players, including Pollard, Ink Williams, John Shelbourne, and later Sol Butler and Dick Hudson, because "they were the best players." H. N. Young recalled that Hammond was prejudiced, being near the stronghold of the midwestern Ku Klux Klan in Indiana, but remembered only a few incidents of racial discrimination directed against the black members of the team.[20]

Pollard later said that he coached the Pros during the 1923 and 1924 seasons because "several of the players wanted me as coach." He admitted that "I only coached Hammond. I didn't play for them unless it was absolutely necessary." When asked if Pollard actually coached Hammond in those years, H. N. Young, who as a boy attended most of the games and practices, stated emphatically, "Yes, he really did coach Hammond, you can put me down for yes." Being a player-coach in the early NFL had its advantages. After the league instituted a salary cap for teams in 1922, some owners got around the restriction by paying superior players an additional sum to coach, an activity not covered under the league limitation. It is probable that at least part of the large football salaries Pollard recalled receiving in the early 1920s can be accounted for by supplements paid him for coaching duties. In fact, Pollard only played in two NFL games for Hammond during the 1923–24 seasons. He played in a season-opening 17–0 loss to the eventual 1923 champion Canton Bulldogs, and a week later in a 7–0 victory over the Dayton Triangles. In the Dayton game, Pollard started and played the whole game at quarterback, making him the first African American to quarterback a team in the NFL. It was a distinction little noted at the time or since.[21]

During early October, Pollard divided his time between coaching the Hammond team and serving as head coach at Wendell Phillips High School on Chicago's South Side. He and his assistant Albert C. Johnson revived the school's football program after a six-year lapse. Wendell Phillips, a de facto black school since World War I, finished a respectable third in Chicago's Class B division, but it is doubtful that Pollard had much time to devote to high school coaching. In mid-October, he received a call from Charley Copley asking him to play for the Gilberton Catamounts in the Coal Region of northeastern Pennsylvania. Pollard accepted the offer and would spend most of his autumn Sundays for the next two years playing in the "Coal League." He most likely agreed to play in Gilberton because of the substantial money involved. By 1923, Hammond was a declining franchise that would average only five league games a year through the 1926 season, its last in the NFL; for the players, this meant few and meager paydays. The Coal League teams, on the other hand, were engaged in a bidding war that would eventually attract some of the top professional football talent of the era. In the fall of 1923, Pollard commuted to Gilberton on Fridays and returned to Chicago on the Sunday evening train. During the week, he did his best to meet his coaching responsibilities at Wendell Phillips and in nearby Hammond. This schedule helps account for H. N. Young's recollection that although Pollard "was around a good part of the time," he was controversial because "he could not always be depended upon to show up when he said he would."[22]

Visiting the depressed anthracite Coal Region today, it seems improbable that the area, roughly seventy-five miles northwest of Philadelphia and encompassing an area of fewer than five hundred square miles, produced some of the finest professional football teams in the country during the early 1920s. But in the post–World War I era, the anthracite coal fields supported nearly three-quarters of a million people, including many Irish, Polish, Lithuanian, Slovak, and Ukrainian immigrants. Life in the mining towns was hard and dangerous. The average miner spent ten to twelve hours in deep shafts a quarter mile or more underground and earned about $5 a day; workers were maimed, crippled, or killed almost every week. Most miners and their families lived in cramped quarters that had few amenities. Saloons, sports, and gambling provided diversion for the many miners who faced back-breaking work, choking dust, and the imminent possibility of death deep underground.[23]

In this environment, sporting events thrived, and interest was heightened by wagers made at the numerous saloons or at the contest itself. Athletic events were loosely organized and almost totally unregulated, giving the region the reputation of supporting "outlaw leagues" in both baseball and football during the 1920s. Some of the major league baseball players whom Commissioner Kenesaw Mountain Landis banned for life in the wake of the Black Sox scandal of 1919, for example, found refuge on Coal Region baseball teams. In football, gamblers, including many of the fans, controlled the games almost as much as did the teams and managers. It was common to see "fellows walking along the sidelines holding their hats filled with money wanting to bet on either team," a reporter from the Philadelphia *Public Ledger* recalled. "There was no tomorrow," Mahanoy City native John Sullivan explained. "Everyday there was somebody being hauled out of the mines, crippled or killed. They lived from day to day." Until the 1920s, many games in the Coal Region were never completed because fans on the losing side would start a riot in the final period so they would not lose their wagers. All this changed when Robert "Tiny" Maxwell, a prominent referee and former Swarthmore College player, was brought in to officiate along with two other nationally known officials, Wilmer Crowell and Charles McCarthy. According to John Sullivan, "Tiny Maxwell turned Coal Region football from chaos into a properly officiated and played game."[24]

Copley, a Mahanoy City native and captain of the neighboring

Gilberton team, had summoned Pollard to the Coal Region in 1923. Gilberton, Shenandoah, Pottsville, and Wilkes-Barre competed to sign the best available professional talent. It is not clear how the competition started, but the causes of the bidding war are easier to discern. Football managers and promoters in these small towns were caught up in the boosterism and sports craze of the 1920s, and attempted to bring prestige and glory to themselves and their communities by buying a winning team. Given the intense interest in football in the area, they hoped to cover their costs through increased attendance. Professional talent was available in part because the NFL, under Commissioner Joe Carr, had some success in restricting team wages through the salary cap. Playing in the Coal Region was attractive for many professionals because they were offered a good wage, around $200 a game, and in the beginning were only expected to report on the day of the game or the day before. Like Pollard, many held other jobs during the week and played in the Coal Region on Sunday. The former Syracuse All-America Joe Alexander worked out an even better deal. In 1923, he ran his medical practice in New York during the week, played for the Frankford (Philadelphia) Yellowjackets on Saturday (Sunday football was banned in Philadelphia), and competed for the Wilkes-Barre team in the Coal League on Sunday. As long as such promoters as Joe Sepauley in Shenandoah and Joe Keating and James Rafferty in Gilberton had the money, some top professionals were willing to forgo play in the NFL to take advantage of the lucrative deals in the Coal Region.[25]

Copley told Pollard not to go directly to Gilberton, but to proceed to Philadelphia, where he would be driven by car to the tiny coal-mining village. A town of several thousand in 1923, Gilberton was nestled in a valley directly over a rich vein of anthracite. The village, crowded with row houses and shanties, was slowly sinking into the mine and periodically flooded, causing residents to nickname the main thoroughfare Duck Street—the Gilberton football team, the Catamounts, was also known as the "Duck Streeters." Yet, the thriving community supported a hotel, two dance halls, and thirteen saloons and speakeasies, the recently enacted Volstead Act having little impact upon the Pennsylvania Coal Region. The neighboring town of Shenandoah was dubbed "the only western town in the east" by New York dailies because of the large number of saloons and the ineffectiveness of federal agents in enforcing Prohibition there. After arriving in Gilberton, Pollard asked about his indirect route to the tiny mining town. Copley explained that Gilberton was playing against Shenandoah on Sunday, and there had been threats to kill Pollard if he dared show up. Escorted by a contingent of police, the Gilberton team made its way the five miles to Weston Place field on a mountain top overlooking Shenandoah. Like many of the Coal League fields, it was designed for baseball, was steeply pitched and full of jack rocks, making it the League's second-worst surface (the worst was Coaldale, where teams played on coal dust mixed with small stones). "Of course," Pollard recalled with considerable exaggeration, "the crowd had never seen a black man before, never." He remembered that "they greeted me with a hail of rocks and bottles."[26]

Possibly rusty or unnerved by his hostile reception, Pollard got off to a slow start in Coal Region football. At Shenandoah, the game was held up while the managers debated whether or not Pollard would be allowed to play. Manager Joe Sepauley of Shenandoah "objected to a team of whites playing against him and feared there might be trouble." After Gilberton threatened to cancel the game if Pollard did not play, he lined up at fullback as Wilmer Crowell informed the Shenandoah players that the first to rough Pollard would be thrown out of the game. At halftime, Pollard and his teammates remained at midfield, fearing that the hostile crowd might injure him if he ventured near the sidelines. Pollard turned in a below-par performance in the 6–0 loss to Shenandoah, and the following Saturday showed "miserable form on several occasions" in a scoreless tie with the highly touted Frankford Yellowjackets in Philadelphia. Amid rumors that he would be released, Pollard played a creditable game at Pottsville's Minersville Park in Gilberton's humiliating 27–0 loss to the Maroons.[27]

After a 6–0 victory over a weaker Mt. Carmel team, in which Pollard scored the only touchdown, and a 3–0 loss to the Wilkes-Barre Panthers, primarily a Sunday version of the Frankford Yellowjackets, Gilberton was set for a rematch with Pottsville at Minersville Park. Pollard's two-touchdown performance against the Maroons, one on a blinding eighty-yard sprint, was the beginning of the Pollard legend in the Coal Region. Reinforced by halfback Steve "Paddy" Sullivan, whom Pollard had brought in from the Hammond Pros, and former All-America and NFL players Joe Alexander and

Walter French, on loan from Wilkes-Barre, Gilberton upset the Maroons 16–7. That evening a hundred jubilant Gilbertonians escorted Pollard to the railroad station at Mahanoy Plane where he caught a sleeper for Chicago. "The lads from Duck," according to the Mahanoy City *Record-American*, "told the train crew in no uncertain terms that Fritz must have a berth in the Pullman and if any attempt was made to draw a color line there would be hell up. Fritz got the berth and the train pulled out amid the cheers of the populace."[28]

In the weeks after the Pottsville game, Pollard became something of a celebrity in Gilberton and nearby Mahanoy City, where the Catamounts played their home games because Gilberton's Stoddard Field was often flooded and known locally as Lake Stoddard. The color line was waived for him at Weeks Hotel in Gilberton and the Mansion Hotel in Mahanoy City, where he stayed before the Sunday games. In Gilberton, Pollard was invited to speak to the children at the village grade school. He regarded the invitation as a great honor until he learned that the authorities only wanted the youngsters "to see what a 'modern Negro' looked like and how he acted." During his weekend stays in the Coal Region, Pollard was reputedly the life of every party in Gilberton and a free-spender in the numerous local saloons.[29]

Toward the end of the season, the major Coal Region teams, with the exception of Coaldale, increasingly padded their lineups with imported professionals, some jumping from NFL teams. For the Shenandoah game at Mahanoy City, Gilberton signed lineman Nasty Nash, who was playing for the Buffalo All-Americans. In a game reminiscent of the earlier chaotic days of Coal Region football, fans swarmed on to the field in the fourth quarter and "the players were enclosed in a veritable human crowd." Gilberton eked out a 5–0 victory on a marvelous forty-seven-yard drop-kicked field goal by Mike "Gyp" Downey. The following week Gilberton traveled to the remote Panther Creek Valley to oppose league-leading Coaldale, which under the direction of coach Jim Gildea was the only major Coal Region team to resist the trend toward imported professionals in favor of local talent.[30]

Pollard later recalled that the only black people ever seen in Coaldale were Pullman porters, and that he was greeted at the train depot by a gang shouting "Don't come here, blackie." He was forced to dress at the depot because the local hotel would not admit him, and he spent halftime at midfield to protect himself from a hostile crowd that was calling him names "I had never heard before." After a disappointing 3–0 loss to the Coaldale Big Green, a fan who was also a local boxer challenged Fritz to a fight. Pollard reluctantly agreed to return Monday night to take on the challenger. Before a packed auditorium in Coaldale, according to Pollard's account, he waltzed through six rounds with the "big bully" who "didn't know a lick about fighting. I didn't try to hurt him seriously," Pollard remembered, "because I was afraid of what might happen to me. I was the only Black man in the whole damn town."[31]

In early December at Mahanoy City, Pollard got a measure of revenge as he led Gilberton to a 7–0 victory over the champion Coaldale eleven. Pollard brought in Clair Purdy to play halfback and Manager Joe Keating borrowed the former NFL player Carl Beck from Pottsville for the rematch. Playing in a sea of mud, "the little brown doll of Brown," as *Record-American* reporter Russ Green called Pollard, "simply ran wild over the field." Pollard made a spectacular seventy-yard run, but the highlight of the game came when Coaldale's team captain Boock slugged Pollard as he slashed his way to the Big Green sixteen-yard line in the second period. Russ Green commented wryly that the punch "landed on Pollard's jaw, to his probable discomfort." After the offending player was banished from the game, Gilberton scored the winning touchdown. By season's end, Gilberton had seven imported professionals on its roster as opposed to one for its opening game if Mahanoy City's Copley, who had NFL experience, were counted as an import. Despite reports that most Coal Region teams were in debt because of the large salaries paid to the outsiders (Joe Sepauley of Shenandoah was rumored to have lost $7,000), there was little evidence that many manager-promoters intended to curtail their bidding war for the best players during the 1924 season.[32]

Pollard played in the Coal Region for a number of reasons. It provided the highest quality professional football available to him on a regular basis. His first love was playing football, and the Hammond schedule offered too few games. It is likely that after the Milwaukee debacle Pollard had been branded a troublemaker in the NFL, and the few teams that might have signed him backed off. He certainly was motivated by the money; he earned at least $200 a game in Gilberton and perhaps as much as $350 when he coached in 1924. This, combined with the amounts Doc Young paid him to coach Hammond and he earned from his investment firm, provided a handsome salary in the 1920s. Being one of a handful of educated, professional African-American athletes who performed well against white competition, Pollard, like Robeson, Ink Williams, and a few others, was part of an elite in black America and expected to enjoy that status. He drove an expensive car, bought only the best clothes, and enjoyed the finest cigars and a fast-paced life-style. At one point in the 1920s Pollard hired a chauffeured limousine for family use and later sent his daughters to an exclusive prep school. Unfortunately, as his son later recalled, money meant nothing to Pollard, and it went through his hands like water. Thus, the $200 or more that he received in silver coins each autumn Sunday in the Coal Region was certainly welcome.[33]

The 1924 campaign would see Coal Region football reach its peak, with several teams on a par with NFL clubs, before it gradually declined. At a meeting in late August in Coaldale set up by Jim Gildea, team managers organized the Anthracite Football League. They made up a schedule and agreed to stop the expensive practices of "player raiding" and hiring outside professionals in midseason by requiring each team to file a list of eligible players at the beginning of the season. With the exception of Coaldale, the teams almost immediately violated the eligibility and raiding agreements. By mid-October, Wilkes-Barre had cancelled most of its league games because its roster had been raided by rival teams, including Gilberton. As the season progressed, most teams reconstructed their lineups with outsiders, many from the NFL.[34]

For the second straight year Pollard got off to a slow start in the Coal League. Arriving in Gilberton in early October and suffering from inflamed tonsils, he found the village almost completely underwater. A dam had burst on the fifth level of the Draper Mine, and most of the town was a "germ-filled, mosquito-breeding destructive lake." Taking refuge in Mahanoy City, he prepared for Gilberton's first league game against Pottsville. Before ten thousand fans at Minersville Park, the Maroons, led by Wilber "Fats" Henry, drubbed Gilberton by a score of 17–0. Playing poorly and carrying the ball sparingly, Pollard was in a foul mood when the contest ended. He told a Pottsville *Republican* reporter that there was dissension on the team and that he intended to quit if changes were not made. He maintained that he was not given a chance to carry the ball and that "there are too many southerners on the club to let me get by."[35]

The southerners to whom Pollard referred were quarterback Lou Smyth and halfback Cecil "Tex" Grigg, both from Texas, who had played the previous season at Canton. Gilberton had also acquired guard Joe Williams, also from the inactive Canton franchise, who played alongside the veterans Nasty Nash, Charley Copley, and Joe Alexander. During the season, Nash, Alexander, Smyth, and Grigg doubled as players for the NFL Rochester Jeffersons. Although most of the Gilberton team was now made up of outside professionals, the local players Barber Marac, Gyp Downey, and Butch Boslego would still start most of the games. John Sullivan remembered that the local boys were quite good. One day at West End Park, Boslego, a small, squat, bowl-legged miner who played helmetless, made a spectacular leaping tackle and threw a big fullback to the ground. "When the play was over," Sullivan recounted with relish, "there was Alexander, the big All-American, staring at little Butch on his back in amazement and admiration." Unlike the imported players who were paid by the game, the local boys were paid from the profits at the end of the season, which meant they received little or nothing. Boslego was killed during the depression in a cave-in at a "bootleg" coal hole, trying to make a few extra dollars.[36]

After the Pottsville game, Joe Keating spiked the rumor that Pollard was about to quit, although he confirmed that Fritz was still not in the best of health for the upcoming game with Shenandoah. Joe Sepauley of Shenandoah brought in two new outside players as well as bleacher seating, at a cost of $3,000, to accommodate the expected overflow crowd at Weston Place. With tickets selling at $1–$1.65, it took a sizable crowd to cover the considerable expense of player salaries, field rental, extra seating, and the opposition's guarantee.[37]

Only a "fair" crowd showed up at Weston Place to watch Shenandoah defeat Gilberton 6–2. Gilberton brought in the former Canton lineman Ben Shaw for the contest, but it was the former Penn State All-America Hinkey Haines who led the Shenandoah attack and was the star of the game. Pollard had another poor game. Reminding its readers that Pollard had started slowly the previous year, the Mahanoy *Press* simply stated that "the colored flash looked awful in the first two games." Pollard redeemed himself the following week before a standing-room-only crowd at Mahanoy City, however, by leading the Duck Streeters to a 14–0 victory over Shenandoah. With Pollard's former NFL teammates Jim Dufft and Rip King added to the lineup, Gilberton overpowered Shenandoah with the help of Pollard's long runs and pass receptions. Despite two losses, Gilberton managers Keating and Rafferty apparently still wanted the Anthracite championship and were prepared to pay for it by importing more big-name players.[38]

By late October, Anthracite League competition heated up both on and off the field. Pottsville was undefeated, Shenandoah and Coaldale had one loss each, and Gilberton had suffered two setbacks. Fans bet heavily on the games, and crowds were becoming more difficult to control. After Coaldale's loss to Pottsville on October 19, for example, someone fired a shot through a window of Pottsville's special train as it left the Coaldale depot. The Big Green Coaldale team was scheduled for a special midweek contest against Gilberton at Mahanoy City on Mitchell Day, a holiday commemorating the birth of former United Mine Workers president John Mitchell. Jim Gildea was jubilant when his "home-grown" Coaldale team defeated Gilberton 9–3 at West End Park. After the Big Green scored its touchdown, Gildea leaped into the air, shouting, "I told you home talent could do it." The Shenandoah *Evening Herald* saw the result of the game as a vindication of Gildea's effort to promote local talent over the imported professional variety. Despite solid performances by Nash, Alexander, and Pollard, Gilberton's title hopes were all but dashed. In hopes of salvaging what was left of the season, the Gilberton managers hired a new coach, Elgie Tobin, who had earlier coached with Pollard at Akron.[39]

After Tobin's arrival, Gilberton played better, if not inspired, football and ended the season on a bright note—at least on the field. When Reading cancelled its game with Gilberton, Tobin scheduled an Armistice Day contest with the NFL Akron Pros. Having been defeated two days earlier by the eventual 1924 NFL champion Cleveland Bulldogs, Akron played uninspired football at Mahanoy City. Most of the Pros played under assumed names, probably to avoid censure from Commissioner Carr for participating in an unauthorized game. Pollard set up one touchdown, scored another, and booted an extra point in a 13–0 victory over his former team. The Mahanoy *Press* noted sarcastically that "Western football is in the retrograde if the Akron team is representative of the class of gridiron aggregations that provide gory spectacles in the Mrs. Sippi Region."[40]

Coal Region football peaked in northern Schuylkill County on November 16, when Coaldale opposed Shenandoah at Weston Place and Gilberton played the undefeated Pottsville Maroons in Mahanoy City. At fields within walking distance of each other, some of the top professional players of the era would engage in gridiron combat. The "Old Rounder," writing for the Shenandoah *Evening Herald*, exaggerated a bit when he wrote that "with two football classics being waged within a few miles of each other, the anthracite region of Pennsylvania will come mighty close to being the center of the gridiron in this good old U.S.A. tomorrow afternoon." Reinforced by Scotty Bierce of the Cleveland Bulldogs, Gilberton fought the Maroons to a scoreless tie on a cold, blustery day before ten thousand shivering fans. The Duck Streeters outplayed the Maroons, but two of Pollard's field-goal attempts were blown wide of the goal post, one by less than a foot. A smaller crowd watched Shenandoah defeat Coaldale, primarily because few Big Green fans showed up, reputedly in protest of Gildea's continued refusal to sign imported professional players.[41]

Gilberton closed out its season with a 17–0 Thanksgiving Day victory over a dispirited Coaldale eleven. Pollard capped off his second campaign in the Coal League with a series of long gains setting up all three Catamount scores. The Mahanoy *Press* expressed "a shade of sorrow" for the defeated Coaldale team because "we realize, as did every other fan present, that Jim Gildea's great Home-Breds are 'thru.'" By season's end, the financial bubble had burst for most of the Anthracite teams that employed large numbers of outside professionals. Joe Sepauley in Shenandoah and Rafferty and Keating in Gilberton were deeply in debt, and those teams could afford few imported professionals in 1925 after a long strike closed the mines. Pottsville was the exception. The Maroons, who won the 1924 Anthracite League title with an impressive 6–0–1 record, would join the NFL in 1925 and post a 10–2 slate before being suspended for playing an unauthorized game. Pollard would remain a favorite in Gilberton and Mahanoy City and return to play again in the still strong, but declining Coal League.[42]

In later interviews, Pollard often skimmed over his playing days in the Coal Region in 1923 and 1924 and focused on his coaching role with the Hammond Pros. By the 1970s or before, he undoubtedly recognized the preeminence of the NFL and realized that his legacy in professional football and any hope he had of being selected to the Professional Football Hall of Fame depended on his association with the league as either a player or coach. In 1923 and 1924, however, he had the energy and resilience to juggle three separate football jobs with some degree of success. How much time he actually spent coaching the Hammond and Wendell Phillips teams is not known, but clearly he gave some attention to those duties. While he pursued his interest in football, moreover, Pollard was also becoming wealthy as president of F. D. Pollard and Company.

RIDING A WHIRLWIND
10

Fritz Pollard became involved in the banking and investment business in Philadelphia when he coached at Lincoln just after World War I. Edward C. Brown, president of Brown and Stevens Bank, was a fan of the Lincoln team and in late 1918 or early 1919 hired Pollard on a part-time basis. Juggling a busy schedule which included coaching, playing professional football, and dental studies at the University of Pennsylvania, Pollard also became a real estate and bond salesman for Brown and Stevens Bank. After quitting dental school in mid-1920 to attend to the needs of his growing family, Pollard was appointed sales manager of the investment department at the bank's main office in a splendidly furnished building at 427 South Broad Street. Pollard would learn the banking business from Brown and his partner and vice president Andrew F. Stevens, who were widely respected in both the black and white communities of Philadelphia, but whose financial practices were unscrupulous.[1]

Dating back to the tragic failure of the Freedmen's Bank in 1874, many African Americans did not trust banks. By the turn of the century or before, however, it was apparent that they needed a source of capital and credit not generally available at white banks, which discouraged or refused their patronage. Between 1899 and 1905, twenty-eight banks, many of them in the South, were established by African-American businessmen. White businessmen often encouraged the black bankers and overlooked their irregular financial practices in the hope of sustaining the segregated system and, from the white perspective, promoting racial harmony. It was under these circumstances that Brown established in 1905 first the Crown Savings

Bank in Newport News, Virginia, and later in 1909 the Brown Savings Bank in Norfolk. Like many African-American bankers, Brown "was primarily interested in real estate promotion and speculation rather than banking." The main problem for black bankers such as Brown was that with so few African-American businesses of any size, most of their assets were tied up in unreliable real estate loans.[2]

When Brown went to Philadelphia in 1916 and established the Brown and Stevens Bank in association with Stevens, the son of a prominent Philadelphia caterer, he used the enterprise as a vehicle to promote speculative ventures in real estate and the entertainment industry. The partners dipped into the assets of the bank to maintain their own high standards of living and to support such risky undertakings as the construction and operation of the opulent Dunbar Theater, a financial failure. During 1919 and 1920, Pollard was undoubtedly engaged in selling public stock in the theater, an offering which was never fully subscribed. While on paper the Brown and Stevens Bank appeared to be prospering (the Philadelphia *Tribune* reported in 1920 that it had assets of more than $1 million and employed 212 people, with salaries amounting to $267,592 annually), the bank was actually in serious financial trouble. Because of the respect Brown commanded in white financial circles and his wizardry in juggling his books, the bank remained open until February 1925, after which the partners accepted a bankruptcy petition. Abram L. Harris, a student of early African-American banking, has declared that "the notorious manipulations that led to the failure of the True Reformers Bank in Richmond, Virginia, in 1910 pale into insignificance when compared with the financial jugglery, the kiting of assets, and the speculative promotions of Messrs. Brown and Stevens." By 1925, Pollard was far removed from Brown and Stevens's collapsing financial empire in Philadelphia. It is unclear whether he was unaware of his former employers' shady fiscal dealings or if he played a knowing part in them. The best that can be said is that Pollard learned the banking and investment business from two disreputable men.[3]

In the summer of 1922, Pollard and his boyhood friend Chick Evans organized F. D. Pollard and Company, with Pollard as president. Pollard recalled borrowing $25,000 from his mother to capitalize the firm, and Evans matched that sum. Evans, one of the most prominent golfers in the country, won the U.S. Open and U.S. Amateur championships in 1916, and because of the war was reigning champion for three years. Although an amateur, he became a wealthy man and was associated with a number of philanthropic causes. During the war, he played in more than four hundred Red Cross matches and later founded the Evans Scholars Foundation, which helped thousands of former caddies to attend college. After losing more than a quarter of a million dollars in the stock market in 1923 and suffering a nervous breakdown two years later, Evans played only a minor role in the operation of the black investment firm.[4]

Pollard set up an office at 608 South Dearborn Street in Chicago's Loop, and by his account the firm flourished until the Stock Market Crash of 1929. Little is known about the daily operation of the business except what Pollard recalled in later years. He pointed out that "blacks knew little about the purchasing of stocks and bonds in those times," and that "we were not only in business but were actually teaching our people about the market." Pollard also recollected that the firm, which had a wholly African-American clientele, was the first of its kind in the Midwest. Evidence suggests that the firm was also engaged in the real estate business, and that Pollard may have occasionally engaged in irregular business procedures. The Chicago *Defender* reported in May 1924, for example, that he was taken into custody on a warrant initiated by J. C. Davis, who alleged that "Pollard fleeced him out of $300 in a real estate deal." Davis charged that he gave Pollard a check as earnest money on a property transaction and that when he demanded its return, Pollard gave him a hot check. The case was apparently settled out of court.[5]

According to family testimony, Pollard was a shrewd businessman, but a risk-taker who often did not follow through on ventures and sometimes engaged in unorthodox business practices. Pollard's daughter Leslie recalled him telling her that as long as he had a blank check in his pocket he always had money. She said that her father often provided the ideas from which others made money, and because they usually did not compensate him, "he took the freedom upon himself to write a check and sign it and was never prosecuted." "Sometimes I think he thought money grew on trees," Fritz Pollard, Jr., stated. "See, during the football season he made a lot of money. But he spent a lot of money. He was the kind of guy that when he had it and you wanted it, you could have it. So when the time came when he didn't have it, you were supposed to give it to him." Pollard's free-and-easy approach to money was a major cause of his marital difficulties in the 1920s.[6]

Since their elopement in 1914, Fritz and Ada's marriage had been difficult. While Pollard was at Brown, Ada had lived in virtual exile in Springfield, Massachusetts, working and raising Fritz, Jr. During Fritz's wartime service, Ada had moved around, staying with friends or relatives in different cities. Then after Leslie was born in New York City in 1919, Pollard decided to send Fritz, Jr., to live with his grandparents in Rogers Park, separate from his three younger sisters. By the time Pollard moved with Ada and the girls to Chicago in 1922, relations between Fritz and Ada were strained. Pollard bought a home for the family in Evanston, but did not live with them for long. In late 1922 or early 1923, he moved into an apartment in southeast Chicago.[7]

Leslie Keeling maintained that the biggest difficulty between her father and mother was over the question of support. "My father handled an awful lot of money in his day," she said. "And he got rid of it twice that fast." Her mother had to find a way to support the family.

> She could not do it with somebody around who was not contributing. And what he did with his money, possibly it was because of the other ladies outside, I don't know that he was a gambling man, what he did with it, how it got away from him, I don't know. But, I do know this, that my father could bring home a pile of money, and if my mother didn't have a way to spend it right fast, he would be back the next day and borrow it all back. My father was not a fighting man, he was a gentle man, but that was the reason of their separation.[8]

Fritz Pollard, Jr., agreed that his mother and sisters' situation was untenable. "He was the type of guy," Fritz, Jr., said about his father, "who would go out and buy a house, put them in it, and go off. And you wouldn't hear from him. And then what used to cause family problems was the fact that here my sisters and my mother were in this house without sufficient income to pay the mortgage money and so forth. I'll bet if he bought one, he bought ten houses."

Leslie remembered living in at least five different houses in Evanston and Chicago before she reached the fifth grade.[9]

While his family lived primarily in Rogers Park and Evanston on Chicago's North Shore, Pollard spent a good deal of his time in downtown Chicago and on the South Side. In his idle hours, he associated with football colleagues. Ink Williams worked for Decca Records, and Duke Slater later became a Chicago judge. Paul Robeson was another close associate, at least until his singing and acting career caused him to spend a considerable amount of time abroad. Because of their education and success in integrated athletic competition, the group of athletes formed an elite in the African-American community. They spent many evenings at Chicago nightclubs and traveled frequently to New York and Philadelphia and other eastern cities. Pollard and his colleagues often flaunted their wealth and status as did many successful black entertainers of the period but his circle of friends and acquaintances was diverse. Fritz, Jr., recalled that his father "knew everybody, all the thugs and everybody else in the twenties. He knew everybody from top to bottom. He was the kind of a person who always had fifteen or twenty people around him, almost like Joe Louis. He was the one that always steered everything."[10]

Despite his prominence and financial success in Chicago during the boom years of the mid-1920s, Pollard's first love was still football. He would play for three different NFL teams in 1925 and serve as head coach for two of them. With a coal strike in eastern Pennsylvania and the Anthracite League in disarray, Pollard rejoined the Hammond Pros as a full-time coach and player. A declining franchise by 1925, Hammond still had a few fine players including Ink Williams, veteran NFL back Guil Falcon, and Pollard's former Brown teammate Dunc Annan. Pollard coached from the sideline and played sparingly in the Pros' season-opening 14–0 loss at Green Bay. After the game, he received a call from Akron Pro owner Frank Nied asking if he would be willing to join Akron again as a player-coach. Doc Young, whose Hammond franchise was struggling financially, agreed to send Pollard, along with Annan and Falcon, to Akron, which had not yet opened its season. Hammond would struggle through the season with an unimpressive 1–4 record but notch its lone win against the eventual 1925 NFL champion Chicago Cardinals.[11]

Reinforced by the Hammond backs and with veteran Al Nesser joining the team early in the season and anchoring a solid line, the recently dormant Akron team emerged as a contender in the NFL race. Pollard, who remained a favorite of the Akron fans, got off to a slow start for the Pros but showed flashes of brilliance in wins over Cleveland and Kansas City and in a scoreless tie with Buffalo. Before an overflow crowd at Canton's Lakeside Field on October 18, Pollard led the Pros to a 20–3 come-from-behind victory over the archrival Bulldogs. During an action-packed second half, he threw two touchdown passes and ran for a third to secure the victory. The Canton *Repository* paid Pollard a rare compliment by noting that "the curly-haired negro, always smiling, played the game of his life and was the central figure throughout the combat." Akron's conquest of the Bulldogs put the Pros on top of the NFL standings in a tie with the Detroit Panthers whom they opposed the following week in Detroit.[12]

The Detroit-Akron clash of October 25 was one of the fiercest contests that either players or game officials could remember. More than a dozen players were injured or knocked out of the game, either permanently or temporarily, during the course of a scoreless tie. Pollard was removed from the game semiconscious in the second period after a thumping tackle, but returned for more action in the second half. Detroit coach and quarterback Jimmy Conzelman, recipient of several bone-crunching tackles, directed the Panther attack in a dazed manner during most of the first half until he was replaced after asking teammates whom they were playing and where. The bitterly fought contest was marred by a number of fistfights and ended in a near-riot when several Akron players attempted to seize the game ball as a trophy. One suspects that the warlike conditions stemmed in part from the bad feeling between Pollard and Conzelman dating back to the 1922 season in Milwaukee. With neither team able to secure a victory, Detroit and Akron remained at the top of the NFL standings with slightly better records than the Frankford Yellowjackets.[13]

Akron won again on the following Sunday with a 17–3 at-home victory over the Dayton Triangles before a surprisingly small crowd of 2,500 at General Field. Pollard passed for one touchdown and set up the second on a thirty-seven-yard run the Akron *Beacon Journal* described as "the most spectacular bit of open field running any Akron player or foe has made this season." Akron's title hopes now hinged on an eastern road trip on which they would oppose Frankford and Pottsville on consecutive days in Pennsylvania. The unusual scheduling was because Sunday football was banned in Philadelphia, and Frankford played all its home games on Saturday. Pottsville was admitted to the league in 1925, in part because it was close to Philadelphia and permitted Sunday ball. Thus, some western teams could meet their road expenses by playing back-to-back games in Philadelphia on Saturday and in Pottsville the following day. The scheduling arrangement worked to the advantage of Pottsville, whose opponents were sometimes exhausted from the previous day's game.[14]

Pollard had one of his finest games as a professional on Saturday November 7 at Yellowjacket Stadium, but his superb performance did not prevent an Akron defeat. Guy Chamberlin's Frankford team tore off seventeen unanswered first-half points before Pollard and the Akron team struck back. Philadelphia sportswriters accorded Pollard the highest praise for his gallant second-half effort. One wrote that "Akron, led by the redoubtable, the valiant Fritz Pollard, ex-Brown University star, the great colored back of other years, who still shines effulgent, a scintillating luminary in the professional football firmament, more than held their own in a fury of a second half rally." According to the Philadelphia papers, Pollard was a one-man gang, circling the ends, smashing off-tackle, and completing most of his twenty aerials with pinpoint accuracy. Pollard's remarkable performance was so widely publicized that the Chicago *Defender*, which rarely covered pro football, carried a feature story on him and the game. Despite his heroics, however, Akron left for the Coal Region that evening pondering a disappointing 17–7 loss to the Yellowjackets.[15]

The following day in Pottsville, Minersville Park was a virtual swamp after two days of heavy rain. Akron management protested long and hard against playing the game, but to no avail. Sensing that the Pros were battered and dispirited after their contest in Philadelphia, Pottsville demanded that the game go on. In a game played in such miserable field conditions that twice the ball floated away from the line of scrimmage, the well-rested Maroons overpowered the Pros 21–0. Unable to run or sidestep in the slimy mud, Pollard watched most of the game from the bench. Akron's hopes for a second professional championship were dashed during that weekend in eastern Pennsylvania. With the title out of reach and the team sustaining injuries to several key players, management declined to schedule any further games. The Pros finished the season with a 4–2–2 record, which put them in a tie for fourth in the final NFL standings. Pollard's season, however, was not quite finished.[16]

Several weeks after arriving back in Chicago, Pollard and the rest of America learned that the University of Illinois football sensation Harold "Red" Grange had signed a contract to play for the Chicago Bears. Grange, whose record-breaking career at Illinois combined with the intense coverage of his exploits by the media, promised to attract large crowds for a series of games hastily scheduled by Bears' owner George Halas. When Pollard read that the Bears were slated to play the Providence Steam Roller in Boston on December 9, he called Steam Roller general manager Charles Coppen offering his services for the game. Like many other well-known professionals, Pollard hoped to cash in on the Grange phenomenon. After negotiations with Coppen, whom he had known from his college days at Brown, Pollard agreed to play in the Boston game for $500 and participate in the Steam Roller's remaining games for an undisclosed sum.[17]

The Providence Steam Roller had been founded in 1916 and was engaged in its first season in the NFL; during the 1917 season, Pollard had served briefly as backfield coach for the team. He arrived in Providence on November 28, 1925, the day before the Steam Roller, which had compiled a more than respectable 5–3 record against NFL competition, was scheduled to play the Cleveland Bulldogs. The game, played at the Cycledrome, which had no end zones because it was designed for bicycle racing, was a kind of homecoming for Pollard. Not only was he greeted warmly by the fans and his former colleagues, but he was also reunited with Ink Williams, who had been traded to the Bulldogs. Both Pollard and Williams played well, if not spectacularly, in a 7–7 tie played on a muddy field before seven thousand fans. The following Sunday Pollard's stellar defensive play failed to compensate for his misguided aerial intercepted for a Green Bay touchdown in a 13–10 victory for the Wisconsin team. Despite the loss, Steam Roller supporters and area fans looked forward to the "big game" against Red Grange and the Bears to be played the following Wednesday at Boston's Braves Field.[18]

Red Grange had taken the professional football world by storm.

Primarily because of his presence on the field, the Bears had drawn unprecedented crowds of forty thousand in Chicago on Thanksgiving Day, thirty-five thousand at Philadelphia's Schibe Park on December 5, and more than sixty thousand at the Polo Grounds the following day. The moneymaking tour, conceived by Grange's agent and partner Charles C. "Cash and Carry" Pyle and George Halas, was both spectacular and successful. Playing six games in thirteen days against NFL clubs and two sandlot teams, the Bears had posted a 5–0–1 record since Thanksgiving. The schedule was also suicidal. Although Grange was only required to play in two quarters per game in exchange for 50 percent of the Bears' share of the gate, which he and Pyle split on a 60–40 basis, the sheer number of games represented too much physical contact for either Grange or his teammates to endure long. The previous Sunday Grange had seriously injured his arm when New York Giant linemen piled on him after a tackle. When he arrived in Boston on Tuesday, Grange's arm was badly swollen, and many of his teammates were bruised and battered.[19]

The game attracted so much attention in New England that Coppen had also signed Don Miller and Jim Crowley, formerly of Notre Dame's famed Four Horsemen backfield, in hopes of boosting the gate. Ticket prices, in spite of the midweek date, were set at $3.50 for box seats, $3 reserved, and $2 for rush seats, nearly double the usual rate. Two radio stations would broadcast the game, making it the first professional contest heard over the airwaves in New England. Despite a contingent of four thousand Providence fans who made their way to Boston, the game attracted a disappointing crowd of fifteen thousand on what turned out to be the coldest day of the year. Steam Roller lineman Bert Shurtleff recalled that the temperature was six degrees below zero and that the field was frozen solid. Whenever possible, runners headed for the sidelines rather than be tackled on the hard turf.[20]

Boston fans gave Grange an enthusiastic reception, with three thousand of them mobbing him before the game and forcing him to warm up in an area the size of a clothes closet, but their adulation did not last long. Grange played the thirty minutes required by his contract, but with limited results. He carried the ball five times for eighteen yards and had one of his three passes intercepted. "My arm was in such pain I couldn't do anything right" he later recalled. The climax of the game came in the third period when Steam Roller punter Red Maloney intentionally booted the ball directly at Grange, who stood dead in his tracks and deliberately allowed the ball to sail over his head and out of bounds. A Providence *Journal* reporter recounted that "the freezing fans, with the fickleness of the mob, rose as one man at the end of the third quarter when a substitute left halfback trotted on to the field and booed and hissed and jeered with cries of 'get the ice tongs'" as Grange left the game. He later recalled that he was booed for the first time in his career in Boston, and learned that pro fans were much more demanding than the college crowds.[21]

Pollard did not enter the game until the fourth period, and thus two of the greatest halfbacks of football's first half-century did not actually oppose one another. He carried the ball only three times for eight yards in an unimpressive effort. The only thing that was normal for Pollard was that he became a special target for Chicago tacklers. The Providence *Journal* reported that "the Bears were so intent on squelching the dusky Fritz that five of the orange-jerseyed athletes piled on the former Brown star. The rough playing cost Chicago 15 yards." Undoubtedly, Pollard blamed Halas for the incident, and it probably contributed to the feud between them which ripened over the years. When the final whistle blew, the Steam Roller had upset Chicago 9–6, ending the Bears' unbeaten string since Grange had joined the team on Thanksgiving Day.[22]

Grange would play in only one more game on the northern tour before his arm injury forced him to the sidelines and the remaining games were canceled. After Grange's injury healed, Pyle's whirlwind exhibition series continued, with the Bears playing games in the South and West through the month of January. Despite the current wisdom that Grange's signing helped put professional football on the map, many contemporary newspaper accounts maintained that he was exploited and that his poor performances were turning the public against the professional game. Pollard played one more game in Providence against the Frankford Yellowjackets. Despite dropping a forward pass for an apparent touchdown, he was the rushing star of the game, reeling off two open-field runs in a 14–6 Steam Roller defeat. The Providence *Journal* noted that "on those two plays Fritz was the Pollard of old, the man that won all-American fame while zigzagging his merry way o'er the chalkmarkers for the near-championship Brown eleven of that season." The writer might have added that Pollard's best playing days were behind him.[23]

Pollard rejoined Akron for the 1926 season as a player-coach. Under the direction of Frank Nied, the Akron team was renamed the Indians, but like many NFL teams that year it struggled financially. Unable to secure an NFL franchise in New York City, C. C. Pyle organized a rival professional football circuit, the American Football League (AFL), with nine teams and Red Grange of the New York Yankees as its featured attraction. In the key cities of New York, Chicago, Brooklyn, and Philadelphia, there was head-to-head rivalry between the leagues. The competition from the new league and poor fall weather combined to create financial woes for many NFL teams in 1926. Akron opened its campaign against the eventual NFL champion Frankford Yellowjackets on a sweltering September day in Philadelphia before a relatively sparse crowd of seven thousand. Playing helmetless and without shin guards because of the intense heat, Pollard provided most of the Indian offense. His second-period, forty-five-yard pass to Hal Griggs for a touchdown was enough to secure a 6–6 tie with the favored Yellowjackets. The Philadelphia *Inquirer* remarked that "Pollard, colored wizard, . . . just tore around, and hot or cold, he was the Akron attack."[24]

Within twenty-four hours, the exhausted Akron team took the field in Buffalo to meet Jim Kendrick's aggregation of former Texas players nicknamed the Rangers. The southern-born Rangers made Pollard a target and caused the Akron *Beacon Journal* to remark that their "playing was so individually dirty that the game degenerated into a rough-house affair in which football was rather forgotten." Tired and bruised, Akron managed only two first downs during the course of a 7–0 loss to Buffalo. The *Beacon Journal* speculated that "if the team loses another game there will probably be a wholesale firing of high-priced men and a general loading up of cheaper talent. We rather believe, that if the Indians were paid by the yard gained instead of the game played the results might be uniformly pleasing all season." It appeared likely that Frank Nied was prepared to unload some of his veteran players such as Al Nesser and Pollard.[25]

By the time the Indians took the field for their home-opener against the Hammond Pros, Nesser had been released and was picked up by the Cleveland Panthers of the AFL. Only a small crowd turned out at General Field to watch the Indians easily subdue the hapless Pros 17–0. Hammond quarterback Dunc Annan hurled numerous aerials to Dick Hudson and Ink Williams, but to no avail. Pollard ran the Akron attack competently for three periods, but the *Beacon Journal* game account hinted that his days as Indian quarterback were numbered. Reporter Blaine Conley praised the work of Pollard's fourth-quarter replacement, Windy Wendler, and stated that the former Ohio State signal caller "is not going to be kept warming the bench much longer if he flashes the same stuff again and convinces Frank Nied, his boss, that such playing is habitual with him." Nied also had to consider paring down player salaries because, as the Canton *Daily News* reported, the small turn out for the Hammond game "made future pro football for Akron look rather dim."[26]

Pollard played his last game for Akron and in the NFL on October 10 against the archrival Canton Bulldogs. Neither Pollard nor his replacement, Wendler, could generate much offense for the Indians as the team managed only two first downs. The Bulldogs were equally ineffective under the direction of quarterback Sol Butler, a former black sprinter from Dubuque College. Defense prevailed as Akron and Canton battled to a scoreless tie. It was perhaps a fitting conclusion to Pollard's NFL career in that he faced his old rival, Jim Thorpe, thirty-nine, one last time in gridiron combat. After the Canton game, Nied gave Pollard, who was thirty-two, his unconditional release as player and coach. An Akron news release stated that Indian management took the action because Pollard "failed to play up to the form expected of him." Pollard was quoted in the article as saying that he had intended to retire after the season and wanted to end his professional career in an Akron uniform. He added that he had "never counted on being fired." Pollard made it clear that he would not sign with any other team and that he was heading home to Chicago.[27]

Pollard's forced retirement at Akron in 1926 marked the height of African-American participation in professional football before World War II. In 1922, 1923, and 1926, five blacks played for NFL or AFL teams. Beginning the 1927 season only Duke Slater of the Chicago Cardinals remained on an NFL roster until he was joined by Harold Bradley in 1928. Again in 1929 only Slater remained. Only three other blacks would play in the league before the color line was drawn in 1933. The decline in numbers of black players

in the NFL was because of the withdrawal of many teams after the
financially disastrous 1926 campaign. While twenty-two teams began
the 1926 season, only twelve competed for the championship the
following year. Williams, Butler, and Hudson played for teams that
dropped out of the NFL and were not signed by other franchises.
There is no evidence of an organized racial barrier, but it is clear
that some teams, such as Hammond and Canton which ceased in
1926, were more willing to hire black players than other teams.
There is also some evidence that racial tensions were becoming more
strained in the NFL by the mid-1920s. Shortly after Pollard's retirement, for example, New York Giant players refused to take the
field in a Tuesday afternoon game against Canton at the Polo Grounds.
Giant management maintained that the large crowd might object to
the presence of Sol Butler on the field. The Chicago *Defender* linked
the protest to a number of southern players on the New York team
including Steve Owen, "Cowboy" Hill, and Cecil "Tex" Grigg. After
a ten-minute delay, Butler withdrew voluntarily, advising his teammates to play and not disappoint the crowd.[28]

Aside from the prevailing racial climate, a number of factors
made it difficult for African Americans to find employment in the
NFL. The most obvious was the small number of blacks who played
football at white colleges, which were the recruiting grounds for
professional teams. Beyond that, most black players had to achieve
All America status just to be considered by the pro teams. Pollard
believed that the increasing acceptance of professional football by
the fans during the 1920s allowed owners to release African-American players who earlier were needed as drawing cards. Major black
newspapers, moreover, rarely covered the professional game, and its
following in the African-American community was limited. Only
occasionally did any number of black fans turn out to see professional games, such as the eight hundred (out of a three-thousand
total) who watched Ink Williams and Sol Butler perform for Hammond against the Chicago Cardinals in 1924. As a rule, black fans,
like white fans, did not have as much faith in professional football
as they did in the college game. Under these circumstances, there
was little incentive for pro football owners to hire African-American
players unless they were clearly superior and could assure victories.[29]

Not long after Pollard returned to Chicago, he received a call
from Charley Copley inviting him to play once again for the Gilberton

Catamounts. Putting aside his self-proclaimed retirement, Fritz jumped at the chance, perhaps for the money. The quality of football in the Coal Region had declined from the peak years of 1923–24, but still remained formidable. Gilberton, Shenandoah, and Coaldale had joined the Eastern Pro League which included teams from Lancaster, Bethlehem, and Newark, New Jersey. Pollard arrived in Pennsylvania in time to provide what little offense the Catamounts could muster in a 14–0 road loss to Lancaster. After a week lay-off due to foul weather, Pollard returned to the scene of his Coal Region football baptism at Weston Place against Shenandoah. Aside from the fact that only Copley and Butch Boslego remained from the fine Gilberton team of two years before, nothing much had changed; almost anything went in Coal Region football. John Sullivan recalled that on Pollard's touchdown sprint which led to a 7–0 Gilberton victory, three Shenandoah tacklers led by Mike Kutsko seized Fritz at the goal line and jammed his face along a sideline made of lime. Fritz was forced to wear dark glasses because of his resulting eye irritation.[30]

Although Pollard had lost a step or two over the years, he was usually swift enough to dominate play in the Eastern Pro League. Shedding his dark glasses and taking his place in the backfield, he ran wild in an easy Gilberton win over Newark. "A phantom as easy to catch as a bolt of lightening, and as easily held," sportswriter Russ Green wrote poetically in the fashion of the day, "the colored quarterback made a cross-continental tour of the combat, crossing and re-crossing the whitewashed horizontals stretching over the field almost at will." On other occasions, Pollard befuddled his opponents. John Sullivan still remembers how he outwitted a powerful Coaldale team on Armistice Day in 1926 to secure a Gilberton victory. With Gilberton trailing 3–0 in the final period, the Catamounts had the ball on the Coaldale eight-yard line with third down and goal to go. Everything appeared to be in confusion, Sullivan said. Pollard was shoving two Gilberton backs into position when, on a prearranged signal, the center snapped the ball to Fritz. "And zip, he gets the ball," Sullivan recalled excitedly, "and he's through the goddamn line for a touchdown. It was the fastest thing I ever saw. The Coaldale rooters called him a son-of-a-bitch and every name in the book."[31]

During the 1926 season, Pollard spent more time in the Coal Region than in previous years and was a prominent figure in Gilberton

and Mahanoy City. On weekdays he often loafed in the lobby of
the Mansion Hotel in Mahanoy City, talking sports and swapping
stories with leading citizens of the coal mining community. He told
his colleagues that he was a dentist in the off-season. But as in
previous years, not all of Pollard's teammates were glad to have him
on the team. In a late-November loss to Bethlehem, for example,
Gilberton center Joe Sheeley continually snapped the ball to Pollard
before the appointed signal, causing several fumbles and numerous
broken plays. Pollard sent Sheeley out of the game, but Catamount
coach "Haps" Frank sent him right back in. The result was, according
to Russ Green, that "Mister Sheeley stayed in the game against
Mister Pollard's wishes and health." After the game, the dispute was
resolved when manager Joe Keating fired Frank, and Sheeley was
benched for the Thanksgiving Day game against Coaldale.[32]

As expected, the holiday contest at Coaldale's Gildea Stadium
was a bruising affair marred by numerous fistfights which the officials
were unable squelch. Big Green defensive stalwarts "Honey Boy"
Bill Evans and Joe Garland covered Pollard the entire game, and he
was fortunate in avoiding serious injury. Like other keen football
observers, John Sullivan marveled at Pollard's ability to protect himself. When Pollard was knocked down, Sullivan noted, "he would
curl up like a turtle. And other times, flat on his back with the
cleats up. Because they were out to kill Mr. Pollard. To get him out
of the game. And how he protected himself. Miraculously so." On
that day, according to Russ Green, the "Little Brown Star of Brown
was a flickering and feeble constellation" in the face of Coaldale's
defensive pressure, and the best Gilberton could manage was a
scoreless game and a tie for the Eastern Pro League championship.[33]

Pollard completed the 1926 season, his last in the Coal Region,
by leading Gilberton against the NFL Pottsville Maroons at Minersville Park. Pottsville had finished third in the NFL race with an
impressive 10–2–2 record including eleven shutouts. There was intense interest in the game in the Coal Region, prompting the Mahanoy City radio station to broadcast the contest. And it was fortunate for many fans that it did. At game time, a howling blizzard
was in progress, and Minersville Park was covered with six inches
of drifting snow. After groundskeepers had cleared the field as best
they could, players on both sides slipped and skidded through four
abbreviated periods. Maroon halfback Tony Latone's one-yard slide

into the end zone in the first period held up for a 6–0 Pottsville victory. While the game was not a true test of football prowess, it did indicate that tiny Gilberton still fielded a formidable football team.[34]

The year 1926 was Pollard's last as a player in professional football, but it was far from the end of his association with the game he loved. Beginning in 1927, he served for two years as an unofficial backfield coach under Dick Hanley, who had been hired as head coach at Northwestern University. Pollard had met Hanley in Pasadena in 1916 when the latter was a star halfback for the Rose Bowl champion Washington State team. They had remained friends through the years as Hanley established his coaching credentials by leading the Haskell Indian Institute of Lawrence, Kansas, to national football prominence during the 1920s. By 1928, however, Pollard's interest in Northwestern football became secondary to his concern about what he perceived to be an effort to eliminate black players from the NFL. Although there is no specific evidence that team owners conspired against African-American players, it is clear that a number of coaches and owners either refused or were reluctant to hire blacks. Owners had two infrequently stated reasons for the paucity of black players. One was, as Halas later put it, that "probably the game didn't appeal to black players at the time." The other was that the mixing of the races often led to ugly incidents on the gridiron.[35]

Beginning in 1928, Pollard organized an all-star black professional football team on Chicago's South Side with the expressed intention of showing that interracial football could be played without ugly incidents. The team, which became known as the Chicago Black Hawks the following season, scheduled games against white professional and semiprofessional teams in the Chicago area. Pollard's South Side eleven was composed of aspiring young players as well as NFL veterans Ink Williams, Sol Butler, and Pollard himself. Duke Slater also played for the team during the 1928 campaign when he was not otherwise engaged with the Chicago Cardinals. While Pollard proved his point that teams with both black and white players could compete without serious incident, the South Side team drew poorly at the gate. For this reason, Pollard and his general manager, Albert C. Johnson, took the Black Hawks on the road during the fall and winter months for the next three seasons. Most games the Black

Hawks played were against white all-star teams in California. With the depression worsening, however, the team disbanded in California during the 1931–32 season due to poor attendance. Many of the players, nearly broke, were stranded on the West Coast for some time. After failing to sell the rights to his life story to a Hollywood movie company, Pollard returned to Chicago nearly penniless in the summer of 1932.[36]

For a number of years, Pollard had been following the progress of his son, who was emerging as a first-class high school athlete. The younger Pollard recalled that although he did not see his father regularly, he was inspired by his athletic accomplishments. "I had two of his scrapbooks which I used to go through daily," Fritz Jr., stated. "What I really wanted to be was Olympic decathlon champion. He tried to discourage me from playing football. He liked the idea of my wanting to be a track man, too." Under the tutelage of Chick Evans, Fritz, Jr., became one of Chicago's fine young golfers by the time he was twelve. While attending Senn High School, he developed into one of the nation's top hurdlers, capturing the national interscholastic high- and low-hurdle championships in his senior year. Along with Marquette University sprinter Ralph Metcalfe, Fritz, Jr., was named to an All-America team selected by the AAU in 1933.[37]

Taking the advice of his father, who said he was too long and lean for gridiron combat, Fritz, Jr., did not play football until he was in high school. He remembered that playing high school football under the watchful eye of his flamboyant, All-America father sometimes proved to be daunting. Before his first game for Senn, his father along with Duke Slater and Paul Robeson stopped by unexpectedly to escort him to the field. The three football greats, who had been out all night drinking and carousing, drove young Fritz to the game in an expensive Italian automobile, demanded that the stadium gates be opened to allow the car in, and then took two turns around the running track in full view of the thousands of fans. That was only the beginning of young Pollard's embarrassment. At halftime as the players were heading for the locker rooms, Fritz, Sr., emerged from the stands, took off his coat, directed his son to midfield, and proceeded to instruct him on open-field tackling before the amused crowd. Fritz, Jr., who stood in awe of his father, dared not object. Despite the disconcerting baptism, young Pollard went on to become a star player at Senn and was named the outstanding back on the 1932 Illinois All-State prep team. His father was justifiably proud and was already talking about Fritz playing football in the East at either Harvard or Brown.[38]

During his years in Chicago, Pollard was not a civil rights activist in the traditional sense, but he did work behind the scenes to improve conditions for his race. According to his daughter Leslie, Pollard was vitally interested in civil rights but was deterred from taking a more active role because of his extensive business contacts with the white community, where such activism was frowned upon. Pollard did, however, engineer one important political advance for blacks in the Chicago area in the early 1930s. He convinced Edwin B. Jourdain, a long-time friend and Harvard Business School graduate, to run for alderman in Evanston, where Fritz's wife and daughters lived. In 1931, Jourdain, a Republican, was elected as the first African-American alderman in the affluent university town. His election received national attention when Jourdain was ousted by the Evanston city council because of allegations of election fraud and forced to run again, which he did successfully the following year. Jourdain and Pollard would also combine to stage the first black college football games at Chicago's Soldier Field.[39]

While Pollard took pride in Jourdain's victory, his own life was in shambles by the early 1930s. The New York Stock Market Crash of October 1929 resulted in economic ruin for him and his investment firm. As with many other banks and investment houses throughout the country, the tumbling stock prices forced Pollard's firm out of business. While little is known about the financial operations of F. D. Pollard and Company, it is probable that the firm engaged in shady if not fraudulent investment practices. As president, Pollard, rather than Chick Evans, was held responsible for some of the losses. He apparently tried to make good on some of these obligations by writing checks which he unfortunately could not cover. The Chicago *American* made light of Pollard's desperate situation in early 1931 when it noted that the "one time all-American colored halfback of Brown University and formerly with the Chicago Cardinals [*sic*] professional football team, showed a burst of his old speed today when he vanished from the Stockyard Court where he was to face a rubber check charge." Pollard eluded his creditors and the law for nearly a year before he was forced to appear in court once again.

According to his son's account of the proceedings, Pollard, always the survivor, told the judge: "There never was a Negro, only he didn't use the word Negro, he said there never was a nigger involved in that much money in the United States. Something to that effect. So the judge let him off."[40]

Pollard was more fortunate than some other Chicago black financiers who were also victims of the deepening depression. Jesse Binga, for example, owner of Chicago's largest African-American bank, was forced into bankruptcy, convicted of embezzlement, and served time in prison. Despite Pollard's success in avoiding a legal conviction, however, he found it increasingly difficult to face friends and business associates who had lost thousand of dollars invested through his company. To sustain himself, he operated a small coal company in downtown Chicago beginning in 1931. He also began to drink heavily, and his already strained relationship with Ada worsened as his resources to support her and the children dwindled. In late 1932, after Fritz, Jr., had completed his last high school football season, Pollard decided to leave Chicago. Engulfed by personal and business problems, Pollard said goodbye to his family and set out for New York, a city that he had first seen as a youthful student some nineteen years before.[41]

New Beginnings

11

During the mid-1950s, Fritz Pollard, Jr., remembered arguing with his father about the athletic merits of then Syracuse University full-back Jim Brown, who was a favorite of the younger Pollard. Fritz, Sr., maintained that Brown had not yet established himself as a premier running back because he had not played and proven his ability before the fans and sportswriters in New York City. For the senior Pollard, "making it" in New York City was the true test of success.[1]

When he arrived in New York during the winter of 1933 in the depths of the depression, Pollard's prospects of making it in the nation's largest city were uncertain. He remembered taking a hotel room and then walking around the city for several days wondering what to do. After several weeks of attempting to make new contacts and renewing old ones, Pollard found a means of making a living. He was able to borrow enough money to start a coal business similar to the one he had run in Chicago. Renting an office in the General Motors Building on Fifth Avenue and hiring a small fleet of trucks on which he had his name emblazoned in large letters, Pollard began selling coal, principally uptown in Harlem. He bought the coal from wholesalers based on his orders and paid drivers to distribute it. Trading on his name, which was still recognized by many black residents of Harlem, Pollard established a functioning if not thriving enterprise during the worst period of the depression. Where he was able to borrow enough capital to start such an enterprise is an interesting question. Joe Mahood, a Brown alumnus and ex-Bruin halfback, remembers hearing that the Columbia University football coach Lou Little, whom Pollard had known in Philadelphia, the New York University gridiron boss John "Chick" Meehan, "and another man, perhaps a Brown alumnus helped put Fritz in business." Pollard's grandson, Fritz Pollard III, said that John D. Rockefeller, Jr., likely made the loan to his grandfather. Fritz III knew of a $29,000 loan Rockefeller made to his grandfather in the 1930s because the elder Pollard "carried around for years a cancelled check which he used in paying back Rockefeller." Young Pollard felt that the loan was made in the early 1930s, and may have been used in opening the coal business. With his immediate financial situation secure, Pollard soon moved uptown into an apartment in an old brownstone on St. Nicholas Avenue in the Washington Heights section of Harlem.[2]

By 1933, Harlem was in transition. The so-called Harlem or Negro Renaissance that had made the primarily black, uptown section of Manhattan a "Negro Mecca" for writers, poets, artists, and musicians, was beginning to wane under the heavy weight of the depression. White interest and money which had helped fuel the diverse cultural activities in Harlem during the 1920s started to recede with the declining stock market. To be sure, whites from downtown continued to flock to the nightclubs and cabarets concentrated in the area around Seventh Avenue, at least until the Harlem Riot of 1935 scared off many of the thrill-seekers. Establishments such as the Cotton Club, Smalls' Paradise, and Connie's Inn catered to white patrons and featured some of the finest shows and most popular black musicians and entertainers in the country. In the early morning hours, whites shuttled into Harlem to experience the sensual shows, the titillating music of the bands of Duke Ellington and Cab Calloway, or the singing, dancing, and comedy of such headliners as Bill "Bojangles" Robinson. Generally excluded from the clubs, either because of a color barrier or the high prices, Harlem residents entertained themselves at "house-rent parties" that provided a means to pay the rent. Cab Calloway recalled that in the 1930s Harlem "was *the* place for a Negro to be. God knows it wasn't such a ball for everyone. There were a hell of a lot of poor Negroes, too. But still, no matter how poor, you could walk down Seventh Avenue or across 125th Street on a Sunday afternoon after church and check out the women in their fine clothes and the young dudes all decked out in their spats and gloves and tweeds and

Homburgs. People knew how to dress, the streets were clean and tree-lined, and there were so few cars that they were no problem."[3]

There was a seamier side of Harlem half-hidden by the glitter of the raucous cabarets and nightclubs and the "clean and tree-lined" streets. Harlem may have been a "Mecca" for American Negroes, but even during the height of the Negro Renaissance and the prosperity of the 1920s, it was in the grip of a depression. In 1928, more than two thousand Harlem families were destitute, with a quarter of them receiving charity. By 1933, economic conditions had worsened considerably. Half of the potential wage earners among Harlem's nearly three hundred thousand black residents were unemployed. Cramped into a small section of uptown Manhattan with a population density almost twice that of the rest of the city, Harlem families "were doubled and trebled in apartments meant for one family." Tenants paid exorbitant rents to landlords, most of whom were white, for dwellings in flagrant violation of city building and sanitary codes. A substratum of Harlemites, perhaps ten thousand, lived below ground in rat-invested cellars and basements, foraging behind restaurants and in garbage cans for their sustenance.[4]

Although he had found a way to pay his bills in the troubled economic times, Pollard was not satisfied with being a coal merchant. During that winter of despair for many Americans, as the nation awaited the inauguration of a new president and perhaps a new direction and new hope, Pollard made every effort to establish or renew contacts with men of prominence who remembered him as a dashing All-America halfback, the man who had almost single-handedly humbled Yale and Harvard some sixteen years before. In early March, he played in an old-timers' basketball game for the Alpha Physical Culture Club at the Renaissance Casino and rekindled friendships with many prominent black New Yorkers including his former star halfback at Lincoln, Francis "Jazz" Byrd. A few weeks later while walking along Fifth Avenue, Pollard happened to meet an old friend from Chicago, Joe Glaser. Glaser was a talent agent and founder of the Associated Booking Corporation, a firm that specialized in representing black entertainers. He was best known as Louis Armstrong's manager and confidant, but he represented many well-known entertainers. After Pollard told him about his difficulty in finding suitable work in New York, Glaser suggested that Fritz try his hand as a booking agent. Pollard took no immediate action on the suggestion, but mulled the idea over.[5]

In early May 1933, Paul Robeson, now an internationally famous singer and actor, returned to New York from Europe, where he had spent much time in recent years, and announced that he would appear in a film adaptation of Eugene O'Neill's play *The Emperor Jones*. Robeson had earlier starred in the play as Brutus Jones in both New York and London. The New York *Amsterdam News* reported that Robeson would receive $30,000 for his performance from independent producers John Krimsky and Gifford Cochran. Pollard met with Robeson shortly after his arrival and convinced his former teammate to find him a job as a member of the film's production staff. Originally, the movie was to have been shot in New York, with the jungle scenes done in Haiti. Because Robeson's contract stipulated that he would not "shoot footage south of the Mason-Dixon line," however, the producers and the director Dudley Murphy decided to film at Paramount's Astoria Studios on Long Island and shoot some exterior scenes in New Rochelle and at Jones Beach.[6]

In later years, Pollard remembered being Robeson's agent during the filming of *The Emperor Jones*. Pollard probably exaggerated his business relationship with his friend. A widely acclaimed international star, Robeson either represented his own interests or worked through his wife Eslanda, whom the New York *Age* reported to be his business manager. In a mid-July article on the progress of the filming on Long Island, *Amsterdam News* reporter Edward Lewis wrote that Pollard and Eslanda Robeson sat next to Dudley Murphy during the shooting, and Pollard was referred to as Robeson's secretary. Apparently Pollard's association with Robeson and the production of *The Emperor Jones* was more as a general assistant rather than an agent. His primary task was to help Murphy with casting and to select and transport people from Harlem to Long Island to appear in bit parts or as extras. Serving as booking agent for actors or extras may have occurred to Pollard as a result of his chat with Joe Glaser, and he may have suggested the idea to Robeson at their earlier meeting. Pollard also supervised Robeson's physical conditioning to prepare the actor for strenuous scenes. Robeson later remarked that it was great fun running and boxing with Pollard and getting himself into shape again. Pollard also appeared briefly in the film as the piano player at a high-class Harlem party.[7]

For Pollard, being connected with the filming of *The Emperor Jones* was a bit of good fortune. He not only renewed his friendship with Robeson and earned some much-needed money but also, by being associated with the widely publicized film, got a start in the talent booking business, a whole new career for him in the future. For some years, with Glaser's encouragement, he occasionally would book black entertainers into nightclubs in New York City and surrounding areas. After a hurried six weeks' shooting, the film was completed in July and released in mid-September by United Artists in a double premier in Harlem and on Broadway. African-American audiences at Harlem's Roosevelt Theatre applauded Robeson's performance but were taken back by his southern drawl and his use of the word *nigger* in a number of scenes. Critics in both the black and white press gave the film mixed reviews but generally praised Robeson's portrayal of Brutus Jones. The negative reviews, more often seen in black middle-class publications, were more critical of O'Neill's story and his use of racial stereotypes than they were of Robeson's performance. Although some experts predicted disaster at the box office, the film played before overflow audiences in New York and proved to be a modest financial success. Due to some distribution problems, especially in the South, and the racial theme of the film, *The Emperor Jones* was seen by a smaller audience than the producers had hoped for. The idea of a black man starring in a film that also featured white actors in lesser parts, according to *Time*, "was indeed something of a filmic revolution" and too radical for many white Americans to accept, at least in 1933.[8]

At the time that *The Emperor Jones* premiered in New York, Pollard was busily engaged trying to convince his son to attend Brown University. For several years, he had sent press clippings about young Fritz's athletic achievements to the Providence *Journal* and to certain alumni interested in Brown football. Fritz, Jr., however, had other ideas. He wanted to attend Northwestern University and had enrolled at the Evanston school in late August. His days there were few, however, because his father "laid the law down" and said "I had to go to Brown." In early September, Pollard sent his son $50 and instructed him to take the next train to New York. Fritz,

Jr., remembered with a smile that it was "the first time I ever got any money from him. And he met me at the train and I never had to spend any more money until we got to Providence." After Fritz, Jr., arrived in New York, Pollard took his son to his downtown office, which Fritz, Jr., remembered as being near Times Square, "where no black had ever had an office." Outside were four or five big trucks with "Pollard" printed on the sides in big silver letters. A short time later, father and son went to Rockefeller Center to see one of the vice presidents of the Rockefeller Foundation. Fritz, Jr., marveled at how his father brushed his way past more than a dozen white employees who tried to stop the two Negroes from approaching the vice-president's office and gaining entrance. After the door opened, the Rockefeller official threw his arms around Fritz, Sr., and the three men entered the office. The restraining force of Rockefeller employees "nearly died," Fritz, Jr., recalled. "When you start pushing executive secretaries and people around in that kind of a maze at Rockefeller Center," the younger Pollard noted in admiration of his father's resolve, "you have to know what you're doing."[9]

Many years later, Fritz, Jr., still had his suspicions about why his father had insisted so adamantly that he attend Brown. "He probably conned the alumni into giving him this office and coal company and so forth in order to get me to go to Brown." "All I know," Fritz, Jr., continued, "there was a lot of money that passed around, but I didn't get any of it. I didn't know anything about it." After several days in New York, Pollard and his son took the train to Providence, where they were greeted at Union Station by a group of alumni and the press. Fritz, Jr., later recalled that with his father "everything was always grandiose, grandiose!" With the delegation of alumni in tow, Providence *Journal* sportswriter Joe Nutter accompanied the Pollards to the campus, took a number of photographs of them tossing a football around, and did a long interview with Fritz, Sr. The younger Pollard also remembered that his father managed to "con the registrar" into enrolling Fritz, Jr., and assigning him one of the best dormitory rooms on campus without ever offering to make any payment for tuition or room. "Here I was living like Rockefeller or something," Fritz, Jr., explained. "No money coming in from anyplace. In two or three days he was gone. Nothing paid." After paying for his train ticket from Chicago and charges for his trunk after it had arrived in Providence, young Pollard had just $8 left from the amount his father had sent him.[10]

Leslie Keeling recalled that one of her father's greatest faults was not following through on things and cited the incident with her brother in Providence as an example. Fritz, Jr., was more philosophical. "See, I knew all the way from a kid the type of guy Dad was," he said. "He never had anything. When he had it, he never had it long." It seems likely that Fritz, Sr., had—or thought he had—an arrangement with some Brown alumni to cover his son's expenses. But no one stepped forward to pay Fritz, Jr.'s fees. One possible explanation is that Brown officials had been scrupulously enforcing regulations pertaining to financial aid to athletes ever since the Carnegie Report of 1929, which had castigated major college athletic programs for questionable and unethical conduct. Joe Mahood, who played at Brown at the time, remembered that as a result of the report athletes were not even allowed to hold jobs as waiters at the football training tables. The other possibility is that Fritz, Sr., never had a solid commitment from anyone that his son's expenses would be paid.[11]

Despite his precarious economic situation, young Pollard got off to a fast start for the Brown freshmen team before he was declared ineligible in mid-October for failure to pay his tuition and room and board fees. After the story of his plight appeared in the city newspapers, he was rescued by his maternal grandfather Joseph Laing, who came to his grandson's room unexpectedly one afternoon. Although Pollard had never before met his grandfather, Laing took him to a local bank and made arrangements to help Fritz, Jr., meet his college expenses. Young Pollard went on to star in several freshmen games before a foot injury sidelined him for the season. His blazing speed as well as his passing and kicking ability invariably reminded veteran gridiron observers of his more famous father, and some predicted that Brown would soon have another All-America halfback named Pollard. During the spring semester, Fritz, Jr., established himself as a world-class track star by capturing the hurdle events at the Boston Athletic Association games in February and equaling a world indoor hurdle record at a Providence meet the following month. Like his father, however, he failed to pay sufficient attention to his studies, was declared athletically ineligible by the end of his second semester, and returned to Chicago. Although Brown encouraged him to return to Providence for another try the following fall, he was embarrassed by the whole episode and decided to pursue his studies and athletic career at another college.[12]

Pollard's handling of his son's initial college experience reveals some things about Pollard as a parent and a man. To say, as Leslie did, that her father often failed to follow through on things is an understatement. He was a demanding and loving parent but often irresponsible. Pollard saw himself as a man with an important mission in life. He could be and sometimes was a loving and devoted parent. Leslie recalled, for example, how he sat the girls down before he left Chicago and explained the facts of life to them. "He knew how to do it," she said. "I don't know anybody who could have done it better." Even Fritz, Jr., despite the Brown episode, clearly loved and admired his father and saw him as a role model and inspiration. Pollard expected his children to live up to the high standards of achievement he and his family had established, whether or not he was around to provide personal guidance. Why he did not establish closer personal ties with them, one of the things he most treasured from his own childhood, cannot be known for sure; perhaps Pollard viewed himself as exempt from the normal parental role.[13]

Pollard was disappointed and embarrassed by his son's financial difficulties at Brown, but he was in no position to provide economic assistance. With the nation in the grips of the worst depression in its history, Pollard, like many Americans, found it difficult to make ends meet. During 1933, he took a job as sports editor of the black weekly New York *News*, a position which his brother Leslie had held two decades before. He covered the black sporting scene in New York and wrote a number of articles on the history of black athletics. The salary was a welcome supplement to the little income he derived from the coal business. By the mid-1930s, the Pollard Coal Company had gone out of business. In later years, Pollard maintained that he gave up the coal company around 1934 or 1935 because he was embarrassed at a social function when a young lady requested that somebody make that "nasty coal man" leave. While the story may have been true, there is also evidence that the Pollard Coal Company was poorly managed and in serious financial difficulty when Pollard quit the business. His interest and experience in the newspaper business dated back to the mid-1920s when his brother

Luther had been part-owner of the Chicago *Whip*, a black weekly; both Fritz and Luther had written for the *Whip* and occasionally contributed articles to other black publications.[14]

When the New York *News* folded in 1935, Pollard founded his own weekly newspaper, the New York *Independent News*, the country's first African-American tabloid. How he raised the money for the enterprise or who may have backed him is not known, but his venture came at an opportune time. The New York *News* had gone out of business, and the city's leading black weekly, the New York *Amsterdam News*, was in the midst of a bitter labor dispute that hurt circulation and forced the paper into receivership by the end of 1935. The New York *Amsterdam News*, renamed the *Amsterdam-Star News* for a time, would regain its former prominence under its new owners P. M. H. Savory and C. B. Powell, but in 1935 the time seemed ripe for a new black newspaper in Harlem.[15]

As Pollard well knew, running a Negro newspaper for blacks was tricky business. Black papers not only competed among themselves, but also with the white dailies which were more widely read by black New Yorkers. Some African Americans, particularly intellectuals, never read the black papers and, according to Claude McKay, many New York Negroes in the 1930s were ashamed to be seen in public with a black newspaper. Successful black publishers focused on events and issues of exclusive interest to the African-American community and provided only a minimum of hard news. New York's major black papers in the 1930s, including to some extent the venerable and conservative New York *Age*, featured sensational stories about crime, scandal, or racial discrimination and prejudice as well as heavy doses of social, religious, theatrical, and sporting news tailored to black interests. The African-American weeklies carried a smattering of national and international news, but usually only when racial issues were involved.[16]

Pollard established offices on West 125th Street in Harlem and quickly made a success of his new venture. The *Independent News* appeared weekly from 1935 through 1942 when the war and a rival tabloid cut into circulation and forced Pollard out of business. At the height of its popularity in the late 1930s, according to Pollard's estimate, the *Independent News* reached a weekly circulation of nearly thirty-five thousand, which would have put it in the ranks of the ten most widely read Negro newspapers in the country. The paper's format was similar to that of the New York *Daily News*, the most widely read white daily in Harlem. Bold headlines proclaimed the week's leading story at the top of the front page, the remainder of which was given over to large photographs of important personalities or events. The body of the paper was largely composed of feature stories and regular columns that dealt with sports, theatrical news, local politics, and social gossip in the black community. Pollard wrote a weekly editorial that focused on the economic and political concerns of Harlem residents.[17]

Given his interest in sports, Pollard's *Independent News* provided what many felt was the most extensive coverage of African-American athletic events in New York. The front page often featured stories and photographs of black sporting personalities and teams. The heavyweight contender and later champion Joe Louis was frequently given front-page coverage, as were the New York Black Yankees and the Cuban Giants, baseball teams in the Negro National League. Pollard also wrote a column, "Sports by Fritz," in which he praised the accomplishments of African-American athletes and promoted such causes as the integration of major league baseball and the NFL. As a writer, Pollard could be insightful and provocative. In one article he analyzed the close bond between the athlete and the entertainer, a connection that was more apparent in the black community than in the white. He noted that black athletes and entertainers had much in common because they formed an elite in black America. They were given wide recognition, their accomplishments were celebrated, and the best of them were usually highly paid. Sports and entertainment represented two of the few endeavors in which relatively uneducated and underprivileged black youths might strive to achieve status and wealth. Beyond this, Pollard recognized that black athletes often needed to be entertainers in order to stand out and achieve success in the white-dominated sports establishment which usually tried to exclude them. In addition to skill, black athletes often needed to perfect some flashy move or technique in order to make themselves stand out in competition with whites.[18]

By the late 1930s, Pollard turned over his sporting column to Joe Lillard, a former NFL player, and focused more of his attention on editorials and political news. He also hired Earl Dancer, a producer, and Billy Rowe, later a famed Pittsburgh *Courier* reporter, to write columns on theatrical and social events. Occasionally, the veteran actress Fredi Washington, who had starred with Paul Robeson in the film version of *The Emperor Jones*, contributed a feature story on Harlem entertainment. Pollard's editorial views were generally progressive on race issues but more conservative on economic and political matters. He was an ardent spokesman for more jobs for African Americans both within and outside of Harlem and supported the "Don't Buy Where You Can't Work" campaign, one of the early black economic protest movements. Pollard was most forceful in his pleas for integration in a variety of fields, ranging from sports to entertainment to industry. During the 1939 New York World's Fair, for example, the *Independent News* played a role in forcing the city to provide more jobs for blacks at the fair and space for an exhibit about American Negroes. Pollard, however, was conservative with regard to political and economic issues. A lifelong Republican and a small businessman himself, Pollard remained unconvinced that the liberal economic and political agenda of the New Deal would benefit him or his race. During the 1940 presidential election campaign, for example, his editorials ran counter to the increasing Democratic tide in Harlem. He advised his readers to defeat Franklin Roosevelt because among other things the president was responsible for stifling the initiative of American capital.[19]

Although Pollard devoted much of his energy toward publishing his weekly tabloid in 1935 and the years thereafter, he remained a close observer of college and professional football. Even before the first edition of the *Independent News* hit the streets in mid-1935, he was concerned, as were other black sportswriters, about the absence of African Americans in the NFL during the 1934 season. Two blacks, Joe Lillard of the Chicago Cardinals and Ray Kemp of the Pittsburgh Pirates (later the Steelers), had played during the 1933 campaign but did not return the following season. When pressed later in the decade, some NFL club owners offered a number of familiar reasons for their failure to sign black players, including the claim that no qualified Negro players were to be found. Owners maintained, however, that no official policy or ban existed against blacks playing in the league. There is still no indisputable evidence that an official or semiofficial color line was drawn by NFL owners after the 1933 season. The veteran Providence Steam Roller official Pearce Johnson has pointed out, for example, that it would have been difficult to have gotten ten NFL owners to agree on such a proposition. Gerald R. Gems has speculated, however, that Boston Redskins' owner George Preston Marshall (who later moved the team to Washington) "may have included an unwritten recommendation for the exclusion of black players" as part of his reorganization plan for the league submitted at the owners 1933 meeting. Gems further suggests that George Halas, "whose influence in league matters was always substantial, may have provided the necessary support. . . . He probably respected Marshall's business acumen, and in a quest for respectability among the working class, perceived it as a sound business decision along with the other changes proposed by Marshall to increase fans' interest." Commissioner Joe Carr, according to Gems's interpretation, "obviously played a role, the significance of which is unknown."[20]

Later in the 1930s, black sportswriters would allege that Marshall, Halas, and Art Rooney of the Pittsburgh Pirates had a "gentlemen's agreement" to exclude blacks from the NFL and that Commissioner Carr had approved the ban. The African-American press maintained that the owners expected to make big money with their new divisional realignment implemented in 1934, and that "in the midst of the Depression it was considered unseemly for a black man to earn more money than a white man, whatever the field of operation." Although the charges may have had some substance, it appears that any gentlemen's agreement was very informal in 1934, yet may have become more standardized later in the decade. It is known, for example, that Ray Kemp was offered a contract by Pittsburgh in 1934, but turned it down so that he could complete his college education. George Halas, moreover, wanted to sign black halfbacks Ozzie Simmons in 1936 and Kenny Washington in 1939, but apparently could not get the consent of fellow owners. In 1934–35, few black sportswriters focused on the apparent problem in the NFL for fear of bringing attention to a color barrier which might or might not exist and perhaps worsening the situation. Pollard generally agreed with that strategy but with his firsthand knowledge of racial attitudes among NFL owners, he expected the worst and was determined to force the issue at least circuitously.[21]

In February 1935, Pollard "planted" a story with Claude Barnett's Associated Negro Press which stated that Fritz, Jr., "was undecided as to whether he will turn professional or wait until after the 1936 Olympics." The article reported "that young Pollard has been offered a swell contract to play professional football with the 1933 championship Chicago Bears." If the senior Pollard hoped to draw Halas out into the open on the color ban issue, his attempt failed. When contacted about the story, Halas denied the report and cleverly pointed out that the NFL "has an unbreakable rule which forbids offers being made to any athlete until his class has graduated." Fritz, Jr., had two years of college athletic eligibility remaining, according to the story. The response was somewhat ironic because Halas was the cause of the "unbreakable rule" when he signed Red Grange in 1925 before his class at the University of Illinois had graduated. Pollard may have been foiled by Halas again, but he was determined not to let matters rest.[22] .

In the late summer of 1935, Pollard accepted an offer to coach a professional, all-black Harlem football team organized and managed by Herschel "Rip" Day, an athletic promoter and Lincoln University alumnus. The team was named the Brown Bombers in honor of the rising heavyweight boxing contender Joe Louis. Day was determined to make the Brown Bombers the finest black pro team in the nation, on a par with Bob Douglas's famed New York Renaissance Big Five basketball team. Pollard was attracted to the offer to coach the Brown Bombers, at least in part, by his concern about the failure of NFL owners to sign black players for a second consecutive season. As he had earlier attempted in Chicago with the Black Hawks, Pollard would try to showcase the best available black football talent and demonstrate once again that blacks and whites could compete on the gridiron without serious incident. Pollard was further determined to schedule exhibition games with the local NFL teams, the Brooklyn Dodgers and New York Giants, to underscore his points. The *Amsterdam News* sportswriter Artie La Mar reported before the Bombers' 1935 season began that "negotiations for night games with the Brooklyn Dodgers and the New York Giants are under way." During the season, Lewis Dial of the New York *Age* printed a rumor, probably started by Pollard, that the Giants had challenged the Bombers to a game in late November. Dial quoted Pollard as saying that if the November date was not acceptable, "a post season game will be arranged."[23]

In fact, neither of New York's NFL teams was interested in playing the Brown Bombers or any other black team. Pollard's negotiations with Giant owner Tim Mara may have been outright unfriendly in that he would later list Mara along with Halas as being primarily responsible for the ban on blacks in the NFL. Even before Pollard began his negotiations with the New York NFL owners, there was some evidence that local NFL teams were conspiring against African-American players. When former New York University star Dave Meyers, a black who had previously played two seasons for the NFL Brooklyn Dodgers, was scheduled to play in an exhibition game against his former team, Dodger management refused to allow him to take the field. Under the subheading, "Prejudice Feared as Former Star Gets Set to Play," the *Amsterdam News* reported somewhat skeptically that the Dodgers refused to allow Meyers to play because he reported late for the game. The story also quoted a Dodgers' official, Dave Driscoll, as saying that the team had "no thoughts whatsoever of signing Meyers" despite a rumor to that effect. Given the fact that Meyers and Pollard were friends (Meyers would play for the Bombers that season), it seems possible that Fritz may have been responsible for promoting the rumor.[24]

Despite Pollard's continuing and ultimately unsuccessful efforts to schedule a game with either the Dodgers or Giants, he and Day were pleased with their success in putting together a first-rate professional team. Pollard brought in former Chicago Cardinal halfback Joe Lillard as the centerpiece of the Bomber backfield and signed Dave Meyers and the former Morgan College star Thomas "Tank" Conrad to help provide a potent offense. The line was anchored by the former Providence Steam Roller end Howard "Dixie" Matthews and consisted of former black stars from both white and black colleges as well as a few noncollege men. Scheduling only white professional teams from the Northeast and playing their games at Dyckman Oval across the river from Harlem in the Bronx, the Bombers got off to a fast start. In the opening game, they humiliated a much-touted team organized by former Army All-America Chris Cagle (28–6) and then proceeded to demolish (27–0) an all-star team led by Cliff Montgomery, who had quarterbacked Columbia University to a Rose Bowl victory a few years earlier. Joe Lillard provided a good part of the offense, but he was ably assisted by wingback Meyers and the six-foot-three, 240-pound fullback Conrad, the "Negro Nagurski." Meyers and Lillard continued to show their previous NFL form, and the massive but quick Conrad was nearly unstoppable on line rushes, but NFL owners showed no interest in the Bomber backfield trio.[25]

After five games the Brown Bombers were undefeated, racking up ninety-two points to their opponents' nine. The winning streak ended on the last day of the season when the New Rochelle Bulldogs, led by Alabama Pitts, defeated the Bombers 7–6. Pitts, a legendary halfback who had played several years for New York's Sing Sing Prison team the Blacksheep and had been recently released by the NFL Philadelphia Eagles, scored the winning touchdown. Although the city's black newspapers gave the Bombers ample coverage and duly praised Pollard and his players, the team struggled financially. The average attendance at Dyckman Oval was about 1,500 per game, hardly enough to cover players' salaries. To create more excitement and help bolster attendance, Pollard instituted a number of trick plays and unorthodox formations, including one called the "aeroplane shift" that the *Amsterdam News* claimed baffled opponents. Midway through the season, Pollard reluctantly agreed to allow the team to sing spirituals and "truck" from the huddle to the line of scrimmage. He told a reporter that he first opposed the singing and dancing routine which the team sometimes used in practice drills, but "then it struck me all of a sudden that it might help them, and it might aid in selling the team to the public." Truckin' and singing became trademarks of the Brown Bombers, but Pollard stopped short of clowning antics, long a part of African-American professional sports and most recently popularized by the black Cincinnati Clowns in baseball. The showmanship the Bombers instituted was popular with the Harlem fans and did increase attendance, but Pollard admitted near the end of the season that "we've lost about $5000 so far." He added, however, that "we're getting new capital in next year and some new players and I'm sure we'll be a big financial success."[26]

Before the next gridiron campaign began, however, Pollard's attention turned to track and his son's quest to make the 1936 U.S. Olympic team as a hurdler. In the fall of 1935, Fritz, Jr., had enrolled at the University of North Dakota and quickly established himself as a star athlete in both football and track. During the early summer of 1936, young Pollard turned in a number of outstanding performances in the 110-meter high hurdles and qualified for the Olympic team in trials at Randall's Island, New York. The team included nineteen African-American athletes (as against four in 1932) and featured the record-breaking sprinter and broad-jumper Jesse Owens. Fritz, Sr., attended a reception honoring the black athletes and saw his son off on the S.S. *Manhattan* bound for Berlin and a hoped-for Olympic triumph. Young Fritz sustained a leg injury during workouts on the Atlantic crossing but recovered sufficiently in Berlin to make the finals in the 110-meter hurdles. Leading most of the race, Pollard grazed two of the last three hurdles and kicked over the final barrier, causing him to stumble and finally lunge toward the tape for a disappointing third-place finish and a bronze medal. Fritz, Jr., later recalled that his relative inexperience in world-class events caused him to overextend himself in the final stages of the race, resulting in his awkward finish. Nonetheless, he and his fellow black trackmen (especially Jesse Owens) were celebrated as the "black auxiliary forces" that the Nazi press claimed were responsible for the American triumph in track and field events. Pollard served on a committee, which included former track star H. Binga Dismond, Bob Douglas, and Bill Robinson, that welcomed the black Olympic athletes back with a parade through Harlem and a testimonial dinner at the Renaissance Casino.[27]

After seeing his son off to the University of North Dakota, Pollard made preparations for a second season as coach of the Brown Bombers. Once again, he was unable to schedule an exhibition game with local NFL teams and was forced to start the season on the road with a series of warm-up games because Dyckman Oval, which was also used by Negro League baseball teams, was not available until mid-October. Starting with a makeshift lineup, the Bombers lost their first four contests. When the regulars arrived for the home-opener against the Newark Bears, however, it became apparent that Pollard had once again put together one of the best minor-league professional teams in the country. In addition to the mainstays of the 1935 team, Lillard and Conrad, Pollard added Morgan College triple-threat sensation Otis Troupe, who would share season scoring honors with Lillard. Pollard also brought in backs Hallie Harding and Oland Dial, who had played with him on the Chicago Black Hawks. The Bombers humbled the Bears 41–0 before three thousand fans at Dyckman Oval and proceeded to dominate the opposition for the rest of the 1936 season, recording six wins, no defeats, and one tie. Considering the rout of the Newark Bears and a 29–0 whitewash of the still highly regarded Frankford Yellowjackets, Pollard could legitimately claim that he had demonstrated that a number of black players were capable of playing in the NFL. Yet, as before, the league owners showed no interest in either scheduling or recruiting players from the Brown Bombers.[28]

Pollard stayed on for another season as coach of the Bombers but became increasingly pessimistic about the prospects of altering what more clearly seemed to be a ban against blacks playing in the NFL. The Bombers enjoyed another successful season in 1937 by posting a 5-2-1 record, including a 29-0 victory over the Jersey City Giants. Pollard continued to showcase some of the best available black football talent from both black and white colleges. With Lillard and Conrad sidelined with injuries around midseason, Pollard inserted the former Hampton Institute wingback Charlie Paige, who became one of the Bombers' running sensations. On the line, Pollard added the former Brown University tackle Vernon Beaubien and center Al Harris, a recent Greensboro A & T standout. The Bombers played before relatively large home crowds in their third season (averaging more than three thousand per game) and drew more than nine thousand in Newark in a 28-14 loss to the Newark Tornadoes of the American Professional Football Association. Pollard was prepared to coach the Bombers for another season before local and national events caused him to change his mind.[29]

Before the opening of the 1938 Brown Bomber training camp at Verplanck, New York, the *Amsterdam News* sports columnist J. Wayne Burrell announced that James Semler, manager of the Black Yankees Negro National League baseball team, was organizing a "big time" black professional football team by the same name. In an interview with Burrell in which Semler conspicuously failed to mention the Brown Bombers, the Black Yankees' manager remarked that "with the exception of one or two players appearing with white professional elevens, there is no place on [sic] the 'big time' for our stars of color." Semler said he was "appealing to the magnates in the two Negro [baseball] leagues and other sportsminded business men to cooperate with him in trying to create a place in the Sun for these Negro gridiron heroes." The implication of Semler's remarks was clear: he was challenging Pollard's team for supremacy among New York's black fans and obviously did not consider the Brown Bombers "big time." In a section devoted to notes and trivia following the interview, Burrell had "FRITZ POLLARD casting a watchful eye toward James Semler's Black Yankee Grid machine."[30]

Semler's remarks must have hurt Pollard, who had organized and coached black all-star teams since the early 1920s and whose Bombers were clearly the outstanding black team in the country. What was worse, it soon became apparent that Semler had made a deal with Cuban-born Alessandro "Alex" Pompez, owner of the Negro National League's Cuban Giants baseball team and a convicted numbers racketeer, to gain exclusive use of Dyckman Oval, which Pompez owned. When Pollard learned that the Bombers would not be allowed to use Dyckman Oval for their home games and realized that no suitable stadium close to Harlem was available, he promptly resigned as coach. He simply stated to the press that he was "no longer connected with the Brown Bombers football team nor any other in any capacity." The Brown Bombers struggled on for several more years as a road team, but could not afford to pay the best black players and never recaptured their past glory before the wartime mobilization forced the franchise to cease. In later years, when an interviewer asked Fritz if he resented the fact that life for young blacks was so much easier than it had been for him, he replied, "If someone has opened the doors for them, more power to them. I did everything I could to open the doors and make it easier for them. When I organized that Brown Bomber team, and there weren't any black boys in the pro leagues, I did that deliberately to show them that these teams could play against a whole black team and not have any trouble or any prejudice, and could draw a good crowd."[31]

Although the organization of the Black Yankees football team and Semler's deal with Pompez regarding Dyckman Oval were the principal factors in Pollard's decision to resign as coach of the Bombers, he may have had other reasons. His main motive for becoming involved with the Bombers in the first place was to pressure NFL owners into signing top-quality black players. The case of the University of Iowa halfback Ozzie Simmons may have convinced Pollard that no matter how good a black player might be, he stood no chance of breaking into the NFL. Largely forgotten today, Simmons, a Texas high school athlete, started in the Iowa backfield in 1934 and quickly electrified the Midwest with his speed and brilliant cutting ability. After Simmons almost single-handedly demolished

Northwestern in an October 1934 game, Pollard's friend the North-western coach Dick Hanley remarked, "I played against Fritz Pollard and he stood out as my all-time carrier—until Saturday. But compared to Simmons, Fritz was just a real good half back."[32]

Pollard probably did not agree with Hanley's assessment, but having seen Simmons perform he agreed that Ozzie was a sure-fire All-America halfback. The five-man Board of Coaches appointed by the American Coaches Association to select the "Official All-American Team" did not agree. Simmons did not make the coaches' All-America team in any of his three superb seasons. In an article on black All-Americans for the *Amsterdam News* in early 1938, Pollard wrote disdainfully, "What excuse the critics offer for not having placed Oze Simmons on the All-American Team the writer does not know. However the writer does believe that he lost his chances because of unfavorable publicity derived from an argument he had with his coach." At the end of the 1936 season, his last at Iowa, Simmons told reporters that he hoped to make $5,000 the following season as a pro and remarked that he had "one or two offers to play in the National pro league in 1937. I understand Negroes may be barred," he added, "and I may not get a contract but I hope I do." Simmons failed to get an NFL contract that year or any other. He played a number of years for the Patterson Panthers of the American Professional Football Association, where he had some memorable clashes with Joe Lillard, who had transferred his allegiance to the Union City Rams. Pollard later arranged for Simmons to become head football coach at Wendell Phillips High School in Chicago after the war curtailed minor-league professional activity.[33]

The failure of NFL owners to sign Simmons, who along with Pollard may have been one of the top open-field runners in the first seventy years of college football, no doubt further discouraged Pollard from continuing his experiment with the Brown Bombers. If Simmons could not get a contract or even a tryout with an NFL team, then what black player could? And there was no shortage of qualified black players coming out of the college ranks by the late 1930s. In 1938 alone, backs Wilmeth Sidat-Singh of Syracuse, Bernie Jefferson of Northwestern, and Kenny Washington of the University of California at Los Angeles (UCLA) demonstrated All-America qualifications. Many experts agreed that Jerome "Brud" Holland of Cornell and Woody Strode of UCLA were the best ends in the country in 1938, but neither was named a first-team All-America by the Board of Coaches, and only Holland was selected starting wingman on another prestigious All-America eleven picked by Grantland Rice. How many players of equal ability were playing at black colleges will never be known, but Pollard had demonstrated with the Brown Bombers that most likely there were quite a few. Pollard could take some pride in the fact that Fritz, Jr., at North Dakota had been named starting halfback on the Little All-America team and had made the second-team backfield on several other major All-America selections, but he did not encourage his son to pursue a career in professional football. By the late 1930s, Pollard, usually an optimist, was disheartened by the chain of events which caused him to sever his on-field connection with the game he loved.[34]

At about the same time that Pollard resigned as coach of the Brown Bombers, black sportswriters were encouraged by the announcement that George Halas had agreed to play a charity exhibition game pitting his Bears against a hastily assembled black all-star team in Chicago. Coached by Duke Slater and Ray Kemp, the black all-stars included such standouts as Tank Conrad, Ozzie Simmons, and Joe Lillard. When the powerful Bears routed the black all-stars 51–0 in late September 1938, some black writers were discouraged but others were heartened by the breakthrough achieved in blacks facing an NFL team. The following year when UCLA sensation Kenny Washington appeared in the College All-Star Game in Chicago, Halas, according to Washington, asked the UCLA star "to stay around Chicago." After waiting for a week, Washington remembered being told by Halas that "he couldn't use me." Apparently Halas had consulted NFL owners concerning the signing of Washington and had been rebuffed. Pollard did not comment on these events at the time but in later years never altered his views on Halas. In a 1970 interview after Halas had integrated the Bears, Pollard stated that "George Halas was one of the toughest, most prejudiced guys I ever knew. But he was a slickster. He would move over and let a black man come in if it was going to help him, financially, as it did."[35]

As the nation moved closer to war, the Brown Bombers struggled as a road team, and fewer black New Yorkers remembered the pioneering integrationist efforts of Fritz Pollard. In the days after Pearl Harbor when rumors of the impending integration of professional football and baseball were rife and black sports commentators praised the latest leaders in the movement, the former Brown Bomber manager Rip Day paid Pollard a tribute in a testy letter to *Amsterdam News* columnist Dan Burley, who had been celebrating recent efforts to integrate professional football as if the movement had just begun. "I still say," wrote Day, "that Fritz Pollard did more to advance the idea of the best-against-the-best-regardless-of-color than any single man in the business."[36]

With his coaching days behind him and war clouds gathering in Europe, Pollard devoted his energies to the *Independent News* and to expanding his business activities. Beginning in the mid-1930s, at the urging of sportswriter Romeo Dougherty, Pollard had begun to contribute feature sports articles to the *Amsterdam News* that were reprinted by other black weeklies. He did a feature story on Joe Louis based on an exclusive interview and continued the practice of free-lance writing on the history of black sports until his retirement in the 1960s. In addition, as a result of his advocacy of the "Don't Buy Where You Can't Work" campaign, Pollard was hired as director of the sales division at the white-owned Bentley's Credit Department Store on 125th Street in Harlem. Although Bentley's general manager H. A. Fisher stated that "we have always believed in the policy of hiring people in the community in which we do the bulk of our business," he also conceded that the hiring of Pollard and several other black employees was a matter of "fair play." A news story covering the event related that "since Mr. Pollard's introduction into the department, the store reports a substantial increase in business."[37]

Never one short of energy or lacking interest in new business ventures, Pollard also became involved with Suntan Studios, a talent agency and rehearsal hall established by his friend Leonard Harper. Harper was a former dancer and singer who had turned to producing shows for such Harlem nightclubs as Elks Rendezvous, Smalls' Paradise, and Murrains. During the late 1930s, he offered Harper the use of a block of vacant offices on the same floor as his *Independent News* operation on West 125th Street near the Apollo Theater to conduct tryouts and rehearsals for the productions. Harper called his rehearsal rooms the Suntan Studios. In his spare time, Pollard sometimes played the piano during the practice sessions and aided Harper in selecting talent for the productions. Little did Pollard suspect at the time, but he would soon become engaged in the entertainment business on a full-time basis.[38]

ANOTHER WAR AND PEACE
12

The historian Richard Dalfiume has noted that the years of World War II, 1939–45, mark the "forgotten years" of the modern civil rights movement. During those years, black attitudes about America changed and important events occurred both at home and abroad which would eventually trigger a mass protest against segregation and discrimination. Even before Europe drifted toward war in the wake of the 1938 Munich Crisis, African Americans were keenly aware of the contradictions involved in America's opposition to the master race ideology of Nazi Germany and the suffocating caste system a majority of blacks faced in the supposedly democratic United States.[1]

In sports, the triumphs of the "black auxiliaries" at the Berlin Olympics and Joe Louis's dramatic victory over the German boxer Max Schmeling in their 1938 rematch emphasized the incongruities between American ideals and practices. The facts that civil rights organizations were stronger and more numerous than a generation before, that the African-American press was more mature and vocal, and that the number of college-educated blacks had increased rapidly all contributed to a more vigorous insistence on fair treatment as the war approached. Given the disappointing results of the almost uncritical commitment to patriotism and victory by black leadership in World War I, a new generation of leaders in the early 1940s led by A. Philip Randolph demanded both victory over fascism abroad and victory over racism at home. Prejudice and discrimination against African Americans remained entrenched both on the home front and in the military services, however, and progress was slow. As the

Swedish-born economist Gunnar Myrdal correctly predicted during the worldwide conflict, "There is bound to be a redefinition of the Negro's status in America as a result of this War."[2]

Pollard, like many African Americans who had served in the military during World War I, was not surprised by the racism and discrimination that the nation's eventual two million black servicemen would face or by the failure of American industry to voluntarily hire blacks in the war plants. His son, a law student in Chicago in early 1942, was one of thousands of black volunteers given the runaround when they applied for commissioned officer programs in the armed forces. Fritz, Jr., attempted to join the army's paralegal branch, but an officer encouraged him to apply for a commission at the Army-Air Corps black Flying Cadet facility in Tuskegee, Alabama, which he did. After losing ten pounds in one day in order to qualify for the program, he reported to Tuskegee. Before his paper work cleared, he was drafted into the army as a private. Unlike World War I, however, when cases of discrimination or the double standard afforded African Americans were often ignored by the black press, African-American weeklies in the 1940s focused on the blatant racial inconsistencies in American society. Commenting on the subject of black athletes in the military, the New York *Amsterdam News* sportswriter Ted Carroll, who assumed that young Pollard had been accepted in the Tuskegee program, pointed out that although Fritz, Jr., and his fellow Flying Cadet and former Northwestern halfback Bernie Jefferson were good enough to risk their lives for democracy, "they have been barred from playing in the pro league!" The new militancy of the black press and civil rights organizations spawned only limited progress during the war, and the elder Pollard was skeptical about the permanency of change. This time, however, the worldwide conflict would generate a fundamental reorientation of racial affairs in America, and it would be Pollard and his contemporaries who would have to adapt to the views and expectations of a new generation of black Americans. All this was in the future, however, as America mobilized for global war in the spring of 1942.[3]

A few months after Japan's devastating attack on Pearl Harbor, Pollard's immediate concern was his future in the newspaper business. "It was a tough life," he remembered, "keeping up with the events in the community, staying up all hours of the night getting the paper together and soliciting advertising. I soon tired of it." In addition, profits from his weekly tabloid began slipping during the wartime mobilization despite the fact that Pollard had switched to a Sunday magazine format in 1940, and increased the price of the paper from 3 to 5 cents. In early 1942, Pollard agreed to give up the *Independent News* and go to work for Charles Buchanan, manager of the Savoy Ballroom, and Adam Clayton Powell, Jr., the flamboyant Harlem clergyman and state legislator, who had organized a rival tabloid, the *People's Voice*. Years later, Pollard recalled that "the man came to me and talked me into giving it up and joining his newspaper. After I had joined his newspaper, why he and myself couldn't get along which he knew in the beginning and all he wanted to do was wipe my paper out." The veteran Harlem sportswriter St. Clair T. Bourne, Sr., could not remember the details of the demise of the *Independent News* but confirmed that in Harlem "a lot of smaller papers were tricked or submarined or bought out by the larger ones." It is not clear whether "the man" Pollard claimed tricked him into giving up his tabloid was Buchanan or Powell, but by early 1942 he was forced out of the newspaper business.[4]

Casting around for a new direction in the spring of 1942, Pollard agreed to serve as vice president of the Negro Major Baseball League of America. Under the direction of R. R. Jackson of Chicago, a former president of the Negro American League, the new organization was designed to elevate black baseball. With the black press as well as a few white sportswriters and politicians intensifying their campaign for the integration of major league baseball, the Negro National and American leagues had come under scrutiny. Critics, including a few blacks, charged that the leagues were run in a slipshod manner. Scheduling was erratic, players, although talented, were not drilled in the fundamentals, umpiring was substandard, and record keeping was haphazard. What was worse, known or suspected gamblers owned a number of the franchises in both leagues. Major league officials often cited these defects as reasons for refusing to accept the two top Negro leagues as part of organized baseball. With reportedly secure financial backing, Jackson and Pollard apparently hoped to establish a first-rate black league as an initial step toward the integration of major league baseball. Six franchises were granted in late March with the expectation that a seventh team would be established in Harlem; league play was to begin in mid-May. For unknown reasons, however, a number of financial supporters backed out and the new league was stillborn. With little hope of reviving the venture until after the war, Pollard turned his attention and energies toward the world of entertainment.[5]

The transition from sports to show business was a natural one; black athletes and entertainers were regarded as heroes in the black press and usually enjoyed uncommon wealth and status in the black community. "Those closest to the ballplayers in lifestyle," Donn Rogosin has written of Negro baseball stars before the war, "were the musicians, and strong friendships developed between the two groups of young male, black achievers." As a former All-America football player, Pollard knew most of the major entertainers of the era. It was his association with the production of *The Emperor Jones*, he said, "that gave me quite a kick-off in the theatrical world."[6]

With the help of Joe Glaser, Pollard had come to know a number of nightclub owners along 125th Street in Harlem, and they began to ask him to send over a singer or a dancer. "Having been a musician for a quite a few years I could pick talent pretty well," Pollard recalled, "so the doors began to open in Harlem. My old friends from downtown would call and would ask me to find some good talent. And I'd find somebody, a good singer, and send him down there." Finally, Pollard began going around to the key nightspots all over New York and in Philadelphia and Atlantic City seeking employment for his clients. As Pollard remembered the process, he would "talk to the head men, most of them acquaintances I'd made while playing pro ball," and "they'd always talk straight to me, no bull. 'We've never had Negro talent here,' they'd say. 'Well, why don't you try it?' I'd ask. We'd sit around, I'd play the piano, and we'd talk. Most of the time they'd help me out." Occasionally, when "the mobsters and gangsters" who usually owned the nightclubs refused his talent, Pollard admitted many years later, he would ask some of his Harlem underworld friends to pay them a visit. "When I would go back there," Pollard related, "they would say, 'Well Fritz, let's try some of your talent.'" By whatever means available, Pollard explained, "that's the way I broke the barriers down" and "booked a lot of talented young blacks in those depression years."[7]

Pollard remembered that during and after the war many big-name entertainers came to Suntan Studios "to rehearse because they could not rehearse downtown. Duke Ellington, Cab Calloway, King Cole, and all the big bands used to come up there and rehearse, which made my studio pretty well known." As a result, Pollard became the booking agent for some of the top black entertainers of the era. In a 1981 interview Pollard could remember only a handful of the famous entertainers that he had booked, nonetheless, the list was impressive: Billie Holiday, Count Basie, Louis Jordan, Fats Waller, Andy Kirk, and Dizzy Gillespie. "There are a lot of people that I don't remember right now," Pollard added in another interview. "Redd Foxx was one of the fellows who I booked along with the gangs of them who have become famous stars now. They used to come up to my studio. Then on top of that, I got in with all the gangsters who controlled these nightclubs. My point in saying that is this," Pollard emphasized: "How could Fritz Pollard get into these nightclubs to book this talent? Who did he know? So I'm just telling who it was. They wouldn't refuse a request from me. . . . I got hundreds and hundreds of acts into places where they never got before."[8]

By 1942, Pollard was spending more time at Suntan Studios developing talent for his booking agency, and the following year, when Harper died, he took control of the operation. In the meantime, however, Pollard had become involved with the distribution and production of Soundies, which would propel him and Suntan Studios into the mainstream of the black entertainment industry. Developed by the Mills Novelty Company of Chicago in the late 1930s, Soundies, or Phonovision, were musical films played in juke box-like movie machines. An automatic phonograph was installed in the bottom of a box about six feet high: at the top was a 21 by 28-inch screen on which three-minute, sixteen-millimeter moving pictures were shown by rear-view projection and synchronized with the music. For a dime a play, a patron at a hotel, tavern, or restaurant could view and listen to up to eight different selections. In later years, Soundies were used as fillers between feature films in movie theaters.[9]

Mills Novelty got the jump on the competition in the musical video business in 1940 when it founded Soundies Distributing Corporation of America and installed James Roosevelt, the president's son, as its head. Despite the popularity of the new entertainment medium, theater owners and juke box manufacturers such as Wurlitzer, Seeburg, and Rockola began a campaign against Soundies, which they saw a threat to their businesses. After Roosevelt resigned as president of Soundies Distributing in late 1940 to join the armed forces, the new industry came under government scrutiny. In late 1941, probably at the suggestion of theater and juke box interests, Senator Burton K. Wheeler threatened an investigation of Soundies, claiming that "some of these 'juke box' pictures they are putting out and which have government priorities, are lewd and lascivious and would not be permitted on any decent stage or motion picture screen in the country." Under pressure from all sides, Mills Novelty, which had about four thousand machines in operation by 1941, turned to Pollard to produce and distribute Soundies featuring black performers.[10]

In August 1942, Pollard signed a contract with Gordon Mills to serve as manager of the New York office of the Soundies Distributing Corporation of America. According to the *Amsterdam News*, Pollard was assured that at least four of the eight selections on each reel would "feature colored artists, thus opening a new and lucrative field for both Negro song writers and musicians." Pollard was quoted in the article as saying that "as soon as technical difficulties are removed his firm plans to go into the production end upon a much larger scale." Soon after he signed the contract, Pollard, along with two associates, William Crouch and John Dorn, the former production manager at Paramount's studios in Long Island where *The Emperor Jones* was made, began to distribute Soundies machines to saloons, pool halls, hotels, and restaurants in both black and white neighborhoods of New York. By early 1943, musical numbers were rehearsed at Suntan Studios and were filmed, under the direction of Crouch and Dorn, at a studio which Soundies Distributing had leased at 198th Street and Decatur in the Bronx. Pollard had little difficulty contracting leading black artists to appear in Soundies because of his many contacts, including his former teammate Jay Mayo Williams, who supervised black talent for Decca Records. Dorothy Dandridge, Duke Ellington, Count Basie, Nat King Cole, Andy Kirk, Louis Jordan, Cab Calloway, and a host of others appeared. With the decline of race movies by the late 1930s, the historian Thomas Cripps has pointed out, Soundies represented one of the few remaining outlets for blacks to produce their own films and "might have revived musical film as a means of black expression."[11]

Leslie Keeling recalled visiting the Bronx studio with her father during the war and watching the Ink Spots record a Soundies number. She never forgot her embarrassment "when my father dressed me down right in their presence" after "I asked to meet the Ink Spots. Because I was a celebrity's daughter," she explained, her father believed that the Ink Spots should have asked to meet her. Leslie remembered her father as a sensitive and loving man, but he set high standards and insisted that the children have "the best of manners." At the family dinner table, she recalled, if any of the girls put their elbows on the table, Fritz would stop eating and talking and look at them. "Although he was a very gentle man, he wasn't mean or anything," she said, "but you knew when you could sense these eyes on you, you were doing something wrong."[12]

In fact, Leslie was a celebrity's daughter. Pollard became a force in the world of African-American entertainment during the wartime years. "I began furnishing all the talent for these colored Soundies," he later recalled with pride. The performers who appeared represented a who's who of black musicians and dancers. In two surviving films, Fats Waller performs "Ain't Misbehavin' " and "Honeysuckle Rose" while flanked by sleek female dancers. Lincoln Perry "Stepin Fetchit" introduces a dance number by Mickey O'Daniel in another short, while Louis Armstrong blares out "Shine" and "I'll be Glad When You're Dead" in two other selections.[13]

But with Soundies coming under increasing attack by theater and juke box interests, the new vogue in entertainment barely survived the war, only to be revived again by others in the 1960s. Thomas Cripps, who has viewed most of the surviving black Soundies, has written that many numbers gave a "false ring of a 'happy Harlem' and the poor production values spoiled spontaneity and left the blacks in the cold again." It was not the poor quality of the black firm shorts that cut short Pollard's tenure with Soundies Distributing, however, but intervention by white interests. "The ofays," Pollard told Cripps in 1970, simply bought up most of the black holdings, thus ending what might have been a productive, long-term venture in the production of musical shorts by black filmmakers. Although his connection with Soundies concluded shortly after the war, Pollard's brief success in booking major black entertainers in the musical shorts made Suntan Studios one of the centers of the entertainment industry in Harlem.[14]

Although he took pride in representing some of the top entertainers of the day, Pollard was even more pleased about Suntan's role in discovering new talent. From the start, the primary objective of Suntan Studios was to develop young artists. "What expenses there were, I paid out of my own pocket," Pollard stated, "and experienced musicians gave unselfishly of their time to help. Frankly, I was not too enthusiastic at the outset, but as time went by, I realized how important the work was and how much the youngsters needed help and I decided to give it my all." After the war, with the aid of his new manager at Suntan, Johnny "Trala" Walker, formerly of Duke Ellington's band, Pollard set up the first black modeling agency in Harlem. He and Walker placed such models as Mary Cunningham and Dorothy Coranaldi at Rose Meta and Sepia Art Models as well as other firms. The list of entertainers developed at Suntan Studios is too numerous to recount but included such postwar stars as movie actress Connie Carroll and singers Mable Lee and Lou Elliott. Even though Pollard was never fully comfortable with his career in the entertainment business, he told *Amsterdam News* reporter Julius J. Adams in 1949 that he intended "to keep up the work as long as there are youngsters who desire to get ahead in the entertainment world."[15]

When World War II ended, Pollard, like many African Americans of his generation, was skeptical about the lasting impact of the progress his race had made as a result of the global conflict. World War I had raised black hopes and expectations only to see them dashed by a powerful postwar reaction of white racism. To be sure, black Americans had been more cautious in extending their full support to the war effort in the second conflict and were more assertive in demanding fair treatment at home and overseas. The threatened March on Washington in 1941 and race riots in Detroit, Harlem, and other cities during 1943 indicated a restiveness with the status quo among African Americans. Similar events on a smaller scale had occurred during and after World War I without fostering rapid change, however. In athletics, dramatic breakthroughs leading to the integration of the major professional sports followed closely the Japanese surrender in Tokyo Bay in 1945. Branch Rickey's signing of Jackie Robinson to play for the Brooklyn Dodgers' Montreal farm team in 1945 was clearly the most heralded and symbolically important. The fledgling National Basketball Association (which grew, in part, out of the Basketball Association of America), the NFL, and its rival the All-America Football Conference also integrated in the immediate postwar years. Many blacks who regarded advancement in sports as a benchmark of progress for their race saw these events as portending a brighter future. Pollard was not so sure.[16]

The desegregation of professional sports culminating with Jackie Robinson's debut as a Brooklyn Dodger in 1947 dramatized Pollard's transition from a leadership role to that of an elder statesman in the movement to integrate athletics. On a larger scale, the postwar civil rights movement exposed a generation gap between an older generation of African Americans and a new one reaching maturity during the turbulent wartime years. No doubt Pollard took pride in the occasional article in the black press that celebrated his pioneering efforts in the early NFL. When Philadelphia Phillies manager Ben Chapman encouraged his team to abuse verbally Jackie Robinson during the 1947 season, for example, *Amsterdam News* sportswriter Dan Burley noted that Jack Johnson, Paul Robeson, and Pollard had received much worse defilement earlier in the century, and that the Dodger first baseman had best accept the harassment as part of the game. More often, however, Pollard was cited in the black press as a footnote in the ongoing saga of sports integration, and his accomplishments were eclipsed by the modern heroes: Jackie Robinson and Larry Doby in baseball, Nat Clifton and William "Dolly" King in basketball, and Marion Motley and Claude "Buddy" Young in football. Pollard was a legend, to be sure, but one whose exploits were only dimly remembered by black sportswriters, and he was largely ignored in the white press.[17]

In the years immediately after the war Pollard was not overly optimistic that the reintegration of professional football, which he enthusiastically endorsed, would become a permanent part of the sport. While watching an All-America Conference game at Ebbets Field in 1947 with Dan Burley of the *Amsterdam News* and Jim Jennings, a white sportswriter for the New York *Daily Mirror*, Pollard recounted how blacks like himself, Paul Robeson, and Duke Slater were brought into the unstable professional league after World War I as star gate attractions. Once the NFL was put on a sound, paying basis, he noted, the remaining black players were given the gate by Tim Mara, George Halas, and the other league owners. Pollard feared that the same pattern would develop with the new All-America Conference, which had taken the lead in integrating pro football. Such fears, however, proved groundless as the black stars in the new league became gate attractions beyond all expectations. The key game, perhaps, was a November 1947 clash between the Cleveland Browns and the New York Yankees. More than seventy thousand fans, including more than twenty-five thousand blacks, jammed Yankee Stadium to watch Cleveland's huge fullback Marion Motley duel with the Yankees' diminutive halfback Buddy Young. The total attendance topped the pro football record established in 1925 when Red Grange and the Chicago Bears had played at the Polo Grounds. Clearly, pro football owners could not ignore the huge turnout and the conspicuously large number of black fans. In later years, Pollard concluded that it was the economic success of early postwar desegregation initiatives, more than any other single factor, which led to the slow but full integration of professional football, excluding coaching and administrative positions, by the early 1960s.[18]

With change in the air during the postwar years, Pollard's personal life underwent a transformation when he married Mary Ella Austin in 1947. Separated from his first wife, Ada, since the early 1920s, Pollard led a fast-paced life during the Roaring Twenties. Although money flowed through his hands, he had made some small effort to support his wife and daughters. After the 1929 Stock Market Crash ruined him financially and led to his eventual move to New York, Pollard was downcast and became a heavy drinker, although the extent of his problem is unclear. Although Fritz's brother Frank was an alcoholic, there is no evidence that Fritz suffered from that disease. Pollard told one interviewer in the 1970s that he was an ex-drunk; other people who knew him in Harlem during the 1930s agreed that he drank heavily but were unaware of a serious drinking problem. His daughter Leslie maintained that her father's excessive drinking was linked to his separation from Ada and the fact that Mary Ella Austin was pressuring him into marriage.[19]

Mary Ella, whom Fritz called Baby, was born in Greenville, South Carolina, and moved to New York after she graduated from high school in the late 1920s. A slim, attractive woman with a nut-brown complexion, Mary Ella worked as a schoolteacher and later a showgirl in the Irvin C. Miller theatrical group the "Desires" for several years. After one performance in the mid-1930s, she met

Pollard and they began to date. A short time later, Mary Ella quit show business and began work at Pollard's *Independent News*, where she wrote feature articles, sold advertising, and did filing until the paper went out of business in 1942. A long-time friend of Mrs. C. B. Powell, whose husband owned the *Amsterdam News*, Mary Ella then got a job as a receptionist at that paper, where she would work for more than twenty-five years. Pollard's daughters, according to Leslie, resented Mary Ella, whom Fritz took to Chicago on at least one occasion, because they held her responsible for breaking up their parents' marriage. Leslie, at least, believed that her father, down deep, always loved Ada. Fritz, Jr., who did not have as close a relationship with his mother as did his sisters, thought Mary Ella had a steadying and "evening influence" on his father. The couple settled in at Fritz's apartment on St. Nicholas Avenue in Harlem and, although he remained energetic and continued to remain constantly active with business ventures, Pollard, who ballooned to 210 pounds in the late 1940s, seemed to thrive on Mary Ella's southern-style cooking and a more stable and orderly domestic environment.[20]

By the late 1940s, Pollard became an elder statesman in Harlem. Former newspaperman Major Robinson recalled that Pollard "had a beautiful personality. You could always talk to Fritz. He always knew somebody. He was one of the ones that stood for something." At the time, Robinson added, "black athletes had more recognition than college professors." Pat Patterson, who knew Pollard only by reputation, remembered that "there were few guys like him," implying that many blacks who had status and money in Harlem "were in numbers or something and that Fritz seemed to be different." Many Harlemites were impressed by rumors that Pollard had connections with the Rockefellers. St. Clair T. Bourne, Sr., explained that the Rockefellers maintained good relations with people like Fritz and Jackie Robinson. Although he had no firsthand knowledge, Bourne assumed that the Rockefellers paid these prominent blacks some kind of retainer or had a similar arrangement. Pollard never mentioned any such understanding, but it is apparent from his relationship with John D. Rockefeller, Jr., and his later association with Nelson Rockefeller and such other Republicans as Richard Nixon and Hugh Scott in the 1950s that he had close ties with the Rockefellers as well as with other GOP leaders. In an era before black consciousness, Pollard's connection with the Rockefellers and his contacts with the white world, according to Bourne, were viewed in Harlem with "half concealed admiration."[21]

As the cold war intensified in 1949 and triggered a period of spy chasing and red baiting in America, Pollard was drawn into a political controversy involving his friend and former teammate Paul Robeson. Beginning in the 1930s, Robeson, who spent a good deal of his time abroad as a celebrated singer and actor, became an extreme antifascist and identified with what he conceived to be progressive political and racial policies in the Soviet Union. Pollard and Robeson met occasionally during the 1930s and 1940s when Robeson visited New York, but whether they exchanged political views is unknown; neither was an avid letter writer. In April 1949, Robeson addressed the Congress of the World Partisans of Peace in Paris and was quoted by the Associated Press (AP) as saying that: "It is unthinkable that American Negroes would go to war on behalf of those who have oppressed us for generations against a country [the Soviet Union] which in one generation has raised our people to the full dignity of mankind." Without checking the accuracy of the AP's quotation, which Robeson's biographer Martin Duberman claims was in error, a cross-section of American black leaders struck out at the once-revered Robeson.[22]

Contacted by the New York *Age*, along with other prominent Harlem spokespersons such as Adam Clayton Powell, Jr., and Walter White of the NAACP, Pollard responded to Robeson's purported remarks with a grandiose statement which had the texture of a football coach humorously rebuking a headstrong lineman. "Paul's at it again, playing Emperor Jones," Pollard began. "He started it after his first trip to England—sometimes he's 'Emperor Jones,' and sometimes he thinks he's the Negro island liberator, Henri Christophe. Despite his spectacular popoffs," Fritz continued, "he's no Commie, in his heart. He just likes to play 'Emperor Jones' and when he does, he's not speaking for American Negroes. I think I can straighten him out." There is no record of what Robeson might have said to Pollard about Fritz's criticism of him or if Pollard actually did try to straighten out his friend. The controversy stemming from Robeson's Paris speech, however, did not seem to affect the friendship. Later that year, they were photographed together with Duke Slater and Joe Lillard as part of a magazine article Fritz wrote naming his choices for the ten greatest African-American football players of all time. Ink Williams and Bob Marshall also made the list. The magazine's editor added a note to the article which in retrospect may shed some light on Pollard's tone in reprimanding Robeson some months earlier. "Few people know," he wrote, that Pollard "taught a lot of the game they knew to Lou Little and Paul Robeson."[23]

One day in 1950 Pollard recalled receiving a call from Fred F. Stoneman, who was under the mistaken impression that Fritz was a tax expert. Stoneman said that he had attended Cornell when Fritz was at Brown and that he had a tax problem. Pollard went over to see him at the Waldorf Astoria Hotel and later recalled, "I figured I'd be able to help him. I knew a lot of people in the tax business" and "I figured it would be worth a thousand dollars for my time." After a discussion of Stoneman's tax difficulties, the Cornell alumnus handed the astonished Pollard $5,000 as a down payment for his services. The next morning Pollard took a train to Washington to consult with a friend and former Holy Cross football player who was the director of Internal Revenue. "I didn't want a job with the Internal Revenue Office," Pollard explained, "but I wanted to find out how I could be a tax consultant." He began to study the tax codes and moved his office from Harlem to the General Motors Building downtown. "I surrounded myself with high-class tax CPAs," Pollard recalled, "and I got into the tax business which I loved. I call it the 'intellectual tax racket,' the kind of work more suited to me." It would take five years and $350,000 to resolve Stoneman's tax difficulties, but in the meantime Pollard became a prominent and prosperous tax consultant in New York City.[24]

As his tax-consulting business grew, Pollard severed his ties with Suntan Studios. He later said that "I decided I wanted to get out of that field because the theatrical world wasn't exactly what I wanted." At his Broadway office, however, he still operated his booking agency, Fritz Pollard Associates, and continued to represent and book a number of top entertainers including Redd Foxx in nightclubs and increasingly in the radio and television industries. Beyond that, Pollard's association with Stoneman led to his involvement with Ardstone Corporation, which also operated out of his Broadway office. Stoneman served as chairman of the board of Ardstone and Pollard was president and treasurer. Although the full scope of Ardstone's activities is not known, it did include a cosmetic firm, Mary Austin Cosmetics, which Fritz named after his wife. All in all, Pollard became a reasonably wealthy man by the mid-1950s, and at the end of the decade moved with his wife into a spacious twelve-room house in New Rochelle in New York's fashionable Westchester County.[25]

Despite his increasing success in business, Pollard was still vitally interested in sports, particularly in the role of the black athlete. In 1952, he organized the Negro Athlete Hall of Fame to celebrate the achievements of African-American athletes past and present. As national chairman of the organization, Pollard recruited an interracial group of more than a hundred former athletes, sportswriters, broadcasters, sports executives, and politicians to serve on an honorary advisory board. The failure of the Negro Athlete Hall of Fame to take root in the 1950s, and its ultimate success under a different name two decades later, demonstrates the rapidly changing racial climate that Pollard and other black Americans confronted during the 1950s and 1960s. In 1973, when Allen Barron, publisher of *Black Sports* magazine, announced the founding of the National Black Sports Hall of Fame, Pollard reflected on his earlier disappointment in trying to accomplish the same objective. "I headed a group that put thousands and thousands of dollars into it but failed," he explained. Opposition "didn't just come from the white community but from the black athletes themselves. They didn't want it; they didn't care for the idea because they felt it was only adding to the separatism that already existed. So I figured the hell with it and dropped the whole idea." With the development of a more intense black consciousness by the early 1970s, few, if any, black athletes objected to a separate organization to honor their achievements. The black hall of fame issue represented one of those frustrating instances where Pollard, as well as many of his contemporaries, were both behind and ahead of the times in the turbulent decades after mid-century.[26]

Although Pollard's Negro Athlete Hall of Fame collapsed in the early 1950s, it did propel him into national Republican political circles. During the 1952 presidential campaign, Pollard wrote to the Republican candidate Dwight D. Eisenhower, an outstanding lineman for West Point before he was injured in 1912, asking him to become an honorary member of the hall of fame. Pollard added that "should you desire not to do this we would appreciate a word of approval from you which we would be permitted to quote in the Negro Press of the Nation." Eisenhower's campaign aides at first drafted a letter praising Pollard's effort but rejecting honorary membership. The letter was revised, however, apparently at the suggestion of campaign aide Herbert Brownell, and Eisenhower accepted the honorary position. Three weeks before the election, Pollard mailed a copy of Eisenhower's acceptance letter to "every Negro newspaper in the Country."[27]

After Eisenhower's inauguration, Pollard sent the president a congratulatory letter stating that "I was very happy to have been one of the players on such a great Republican team, of which you have become its leader, its quarterback and captain." Pollard added that "I would deem it an honor and privilege if it were possible for me to assist you and your cabinet in furthering your work with the Negro population throughout the country." In 1955, the former West Point All-America halfback and later NFL standout Elmer Oliphant, an Eisenhower confidant and one of the early supporters of the Negro hall of fame effort, urged the president to make use of Pollard's talents in the upcoming presidential election. Eisenhower encouraged Oliphant to contact Pollard, which he did, and Fritz responded by doing a number of sports-oriented television spots on behalf of Eisenhower during the 1956 campaign, praising the president's civil rights policies.[28]

Immediately after the election, Eisenhower sent Pollard a note thanking him for helping in the landslide victory over Adlai Stevenson. With the civil rights struggle emerging as an increasingly important political issue by the late 1950s, Pollard became a minor player in national Republican politics. He attended numerous national Republican functions and was often consulted by and photographed with such party notables as Richard Nixon and Hugh Scott. In the late 1950s, Pollard campaigned actively for Nelson Rockefeller in his bid for the New York governorship and later became an ardent supporter of the governor's quest for the presidency. When asked about the elder Pollard's role in politics, Fritz, Jr., who was appointed to a State Department post during Lyndon Johnson's administration and retained the position under the Nixon administration, simply remarked that his father "liked to dabble in politics."[29]

During the 1950s, Pollard began to be recognized for his pioneering efforts in collegiate and professional football more than three decades before. In 1950, one national sports publication named him along with Jim Thorpe, Red Grange, and Bronko Nagurski to its all-time college backfield. The previous year an *Ebony* magazine poll of thirty-eight of the nation's leading sports editors from both black and white publications listed Pollard as one of ten greatest Negro athletes of all time. He was the only football player named. For Pollard, however, the most moving tribute was his induction, with the second group of selectees, into the National Collegiate Football Hall of Fame in 1954. Pollard became the first African-American to be enshrined in the college hall of fame. Accompanied by his wife, son, and sister, Ruth Dobson, Pollard journeyed to Providence where he was to be initiated into the hall of fame during halftime of the Brown-Springfield College football game. During the ceremony and the banquet which preceded it, Pollard, tears streaming down his cheeks, was so choked with emotion that he could barely thank his former teammates, guests, and the thousands of fans who came to pay him honor. Boston sportswriter Bill Cunningham, who made the hall of fame presentation, recalled that after Fritz broke down sobbing he squeezed Cunningham's hand and said, "This is the greatest thing that's ever happened to me and I'm sorry I made a fool of myself." Cunningham, with tears in own eyes, replied, "you didn't make a fool of yourself, you did one of the finest and paid one of the greatest tributes to sport and to Brown University in that moment that any man could possibly have done."[30]

The following winter, Pollard, the other surviving members of Brown's 1916 Rose Bowl team, and their wives traveled to Pasadena as guests of the Tournament of Roses Committee to mark the fortieth anniversary of the first modern Rose Bowl game. A similar contingent of former Washington State players met them, and the aging gridiron stars traded stories about the game on the rain-swept, mud-soaked field in 1916. The 1956 game between Michigan State and UCLA was a far cry from the sparsely attended World War I-era contest, as more than a hundred thousand fans jammed the giant Rose Bowl and millions more watched on television. During the halftime ceremonies, former Washington State and Brown players as well as tens of thousands of fans paid homage to the first black man to play in the Rose Bowl. Pollard, whose spectacular feats on the gridiron and lifetime of pioneering achievements in interracial affairs had been previously largely ignored by the white world, was suddenly receiving long-overdue recognition. The quickening pace of the postwar civil rights movement was undoubtedly responsible in part for his newly gained acclaim. During the 1950s, those middle-class whites who were generally sympathetic with the goals of the civil rights movement often lauded blacks who reflected their white values and thus appeared nonthreatening. Pollard was a personable, educated, politically moderate, and distinctly middle-class Negro with whom many whites felt comfortable. At the time, Pollard was delighted with the various honors and awards, but he had no intention of resting on his laurels and at nearly sixty-two was a long way from retirement.[31]

BITTERSWEET YEARS

13

Soon after he returned from the Rose Bowl trip in January 1956, Pollard directed his energies toward the production of an all-black motion picture, *Rockin' the Blues*. "I met some high-class men, millionaires, and whatnot" in the tax business, he remembered, "and right away they wanted me to make some moving pictures." Although he wanted to remain a tax consultant and had no intention of returning to the entertainment business on a full-time basis, Pollard was willing to invest some of his money and skills in the venture. Setting up Austin Productions as a subsidiary of Fritz Pollard Associates, Pollard eventually raised $350,000 to film the production during the spring and summer of 1956 at the former Soundies studio in the Bronx.[1]

Designed to take advantage of the rock and roll craze that was sweeping New York and the nation, *Rockin' the Blues* featured eighteen rock and roll numbers staged by the veteran producer, Irvin C. Miller, famous for his Brown Skin Models reviews and who had earlier employed Mary Ella. The New York *Age* reported that "the picture could be described as a stage show on celluloid." A slim plot was held together by veteran comedians Mantan Moreland, who until his later years was best known for his stereotyped role as the terrified, bug-eyed chauffeur who often uttered the line "Feets do yo' stuff!" in a series of Charlie Chan films, and Flournoy Miller, Irvin Miller's brother, who had combined with Sam Lyles, Noble Sissle, and Eubie Blake to create and perform in the smash 1920s theatrical hit *Shuffle Along*. In keeping with his previous tradition at Suntan Studios, Pollard, with the aid of his associates, made every effort to introduce new black talent in the seventy-minute, wide-screen feature film. Pollard and his cohorts succeeded admirably both at the box office and in promoting the careers of aspiring young artists in what one critic acclaimed as "one of the most successful pictures by a Negro producer."[2]

Rockin' the Blues premiered at Harlem's famed Apollo Theater in mid-October 1956 before a gala audience of notables from the entertainment world and the news media. One reviewer described the film as "the last word in the current spectacular demand for rock 'n' roll entertainment." According to Pollard and several news-paper sources the film was a financial success but no artistic triumph. What was more important for Pollard, *Rockin' the Blues* helped launch the careers of a number of previously unknown young artists. Connie Carroll, whom Fritz had tutored at Suntan Studios, sang three new songs in the film and went on to a distinguished career in the movies, television, and as a recording artist. Immediately after the premiere, the rock and roll disc jockey Alan Freed signed the scintillating quartet the Harptones to appear in a number of his New York productions. Two other quartets, the Hurricanes and the Wanderers, received important exposure from their appearance in the film. The Five Miller Sisters, Pearl Woods, Elyce Roberts, and Linda Hopkins also found themselves in demand on radio, television, and in nightclubs as a result of their performances in *Rockin' the Blues*. One reviewer pointed out that the important thing about the film project was "the need to give young and still unrecognized talent a chance to prove themselves, to exhibit their talents and to make a livelihood from their chosen calling." He concluded that "Fritz Pollard has done that very thing and his confidence, his objective has been more than gratified. He proved that a Negro can be a successful producer by hard work, know how, and imagination."[3]

Although he had apparently agreed to produce a series of films along the same line, *Rockin' the Blues* was Pollard's last major venture in the movie business. He much preferred the "intellectual tax racket," as he called it, and during the 1950s developed a following of loyal and wealthy clients. By the 1960s, Pollard was so well known and successful in the field that the tax expert D. X. B. Schwartz, who published *Daniel Tax Savers*, a book widely recommend by certified public accountants and tax attorneys, persuaded Pollard to assist him as a consultant. Although he considered himself semiretired after 1961, Pollard continued to serve as president and treasurer of Ardstone Corporation until the mid-1960s. He took the train into the city three or four times a week to see tax clients, to attend to corporation business, and to book a small number of entertainers whom he continued to represent. In addition, Pollard periodically wrote a nationally syndicated sports column for African-American newspapers, which emphasized the accomplishments of the great black athletes of the past. For a man who celebrated his seventieth birthday in 1964, Pollard remained extremely active.[4]

As he began his years of semiretirement in the 1960s, Pollard became more nostalgic and returned more frequently to the scene of some of his earlier great accomplishments, Brown University. After leaving Brown in early 1918 to join the war effort, he had returned to Providence infrequently during the next two decades although he had, however, made contacts with some important alumni, particularly through the Rockefeller Foundation. Pollard was somewhat angry about what he considered to be mistreatment of Fritz, Jr., by alumni and university officials after the younger Pollard dropped out of Brown, but he made at least one visit to the school during the 1940s. It was the National Collegiate Football Hall of Fame induction ceremony in 1954, and the subsequent trip with his former teammates to Pasadena that seemed to rekindle in Pollard a strong identification with Brown.[5]

During his 1954 trip to Providence, Pollard met Jay Barry, a Brown alumnus and expert on the school's football history, who worked for the *Brown Alumni Monthly*. Barry was helpful in supplying Pollard with photographs and equipment from Fritz's playing days at Brown that college hall of fame officials had requested for display at a building they hoped to construct in New Brunswick, New Jersey. The two men became friends and began to correspond regularly. Barry was clearly charmed by Brown's greatest football player and encouraged Pollard to play a greater role in university activities. In 1958, for example, Barry suggested that Pollard write a congratulatory letter to Brown quarterback Frank Finney, who had just broken one of Fritz's long-standing scoring records. Eleven years later, after almost yearly visits to Providence, Pollard received the extraordinary honor of being named a class marshal of the Class of 1919 during commencement ceremonies and leading his classmates in the graduation procession despite the fact that he was not a Brown graduate. Barry also took it upon himself to publicize Pollard's career and recommend the former All-America for a number of awards and honors. Among many honors, during the 1960s and early 1970s, Pollard became the first black elected as a member in residence to the Brown Club of New York, was made a member of the Rhode Island Heritage Hall of Fame, and was named to the Washington D.C. Touchdown Club Hall of Fame.[6]

By the late 1960s, Pollard began supplying Barry with material on the history of African-American athletes, more particularly on his own struggles to break down racial barriers in college and professional football. Barry decided to write a biography of Pollard, and the two men exchanged letters and held numerous conversations, including Barry's two long, taped interviews with Pollard in 1970. Despite several contract offers for a similar project from other sources, Pollard remained committed to Barry's project (which was never completed) despite his occasional mild irritation at its slow pace. In the mid-1970s, Pollard agreed to cooperate in the filming of his life story, which Barry and his college classmate Wheaton Holden hoped to produce for television. The film project was completed in the early 1980s, but it never aired.[7]

During their many conversations, some of which took place at Brown football games, Pollard and Barry discussed a wide range of subjects, including the state of college football. Pollard did not run the modern game down in favor of the earlier way of playing, but he did have certain reservations about contemporary football. To his mind, the purpose of college football and athletics was to build character: "to teach boys discipline and how to conquer the hard knocks they're going to get in later life." He was particularly critical of modern equipment and the trend toward two-platoon football. "I think that putting on a lot of heavy equipment on fellows has had the tendency to keep them from training," he told Barry. "We played 11, 12, and 13 men and if anyone else got in the game they were just lucky. We played 60 minutes. If we got hurt, we had time out but we patched it up and went back." When asked several years later to compare O. J. Simpson with the great backs of his era, Pollard agreed that the University of Southern California All-America halfback was a great runner but refused further comparison. "Today," Pollard said, "when the runner's team loses the ball he just goes to the bench and rests while his defensive platoon gets the ball back for him. The Old Indian [Jim Thorpe] and I almost always played 60 minutes, which made it tougher to be fresh when you ran with the ball."[8]

As he approached his seventy-fifth birthday, one of Pollard's fondest dreams was that his grandson, Fritz Pollard III, attend Brown University and play football. The youngest Fritz, accompanied by his father, had traveled to Providence in 1967 to witness his grandfather's induction into the Rhode Island Heritage Hall of Fame. On their trip from Chicago to Rhode Island, Fritz, Jr., and his son stopped over in New York to visit with Fritz, Sr., and Mary Ella and escorted the senior Pollard to Providence. During their visit in New York, Fritz, Sr., took his son and grandson to Rockefeller Center, where he introduced them to Nelson Rockefeller. "We breezed right through," Fritz III recalled, "I was impressed."[9]

On the same trip, Fritz, Sr., took his grandson to meet Paul Robeson, whose health was rapidly deteriorating. At the time, the twelve-year-old boy was already a strapping 185-pounder. Fritz III went on to establish a fine scholastic record in high school and was named to all-state teams in football, basketball, and track in Maryland, where his family had moved after Fritz, Jr., was appointed to a position in the State Department. Young Fritz was also named to several high school All-America teams. By the time he graduated from Montgomery Blair High School in Silver Spring in 1972, Fritz III was an athlete with awesome potential. He was six feet six, 230 pounds, and still growing; he could bench press more than six hundred pounds and run the hundred-yard dash in under ten seconds. Although he received hundreds of scholarship offers from major athletic schools such as Penn State, Michigan State, and Georgia Tech, young Fritz later told Providence *Journal* reporter John Hanlon that "always in my family it was Brown. So I never thought of others." Hanlon reminded Fritz III that "your grandfather once said his last ambition was to see you at Brown. He might have shot you if you'd gone elsewhere." "I think he might have, too," young Pollard replied.[10]

Fritz, Sr., was indeed determined that his grandson attend Brown. "Dad made me send him to Brown," Fritz, Jr., later recalled. "I wanted him to make his own choice because I know what happened to me when Dad made me go to Brown." The senior Pollard had his way, however. When Fritz III gained early admission to Brown

as a premedicine applicant in late 1971, the elder Pollard became
furious when the university required an economic disclosure statement in order for his grandson to qualify for scholarships or financial
aid. "I am not going to allow him [Fritz, Jr.] to make any of these
papers out," he wrote to Jay Barry, "and if Brown University wants
my grandson, they will have to accept him as a regular scholarship
student without our filling out any financial reports regarding our
family. I have already personally agreed to give them $5,000, but if
they are going to insist on wanting an investigation of our family
financial background; I shall be forced to turn it down." He was
apparently unaware that many schools, including all Ivy League
colleges, required a financial statement from scholarship applicants.
To resolve the impasse, Pollard proposed that he make a gift of his
house in New Rochelle to the university while retaining a life interest
in the residence for his wife and himself and use the ultimate proceeds
from the gift to pay some of his grandson's expenses at Brown.
While university lawyers studied the proposal, young Frederick
Douglass Pollard III enrolled at Brown in the fall of 1972, and
became the third Pollard by that name to attend the school.[11]

During his freshman year, Fritz III filled out to six feet eight
and 240 pounds but sat out the football and basketball seasons
because of his demanding academic schedule and a nagging high
school knee injury. In the spring, he threw the discus for the Bruin
track team and had hopes of making the U.S. Olympic team in 1976.
Brown track coach Ted McLaughlin believed that young Pollard
had not even begun to reach his full potential and that he "could
become the best Brown has had in the event." Fritz III maintained
a respectable 2.5 average in the demanding premedicine program,
but an aggravation of his knee injury forced him to have surgery
during the fall of 1974. After completing his second year at Brown,
he dropped out of school and returned home to Silver Spring,
Maryland. Asked whether his grandfather's imposing stature at Brown
had anything to do with dropping out of school, Fritz III said, "No.
It didn't have anything to do with him," and explained that he was
only sixteen when he entered Brown, and he was immature and
homesick. The knee injury was a factor in dropping out, as was the
fact that his father was paying his expenses at Brown in spite of all
the scholarship offers from other schools. Fritz III also felt uncom-
fortable with the militant attitude of some of the black students

who attended Brown at the time. When asked whether he would attend Brown if he were making the choice again, Fritz III said, "I think I'd still go to Brown."[12]

Fritz, Sr., was undoubtedly disappointed about his grandson's decision to leave Brown but never commented publicly about the development. By the mid-1970s, he was slowing down his pace as a semiretired businessman. When his wife retired from the *Amsterdam News* in 1975, Pollard made the decision to join her in retirement. "I thought about continuing with my work," he said. "But one day she said to me, 'You know Fritz, you aren't as young as you used to be.' And you know, she was right. So I quit working the next day." Pollard gave up the almost daily commutes to New York City and settled down to a quieter life in New Rochelle. Nearly eighty years old, he could have easily passed for a man twenty years younger. He kept in shape by walking a mile with his German shepherd Cappy each morning and told a reporter in 1977 that "for an old man, I guess I feel pretty good." He did feel the strain of retirement, however, after a lifetime of feverish activity. He told reporter Ron Rapoport, who visited him in 1976, "I don't know what to do with myself. My wife's retired and she's home all the time. I have to stay out of the way." Pollard was so grateful for Rapoport's visit that he offered him a twenty dollar bill for tobacco money as the sportswriter was leaving. Rapoport refused it, saying "you've given me more than money already."[13]

In fact, Pollard did remain reasonably active throughout the 1970s. He and Jay Barry met or telephoned regularly to discuss Jay's book or the film project, and they also tried to interest Brown officials in dedicating a wing to Pollard in the proposed university athletic complex. According to Fritz, Jr., his father "was always scheming something. Sometimes Dad got some grandiose ideas and thought people were doing this for nothing. My reading is that when they get wings or something all this is donated. . . . I tried to tell him this." The Fritz Pollard wing was never built, but in the early 1980s the Brown Athletic Department did establish a football award in honor of the school's greatest player.[14]

Pollard, to be sure, did receive many other awards and honors as he passed his eightieth birthday. In 1976, he was rewarded for his many years of service to the Pop Warner Little Scholars scholarship program by being named to the organization's bicentennial

All-America team. NFL Commissioner Pete Rozelle sent a congratulatory telegram to Pollard at the Pop Warner induction banquet in Philadelphia, noting "how fitting to be named to an All-American eleven again in this bicentennial year some six decades after your initial selection as an undergraduate at Brown." Two years later, Pollard followed in the footsteps of Paul Robeson in receiving the prestigious Whitney M. Young, Jr., Memorial Award from the New York Urban League.[15]

After Frank Robinson was named the first black manager in major league history in 1974 by the Cleveland Indians, speculation mounted over when the NFL would join professional baseball and basketball (Bill Russell coached the Boston Celtics beginning in 1967) in hiring a black head coach. Some sportswriters were surprised to learn that the NFL had already broken the coaching color barrier more than five decades before when Pollard coached at Akron. A number of prominent sportswriters interviewed him and wrote feature articles about Pollard's being the first black head coach in a major American professional sport. Although he thrived on the attention, most of the articles were superficial and revealed more about the sparsity of accurate published records concerning early professional football than about Pollard's pioneering effort to integrate the fledgling NFL. Compounded by Pollard's increasing memory lapses, most of the articles were replete with errors concerning which teams Pollard coached and played for, his achievements in breaking down racial barriers, and his overall contributions to early pro football. The prolific author James A. Michener did little better when he interviewed Pollard as part of a Public Broadcasting Service television program in 1980 on "The Black Athlete." Although *Sports Illustrated* reporter Joe Jares called the segment featuring Pollard one of the bright spots in an otherwise lackluster show, Michener, author of the recently published book *Sports in America*, had little idea of Pollard's place in American sports.[16]

During the 1970s, Pollard began to express some bitterness about his treatment as a player and coach many decades earlier and about what he perceived to be the continuing failure of many in the sports community to recognize the full significance of his accomplishments. It was a surprising reaction because Pollard had previously minimized the racial hatred he had endured and the barriers he had surmounted. The nationally syndicated sports columnist Jerry Izenberg, one who did recognize Fritz's achievements, may have summed up Pollard's feelings in a 1978 article entitled "A Genuine Unknown Hero." "Fritz Pollard doesn't get around much these days," Izenberg wrote. "You would think that perhaps more people would come to him but the young of all colors and generations always act as though they invented the games we play, the barriers we break and the hurdles we clear. At a time when a social and cultural revolution cries for black heroes to place alongside the white ones in school books, it is a shame and a scandal (and their loss—not his) that more young people do not even know his name." After recounting Pollard's illustrious career, Izenberg noted that "those numbers add up to nothing in Canton, Ohio. He is not a member of the pro football hall of fame. That is an incredible oversight—almost as incredible as the chain of events which form Pollard's own personal history."[17]

Pollard made several visits to the Professional Football Hall of Fame in Canton during the 1970s, and gave a number of interviews on his playing days in the early NFL. The Hall of Fame Veterans Committee, however, which is responsible for sending names of deserving old-time players to a board of selectors, did not deem Pollard's achievements in the pro game as worthy of a nomination for induction into the hall. Perhaps scheming to win favor, Pollard in one interview seemed to downplay the racial abuse he had experienced during his pro football career. "There weren't any really *bad* situations," he told Jim Campbell. "About the worst thing that would happen was sometimes when we played an away game the local fans would start to sing 'Bye, Bye Blackbird.'" Despite his modest and congenial approach in Canton, Pollard was less composed when he spoke to the black writer Carl Nesfield about being snubbed by the Hall of Fame. Referring to his aborted effort to establish a Negro sports hall of fame in the 1950s and the opposition of black players to the idea at the time, Pollard fumed that black athletes "told me they didn't want to be in a segregated Hall of Fame. But I see that today they are willing to be in a white segregated Hall of Fame." There was no question that the "white segregated Hall of Fame" Pollard mentioned was the one in Canton. Nesfield concluded a two-part article on Pollard by saying that "if he has one disappointment, looking back over his illustrious life, it is the lack of recognition for his achievements in professional football. He feels that he, Ink Williams, Paul Robeson and Duke Slater should have made pro football's Hall of Fame at Canton, Ohio." As a player and a coach, Nesfield wrote, "Fritz should be in there twice. . . ."[18]

The increasing bitterness or disappointment which Pollard expressed publicly during the mid-1970s may have been triggered in part by the death of his friend and former teammate Paul Robeson. Pilloried by government officials and the white press for decades as an alleged communist, the once powerful athlete's health had deteriorated, and he died in Philadelphia in early 1976. Pollard served as a pallbearer at his funeral in Harlem and undoubtedly was moved by the passing of his friend, who had been shunned by the sports establishment to a greater extent than any other black athlete in this century. Several months after Robeson's death, in Pollard's interview with Ron Rapoport, he lashed out at George Halas, accusing him of raising the color barrier in the NFL and claiming that the former Chicago Bears' coach was "as prejudiced as hell." Then after a reference to Robeson's death, Pollard indicated that he still faced prejudice. "When I go to the Touchdown Club and other things, they don't want me," Pollard said. "Who?" Rapoport asked. "Oh, the management and the fans are all right," Pollard replied, "but the other honored guests don't want me."[19]

What was even more surprising, Pollard began making critical remarks about Brown University, which he had previously lauded for giving him his great opportunity in life. "I don't like to say this," Pollard told Rapoport, "but back in those days Brown was prejudiced as hell." He recounted how he succeeded in gaining acceptance at Brown only to be "niggerized" at Harvard and Yale. Rapoport asked Jay Barry to comment on Pollard's acerbic remarks. "I've started hearing discrimination stories from Fritz only recently," Barry stated. "He's saying some things now that he never said before. . . . It could be he always knew them, but didn't want to say them, or it could be that he's embellishing."[20]

Pollard's daughter Leslie was more certain about the source of her father's acrimonious comments. "He was bitter," she said. "We all were bitter, this is deep down in you, but you have to live on — you don't carry that on the tip of your nose. My brother does the same thing," Leslie added. "He contains his [bitterness] very well, too." Fritz, Jr., did not mention the senior Pollard's latter-day remarks in a 1987 interview, but he conceded that his father had endured much worse racial abuse than he usually acknowledged. "You had to talk a long time to get it out of him," he said. Fritz, Jr., attributed his father's custom of minimizing the obstacles he had faced in his long athletic career to the survival skills taught to all members of the Pollard family. "Dad was very much aware. They all were," Fritz, Jr., said. "They tried to keep it from me. But they all knew how to handle the situation. They were good learners. So that they didn't get into the ordinary squabbles that you get into because of the differences in the races. They all knew how to make friends and keep friends race-wise. He was a real survivor, that guy. You take into consideration his size and everything he'd been through. You have to take your hat off to him, there's no question about that." Fritz Pollard III also recognized that in later years his grandfather "started to get a little bitter." He said that the senior Pollard was upset by not being better recognized by fellow blacks and black athletes. It was not so much bitterness, Fritz III determined on second thought, but "disappointment that his achievements were not recognized."[21]

In 1979, Ada Pollard died in Chicago, where she had lived for many years with her daughter, Leslie. Fritz did not attend the funeral because of his own failing health. In one of his last interviews in 1981 with Jay Barry, who was still working on the film of Pollard's life, Fritz found it difficult to remember names and events and often had to be prompted by his wife or Barry. Pollard was suffering from arteriosclerosis. Despite his failing memory, which became progressively worse during the 1980s, Pollard could sometimes overcome even this obstacle when he was sufficiently motivated. Fritz, Jr., recalled with some amazement that when Mary Ella was hospitalized in 1982, his father, who had extreme difficulty in remembering, managed to get into his car, smash his way out of the garage, and drive around New Rochelle in search of the hospital. "The vitality," Fritz, Jr., marveled, "everything about him was extraordinary."[22]

The following year after Mary Ella had died, Pollard went to live with Fritz, Jr., and his wife in Silver Spring. As he entered his ninth decade, Pollard's health continued to deteriorate but according to his son, he maintained a remarkable energy for life. "He was so stubborn," Fritz, Jr., recalled. "You never knew whether he was sick or not sick. Because his mind was failing him, some things he just did so automatically that there wasn't any way to describe it." In the spring of 1986, Fritz, Jr., admitted his father, who had contracted pneumonia, to a Silver Spring hospital. Frederick Douglass Pollard, Sr., aged ninety-two, died there on May 11, 1986. Reflecting on his father's small size and lifetime of accomplishment, Fritz, Jr., said: "A guy that did everything he did and did it in the way he did it, he couldn't be small. He was larger than life in a sense. He was that way until he died."[23]

The Pollard children received tributes honoring their father from around the country, but even in death Pollard stirred some of the turmoil and contention that marked his extraordinary athletic career. Soon after his death, the Chicago *Sun-Times* ran a story on Pollard by Ron Rapoport under the headline, "Pollard Died Hating Halas." Although the article was primarily a summary of Rapoport's 1976 story about Pollard, his death and the subsequent story reignited the long-standing controversy surrounding Pollard and Halas and sent shock waves through Chicago. Leslie Keeling remembered that "when Dad passed, they would not announce it on the TV. They would not announce it on the radio. I called them personally, myself, and I told them that when every Tom, Dick, and Harry dies, you announce it on TV. They absolutely refused." When asked the reason for the slight, Leslie said she thought "it was because he spoke out against Papa Bear, George Halas." Halas had died several years before, but perhaps his Chicago Bears organization still held a grip on a segment of the Chicago media. "I thought it was quite a slap in the face," Leslie said, "and I'll never forget it." It was perhaps fitting that even in death Fritz Pollard continued to agitate some small part of the white sports establishment.[24]

EPILOGUE:
POLLARD ON BALANCE

Ordinarily, historians do not consider African-American athletes as leaders in the civil rights movement that emerged in the United States in the wake of the Civil War and Reconstruction. During the first seventy-five years after black emancipation, such figures as Frederick Douglass, Booker T. Washington, W. E. B. Du Bois, Marcus Garvey, Walter White, Mary Bethune, and A. Philip Randolph as well as many others shaped the agenda and provided the leadership in the struggle of black Americans to gain their full rights under the Constitution. The civil rights movement, however, also has been the struggle of millions of largely unknown African Americans who have had the courage to challenge the presumed inferiority of their race and combat the racial barriers imposed against them. They challenged white racism in confrontations, generally unrecorded, in small towns, on assembly lines, in hotels and restaurants, on public conveyances, and a variety of other locations. Few historians have focused on the masses of black Americans who have carried on this heroic struggle.[1]

Given equal opportunity, black athletes' performances against their white counterparts could be judged on merit. African Americans seemed to sense that athletics represented one of the few areas in society where blacks could compete with whites under equal or nearly equal conditions. In his history of African-American athletics, the tennis great Arthur R. Ashe, Jr., points out without too much exaggeration that early prominent black athletes "have been the most accomplished figures in the Afro-American subculture. They were vastly better known in their times than people such as Booker T. Washington, William E. B. Du Bois, or Marcus Garvey. They inspired idolatry bordering on deification, and thousands more wanted to follow."[2]

Some of the great black athletes of the past are still remembered and recognized by historians as symbolically important in the civil rights struggle. The names of Jack Johnson, Joe Louis, Jesse Owens, and Jackie Robinson are known and honored today. Their continuing prominence is a product of the international impact of their sport and accomplishments and the times in which they achieved their fame, or a combination of the two. Johnson, Louis, and Owens competed magnificently before a world audience, while Robinson's integration of America's national pastime during the turbulent and tension-filled cold-war years propelled him to lasting glory. Pollard was not in the same category as these paragons. His sport was not international in scope; in the case of professional football, it was not even national. He was not known widely in the white community except for a brief fleeting moment during his All-America season in 1916, before the war dimmed his prospects of lasting fame. Pollard was an athletic trailblazer in the mode of such earlier outstanding black athletes as jockey Issac Murphy, Harvard football All-America William Lewis, and Olympic sprinter Howard P. Drew, whose pioneering feats were all but forgotten as the pace of the civil rights movement accelerated in the 1930s and 1940s.

When asked why his father or Paul Robeson did not have the impact on American sports that Louis, Owens, or Robinson later did, Fritz Pollard, Jr., replied, "I don't know. Timing, I guess." Jack Johnson seemed to surmount the times in which he lived, but even Arthur Ashe recalled that as a boy in the 1950s he idolized Jackie Robinson but had never heard of the great black heavyweight champion. There is little doubt that timing was important. The African-American press in the early part of the century could barely sustain a black sports hero in the black community, much less propel him to national prominence. While the Pittsburgh *Courier* and other black papers would send reporters to cover each of Jackie Robinson's games in 1947, Pollard and Robeson's All-America exploits a generation before were reprinted in the black press from articles in the white dailies, if African-American weeklies covered them at all. Football coverage was particularly poor in the black papers because they hit the streets on Thursdays, several days ahead of the weekend games. Pollard became a hero in the black community but understandably his stature, at least for readers of the black press, was shrouded in legend rather than the product of the written record.[3]

World War I and Pollard's apathetic approach to academic pursuits deprived him of an opportunity to become a three-time All-America halfback. Would such an achievement have made him a nationally recognized football legend? Given the temper of the times, such a question remains unanswerable. Pollard's career in postwar professional football presents another problem of timing. Early pro football was a regional sport largely ignored by major newspapers and sportswriters of the era. It was so poorly organized and promoted that many of Pollard's finest accomplishments remain unrecorded in published sources. Major black newspapers, which by the early 1920s had sufficient resources to cover national sporting events such as the Black World Series in baseball and the Lincoln-Howard football classic, imitated the white dailies in ignoring or disparaging pro football. This is surprising because at least in retrospect the integration of the early NFL, which Pollard had no small hand in promoting, represents one of the significant breakthroughs for black athletes in that era. To his credit, Pollard seemed to understand its significance and pursued the issue for several decades after his retirement as a player. African-American weeklies such as the Chicago *Defender*, which had a progressive reputation, seemed more intent, at least in the early 1920s, on establishing a claim to respectability by mimicking the general disdain or disinterest of the white dailies for the pro game. During these crucial years, black sportswriters failed to publicize the exploits of the half-dozen players of their race in the NFL and lost a significant opportunity to nurture a stronger following of professional football in the black community.

Pollard's own motivation is complex in pursuing a career in sports that caused him constantly to confront racism and challenge racial restrictions. Above all, it had to do with his family and the athletic tutoring he had received from his father, brothers, and sisters. He had natural ability to be sure, but he also had the role models provided by his brothers Luther, Leslie, and Hughes. For the Pollard boys, as well as for other black Americans in the early twentieth century, sports was a vehicle to success, fame, and fortune. Pollard was motivated by the success of Jack Johnson but schooled by his brothers on how not to repeat the mistakes of the heavyweight champion. Fritz was not reckless or radical in confronting the white establishment or the many racial obstacles that stood in his path. He and his family's values were distinctly middle class and might be described as bourgeois or conservative by future generations of African Americans. Yet, Pollard had also absorbed the pioneering spirit of the Pollard family and time and again demonstrated a sense of mission in assaulting racial barriers in athletics as well as in the world of business. In almost every interview he gave, Pollard traced the source of his motivation and strength to his remarkable family.

Pollard's career seems to both support and undermine the theories of the black sociologist E. Franklin Frazier and others who have attacked the black middle class for its emulation of white values and its lack of racial solidarity. Clearly, Pollard was an elitist who aspired to a life of status and material comfort. He played pro football, at least in part, because of the lucrative salary, the status it gave him, and the life-style it afforded. He had been well taught how to coexist in the white world and, if need be, to manipulate it to his advantage. Pollard was a schemer who used his considerable skills to salvage his own career on a number of occasions. Yet, as his daughter Leslie said, he cared deeply about civil rights issues and worked throughout his career for the betterment of his race. As a football player, he risked life and limb and endured gross verbal abuse to make the point that a black man could play a white man's game. In his business career, which was usually dependent on white sufferance, Pollard, unlike many organizational civil rights leaders, was forced to work behind the scenes to accomplish his integrationist objectives. Although politically and economically conservative by today's standards, Pollard cared no less deeply than other advocates of civil rights causes and racial progress. He, like other middle-class black Americans, was constantly torn between advancing his own interests in a white-dominated America and promoting the well-being of his people. More often than not he was able to do both.[4]

Despite these limitations, Pollard, both as an athlete and businessman, established more "firsts" for his race than perhaps any other African American in this century. In his declining years, he reflected on his career and wondered why he had not stuck to one enterprise instead of switching from one career to the next. He told Jay Barry that "I have often felt that I have let Brown University down by not continuing to build up the businesses and opportunities that I know were caused by my going to Brown and caused by

Brown men. I think I was kind of chicken leg." Yet, it was Pollard's venturesome spirit, sometimes prompted by necessity, which caused him to establish separate careers in athletics, finance, journalism, and entertainment and put him on the cutting edge of racial breakthroughs in a variety of areas. Fritz Pollard, Jr., echoed the comments of a number of people who knew his father or had seen him play when the younger Pollard stated emphatically: "He was really the pioneer. He was a *real* pioneer."[5]

That Pollard is not better known today for his pioneering efforts is in part due to the times in which he lived, the sport with which he was associated, and most of all because in the earlier part of this century black achievements deemed not important by the white press were usually forgotten. Even today, Pollard is denied his rightful place in the Professional Football Hall of Fame in Canton, Ohio. The facts that he was the first important African-American professional player, the first black head coach, the first black quarterback, and one of the greatest runners in the early pro game speak for themselves. Beyond this, he led a sustained effort to maintain integration in the NFL and later fought to break down the color barrier when it was raised in the 1930s. Pollard devoted more than fifteen years to professional football as a player and a coach. His pioneering integrationist efforts alone, which included bringing at least a half-dozen black players from white colleges into the NFL as well as his stints as player-coach and a coach with the Chicago Black Hawks and Brown Bombers, entitle Pollard to serious consideration by the Professional Football Hall of Fame Veterans Committee. Since the mid-1980s, Pearce Johnson, associated with the one-time NFL Providence Steam Roller franchise since 1916, has lobbied for Pollard's admittance into the pro shrine—a recommendation that has gone unheeded.

Whether or not Pollard is so honored in Canton in the future, his life, his pioneering endeavors, and his accomplishments in a variety of fields will stand as testimony to the courageous struggle of black Americans in this century to gain full dignity and citizenship under the law. Most Americans have never heard of Fritz Pollard; if they have, he remains a fuzzy image from the distant past. As Fritz Pollard, Jr., said with a touch of sadness while reflecting on his father's illustrious career, "If he had been white, everyone in the world would have known about him. That's the kind of personality he had."[6]

NOTES

PROLOGUE

1. New Orleans *Times-Picayune*, September 24, 1978; *The Gramblinite*, September 29, 1978.

2. Supplementary material from the New York *Times* News Service and the Associated Press, September 22 and 23, 1978; New Orleans *Times-Picayune*, September 24, 1978; *Newsweek*, September 25, 1978, 68.

3. St. Louis *Sentinel*, September 21, 1978; Staten Island *Advance*, September 24, 1978; Seth Moseley 2d, "Fritz Pollard, All-American," Westchester *Standard-Star*, January 7, 1979.

4. *The Gramblinite*, September 29, 1978.

5. Jerry Izenberg, "A Genuine Unknown Hero," New York *Post*, April 11, 1978; author interview with John Sullivan, September 28, 1987; letter to the editor, New York *Times*, June 22, 1986.

CHAPTER 1. THE REMARKABLE POLLARDS

1. Jay Barry interview with Fritz Pollard, July 1970, Brown University Archives, hereafter cited as Barry interview with Pollard; "Anniversary, Township of Rogers Park Annexation to the City of Chicago," *Lerner Home Newspapers*, April 3, 1968, Chicago Historical Society.

2. "Luther Pollard Family Notes," undated copy, Brown University Archives, Providence, Rhode Island.

3. Dudley Taylor Cornish, *The Sable Arm: Negro Troops in the Union Army, 1861–1865* (New York: Longmans, Green, 1956), 69-78; Albert Castel, "Civil War Kansas and the Negro," *Journal of Negro History*, 51

(April 1966): 125-38; author interview with Leslie Keeling and Eleanor Towns, July 17, 1987.

4. Castel, "Civil War Kansas," 135; "Luther Pollard Family Notes."

5. Barry interview with Pollard, July 1970; "Luther Pollard Family Notes"; on Revels and Bruce, see Allen Johnson and Dumas Malone, eds., *Dictionary of American Biography*, 20 vols. and suppls. (New York: Charles Scribner's Sons, 1928–58), 15:513, suppl. 3:180; author interview with Leslie Keeling and Eleanor Towns, July 17, 1987.

6. Barry interview with Pollard, July 1970; "Luther Pollard Family Notes."

7. Barry interview with Pollard, July 1970; Edgewater *News*, January 25-26, 1986.

8. Barry interview with Pollard, July 1970; Gail Danks, *The Rogers Park Community* (Chicago: Center for Urban Policy, Loyola University of Chicago, 1982), 3-6; Dominic A. Pacyga and Ellen Skerrett, *Chicago: City of Neighborhoods, Histories, Tours* (Chicago: Loyola University Press, 1986), 128-31; Stephen Bedell Clark et al., *The Lake View Saga* (Chicago: Lake View Trust and Savings Bank, 1985), 9; "Anniversary, Township of Rogers Park," *Lerner Home Newspapers*, April 3, 1968; Michael H. Ebner, *Creating Chicago's North Shore: A Suburban History* (Chicago: University of Chicago Press, 1988), 24-27.

9. Bessie Louise Pierce, *A History of Chicago*, vol. 3: *The Rise of a Modern City, 1871–1893* (Chicago: University of Chicago Press, 1975), 48-50; Carl G. Hodges et al., comp., *Illinois Negro Historymakers* (Chicago: Illinois Emancipation Centennial Commission, 1964), 27-28; "Colored Chicago," *Crisis*, September 1915, 234-36; Illinois Commission on Race Relations, *The Negro in Chicago: A Study of Race Relations and a Race Riot* (Chicago: University of Chicago Press, 1922), 232-35.

10. Barry interview with Pollard, July 1970; Edgewater *News*, February 25-26, 1986; author interview with Leslie Keeling and Eleanor Towns, July 17, 1987.

11. J. H. Harmon, Jr., Arnett G. Lindsay, and Carter G. Woodson, *The Negro as a Businessman* (College Park: McGrath Publishing, 1929), 12-13; Carl Nesfield, "Pride Against Prejudice: Fritz Pollard, Brown's All-American Pre-World War I Vintage," pt. 1, *Black Sports*, November 1971, 17.

12. Barry interview with Pollard, July 1970.

13. Ibid.

14. Ibid.

15. Edgewater *News*, February 25-26, 1986; Barry interview with Pollard, July 1970; author interview with Fritz Pollard, Jr., June 12, 1987; author interview with Leslie Keeling and Eleanor Towns, July 17, 1987. On African Americans and skin color, see Lawrence W. Levine, *Black*

Culture and Black Consciousness: Afro-American Folk Thought from Slavery to Freedom (New York: Oxford University Press, 1978), 284-93; W. Lloyd Warner, Buford H. Junker, and Walter A. Anderson, *Color and Human Nature: Negro Personality Development in a Northern City* (Westport: Negro Universities Press, 1970); and Leon F. Litwack, *Been in the Storm so Long: The Aftermath of Slavery* (New York: Random House, 1979), 513-14. Litwack points out that "too much emphasis should not be given to skin color as a factor in diminishing black solidarity."

16. Edgewater *News*, February 25-26, 1986; Barry interview with Pollard, July 1970; author interview with Fritz Pollard, Jr., June 12, 1987.

17. Author interview with Leslie Keeling and Eleanor Towns, July 17, 1987; author interview with Fritz Pollard, Jr., June 12, 1987.

18. Barry interview with Pollard, July 1970 and November 23, 1974; author interview with Leslie Keeling and Eleanor Towns, July 17, 1987; Ebner, *Creating Chicago's North Shore*, 212.

19. Barry interview with Pollard, July 1970 and November 23, 1974; Harry T. Sampson, *Blacks in Black and White: A Source Book on Black Films* (Metuchen: Scarecrow Press, 1974), 56-59; "6th Annual Field Day of the Cook County High School Athletic Association, June 16, 1894," in Neighborhood Research Collection, Sulzer Regional Library, Chicago Public Library System; author interview with Fritz Pollard, Jr., June 12, 1987.

20. Barry interview with Pollard, July 1970 and November 23, 1974; Nesfield, "Pride Against Prejudice," pt. 1, *Black Sports*, November 1971, 17. Information on Leslie Pollard was supplied by Kenneth C. Cramer, archivist, Dartmouth College Library, Hanover, New Hampshire. Also see Ocania Chalk, *Black College Sport* (New York: Dodd, Mead, 1976), 145, 151, 164-66, 184.

21. Author interview with Fritz Pollard, Jr., June 12, 1987; Barry interview with Pollard, July 1970.

22. Barry interview with Pollard, July 1970; author interview with Fritz Pollard, Jr., June 12, 1987; author interview with Leslie Keeling and Eleanor Towns, July 17, 1987. Fritz Pollard repeated the story about Hughes getting him his first break in the Hyde Park game many times. The story appears to be substantially correct, although some particulars of the account are inaccurate. The Hyde Park game was actually Lane's second game. Lane defeated Thornton Township High School 16-0 on September 25, 1909, with Fritz playing left end and scoring a touchdown. The *Tech Prep*, Lane's monthly newspaper, described the game as "mostly a try out." Pollard often said he was a freshman at the time, but he was in fact a sophomore. The *Tech Prep*, October 1909, 17; issues of the *Tech Prep* for 1908-12 are in the Brown University Archives.

23. Author interview with Fritz Pollard, Jr., June 12, 1987; Barry interview with Pollard, July 1970.

24. Ibid.

25. Author interview with Fritz Pollard, Jr., June 12, 1987.

26. Ibid.

27. Ibid.

CHAPTER 2. LEARNING TO SURVIVE

1. Allan H. Spear, *Black Chicago: The Making of a Negro Ghetto, 1890-1920* (Chicago: University of Chicago Press, 1967), 11-27; St. Clair Drake and Horace R. Cayton, *Black Metropolis: A Study of Negro Life in a Northern City*, vol. 1 (New York: Harper Torchbooks, 1962), 8-10, 47-57.

2. Ibid.

3. Spear, *Black Chicago*, 20, 41-45; Illinois Commission on Race Relations, *The Negro in Chicago: A Study of Race Relations and a Race Riot* (Chicago: University of Chicago Press, 1922), 112-13.

4. Ibid.

5. Commission on Race Relations, *Negro in Chicago*, 438-45.

6. Author interview with Fritz Pollard, Jr., June 12, 1987.

7. Barry interview with Pollard, July 1970.

8. Ibid.

9. Michael H. Ebner, *Creating Chicago's North Shore: A Suburban History* (Chicago: University of Chicago Press, 1988), 161; Barry interview with Pollard, July 1970.

10. Barry interview with Pollard, July 1970.

11. Ibid.; Alexander M. Weyland, *The Saga of American Football* (New York: Macmillan, 1955), 472. North Division High School was renamed Waller High School in 1908 and is now Lincoln Park High School.

12. Lawrence Levine, *Black Culture and Black Consciousness: Afro-American Folk Thought from Slavery to Freedom* (New York: Oxford University Press, 1977), 430-32; Randy Roberts, *Jack Dempsey: The Manassa Mauler* (Baton Rouge: Louisiana State University Press, 1979), 24; Spear, *Black Chicago*, 47-48; Randy Roberts, *Papa Jack: Jack Johnson and the Era of White Hopes* (New York: Free Press, 1983); Jeffrey T. Sammons, *Beyond the Ring: The Role of Boxing in American Society* (Urbana: University of Illinois Press, 1988), 34-53.

13. Author interview with Fritz Pollard, Jr., June 12, 1987; Sammons, *Beyond the Ring*, 40-47.

14. Author interview with Fritz Pollard, Jr., June 12, 1987.

15. Scott Rappe, *75 Years of Achievement: A History of Lane* (Chicago:

Lane Technical High School, 1983), 3-6; *Year Book, 1910* (Chicago: Lane Technical High School, 1910), 25.

16. Pollard's high school transcript and the *Tech Prep: Senior Class Issue, 1912* are in the Brown University Archives, Providence, Rhode Island.

17. Barry interview with Pollard, July 1970.

18. Spear, *Black Chicago*, 44-45.

19. Commission on Race Relations, *Negro in Chicago*, 253-56.

20. *The Oski-Wow-Wow: A History of Hyde Park High School Athletics* (Chicago: Hyde Park High School, 1924), 8-19, Chicago Historical Society.

21. *Oski-Wow-Wow*, 8-19; Gerald Gems to author, September 5, 1989.

22. Barry interview with Pollard, July 1970; *Tech Prep*, October 1909, 17.

23. Ibid.

24. Barry interview with Pollard, July 1970.

25. Barry interview with Pollard, July 1970; Ronald A. Smith, "Harvard and Columbia and a Reconsideration of the 1905–06 Football Crisis," *Journal of Sport History* 8 (Winter 1981): 5-19; Benjamin G. Rader, *American Sports: From the Age of Folk Games to the Age of Spectators* (Englewood Cliffs: Prentice-Hall, 1983), 140-44.

26. William J. Baker, "Sports at the Crossroads," in *Sports in Modern America*, ed. William J. Baker and John M. Carroll (St. Louis: River City Publishers, 1981), 43-44; Rader, *American Sports*, 140-44. Marc S. Maltby dates the term *gridiron* to an earlier rules change in the 1880s, see "The Origins and Early Development of Professional Football, 1890–1920," Ph.D. diss., Ohio University, 1987, 63.

27. Rader, *American Sports*, 142.

28. *Tech Prep*, October 1909, 18. The University of Chicago was one of the few midwestern colleges that supported the pre-1906 rules which were preferred by most northeastern coaches.

29. George Halas, *Halas by Halas: The Autobiography of George Halas* (New York: McGraw-Hill, 1979), 23-24.

30. *Tech Prep*, October 1909, 19.

31. *Year Book, 1910*, 105-6.

32. *Tech Prep*, April 1911, 22-23; Barry interview with Pollard, July 1970.

33. Terrence Cole, "The Great Indoors: The Story of Indoor Baseball," a paper delivered at the convention of the North American Society of Sport History, Clemson University, May 28, 1989; Halas, *Halas*, 24; *Tech Prep*, 1909–12.

34. Barry interview with Pollard, July 1970; *Tech Prep*, October 1910, 33-37.

35. *Tech Prep*, December 1911, 25, 28.

36. Ibid., 20.

37. *Tech Prep*, October 1911, 18, and December 1911, 25; Barry interview with Pollard, July 1970.

38. Barry interview with Pollard, July 1970. It is not clear which game Pollard is referring to here. The *Tech Prep* does not record any games played against teams in southern Illinois. It does, however, give only sporadic coverage of non-league games. Lane did play Thornton Township High School in Harvey, Illinois, during the 1909 season, about twenty-five miles south of Chicago. Because Hughes played in that game, a plot to exclude Fritz seems unlikely. It is possible that Fritz got his directions mixed up because Lane did play a number of road games with teams to the north and west of Chicago.

39. Barry interview with Pollard, July 1970.

40. *Tech Prep*, November 1910, 29.

41. *Tech Prep*, June 1912.

42. Author interview with Fritz Pollard, Jr., June 12, 1987; Barry interview with Pollard, November 1970.

CHAPTER 3. THE TRAMP ATHLETE

1. Benjamin G. Rader, *American Sports: From the Age of Folk Games to the Age of Spectators* (Englewood Cliffs: Prentice-Hall, 1983), 136-37; Jay Barry Manuscript, two draft chapters for a book, containing many direct quotes from unrecorded interviews with Pollard, Brown University Archives, Providence, Rhode Island, hereafter cited as Barry Manuscript.

2. Barry Manuscript. On early African-American college football stars, see Ocania Chalk, *Black College Sport* (New York: Dodd, Mead, 1976), 140-70 and Arthur R. Ashe, Jr., *A Hard Road to Glory*, vol. 1: *A History of the African-American Athlete, 1619–1918* (New York: Warner Books, 1988), 89-98.

3. Barry Manuscript.

4. Ibid.; Barry interview with Pollard, July 1970 and November 1970.

5. Barry Manuscript; Ronald A. Smith, "Harvard and Columbia and a Reconsideration of the 1905–06 Football Crisis," *Journal of Sport History* 8 (Winter 1981): 5-19; Howard Roberts, *The Big Nine: The Story of Football in the Western Conference* (New York: G. P. Putnam's, 1948), 85-95.

6. Barry Manuscript; Barry interview with Pollard, July 1970. Semipro football teams are commonly defined as teams on which only some of the players are paid, whereas professional football designates teams on which all players are paid.

7. Ibid.

8. Ibid. Barry interview with Pollard, July 1970.

9. Ibid.

10. Ibid.

11. Barry interview with Pollard, November 1970; Barry Manuscript.

12. Barry Manuscript. On Elmer T. Stevens, see *Historical Catalogue of Brown University, 1764-1934* (Providence: Brown University, 1934), 492.

13. Barry Manuscript. The Van Wyckle Gates still welcome students to the Brown University campus.

14. Ibid.; Barry interview with Pollard, July 1970.

15. Ibid.

16. Ibid.

17. Ibid.; Barry interview with Pollard, July 1970.

18. William Kirk, *A Modern City: Providence, Rhode Island and Its Activities* (Chicago: University of Chicago Press, 1909), 43; Barry interview with Pollard, July 1970; *The Providence Directory and Rhode Island Business Directory, 1913* (Providence: City of Providence, 1913); author interview with Mable Abrams, July 28, 1987; Charles V. Chapin, *Index of Births, Providence: 1891-1900*, vol. 11 (Providence: City of Providence, 1905).

19. Information on the career of Daniel Laing, Jr., is based in part on materials provided by Kenneth C. Cramer, archivist, Dartmouth College Library; *Dartmouth College and Associated Schools General Catalogue, 1769-1940* (Hanover: Dartmouth College, 1940); author interview with Leslie Keeling and Eleanor Towns, July 17, 1987; Providence *Journal*, August 5, 1880 and September 13, 1924.

20. Rowena Stewart, *A Heritage Discovered: Blacks in Rhode Island* (Providence: Black Heritage Society, n.d.); Kirk, *A Modern City*, 43, 61-62; author interview with Mary Jennings, July 27, 1987.

21. Providence *Journal*, August 5, 1880; *The Providence Directory* for 1883-1914; *Rhode Island Marriage Index—Males, 1886-1900* (Providence: City of Providence, 1985); author interview with Leslie Keeling and Eleanor Towns, July 17, 1987; author interview with Mary Jennings, July 27, 1987; Barry Manuscript; author interview with Mable Abrams, July 28, 1987. *The Providence Directory, 1914* shows that Joseph Laing had moved to 89 Cushing Street, which was the residence of Anna Robinson, a widow. Joseph Laing's mother, Anna, who had previously resided with him, is listed as living at 45 E. Transit Street, which was the Home For Aged Colored Woman. The *Directory* does not indicate if Anna Robinson was white or African American.

22. Barry interview with Pollard, July 1970; Barry Manuscript.

23. Barry Manuscript.

24. Ibid.; Allison Danzig, *The History of American Football: Its Great Teams, Players, and Coaches* (Englewood Cliffs: Prentice-Hall, 1956), 242-43.

25. Barry Manuscript; Barry interview with Pollard, November 1970.

26. Barry Manuscript.

27. Ibid. On Lewis, see Bob Royce, "All-America Bill Lewis," *College Football Historical Society* 2 (August 1989): 8-9.

28. Barry Manuscript; Barry interview with Pollard, July 1970.

29. William J. Baker, "Sports at the Crossroads," in *Sports in Modern America*, ed. William J. Baker and John M. Carroll (St. Louis: River City Publishers, 1981), 44; Allison Danzig, *Oh, How They Played the Game: The Early Days of Football and the Heroes Who Made It Great* (New York: Macmillan, 1971), 216-30; Barry Manuscript; Barry interview with Pollard, July 1970. On the rise of the professional coach in eastern college football, see Ronald A. Smith, *Sports and Freedom: The Rise of Big-Time College Athletics* (New York: Oxford University Press, 1988), 154-64.

30. Barry Manuscript; Barry interview with Pollard, July 1970.

31. Ibid.

32. Ibid.; on Hill, see the *Historical Catalogue of Brown University, 1764-1894* (Providence: Brown University, 1894), 316.

33. Barry Manuscript; Barry interview with Pollard, July 1970; author interview with Fritz Pollard, Jr., June 9, 1988.

CHAPTER 4. BROWN, 1915

1. John Hope Franklin and Alfred A. Moss, Jr., *From Slavery to Freedom: A History of Negro Americans*, 6th ed. (New York: Alfred A. Knopf, 1988), 292-93; Randy Roberts, *Papa Jack: Jack Johnson and the Era of White Hopes* (New York: Free Press, 1983), 198-203; David M. Chalmers, *Hooded Americanism: The History of the Ku Klux Klan* (New York: New Viewpoints, 1981), 28-38.

2. Barry interview with Pollard, November 1970; Irving Berdine Richmond, *Rhode Island: A Study in Separatism* (Boston: Houghton-Mifflin, 1905), 308-42; Richard Barrett, *Good Old Summer Days: Newport, Narragansett, Saratoga, Long Branch, Bar Harbor* (New York: Appleton Century, 1941).

3. Barry interview with Pollard, July 1970; Paul Robeson, *Here I Stand* (London: Dennis Dobson, 1958), 30-31; Shirley Graham, *Paul Robeson: Citizen of the World* (Westport: Negro Universities Press, 1971), 67, 70-71; Martin Bauml Duberman, *Paul Robeson* (New York: Alfred A. Knopf, 1988), 11-12; author interview with Andrew Buni, June 14, 1988.

4. Watson Smith to author, February 28, 1987; W. H. Hurlin, ed., *The Hand-Book of Brown University, 1915–16* (Providence: Brown Christian Association, 1915), 5; Jay Barry and Martha Mitchell, *A Tale of Two Centuries: A Warm and Richly Pictorial History of Brown University, 1764–1985* (Providence: Brown Alumni Monthly, 1985), 127-29. At the time, Brown was among the top twenty-five universities in terms of total enrollment, despite being a small college by today's standards.

5. Author interview with Wardwell Leonard, July 22, 1987; Watson Smith to author, February 28, 1987.

6. Harvard Sitkoff, *A New Deal for Blacks: The Emergence of Civil Rights as a National Issue*, vol. 1: *The Depression Decade* (New York: Oxford University Press, 1981), 31; Marcia Graham Synnot, *The Half-Opened Door: Discrimination and Admissions at Harvard, Yale, and Princeton, 1900–1970* (Westport: Greenwood Press, 1979), 47-52; Richard Morton Smith, *The Harvard Century: The Making of a University to a Nation* (New York: Simon and Schuster, 1986), 46, 86-87. Dartmouth was the most liberal with regard to admitting African-American students, while Princeton did not accept its first black student until the late 1940s.

7. Author interview with Martha Mitchell, July 28, 1987; *Brown Daily Herald*, 1909–11; author interview with Wardwell Leonard, July 22, 1987; Watson Smith to author, January 30, 1987.

8. *The Brunonian*, 1915–16 and *Brown University Financial Records*, 1915–16, both in the Brown University Archives, Providence, Rhode Island.

9. Barry interview with Pollard, July 1970; author interview with Wardwell Leonard, July 22, 1987.

10. Barry interview with Pollard, July 1970; Benjamin G. Rader, *American Sports: From the Age of Folk Games to the Age of Spectators* (Englewood Cliffs: Prentice-Hall, 1983), 142-43; Barry Manuscript.

11. Barry Manuscript.

12. Ibid.

13. Ibid.; Jay Barry, "Brown's Edward N. Robinson Enters Football Hall of Fame," *Brown University Football Program*, October 8, 1955, 5, 40, in the Brown University Archives; taped interview with Wallace Wade, February 23, 1985, Brown University Archives; author interview with Wardwell Leonard, July 22, 1987; Barry interview with Fred and Charlie Huggins, December 28, 1974, Brown University Archives.

14. Barry Manuscript.

15. Fraser is quoted from the Barry Manuscript; Barry interview with Fred and Charlie Huggins, December 28, 1974.

16. Barry Manuscript; Barry interview with Pollard, July 1970.

17. Ibid.

18. Barry Manuscript.

19. Ibid.

20. Robert Van Gelder, "Robeson Remembers," New York *Times*, January 16, 1944; Duberman, *Robeson*, 19-24; Jack W. Berryman, "Early Black Leadership in Collegiate Football: Massachusetts as a Pioneer," *Historical Journal of Massachusetts* 9 (June 1981): 17-28. Pollard's first days of practice at Northwestern and Dartmouth seem to confirm Berryman's implication that black players gained easier acceptance at colleges with longer traditions of including African Americans on their football teams.

21. Barry Manuscript; Barry interview with Pollard, July 1970; *Brown Daily Herald*, November 12, 1915.

22. Barry Manuscript; Providence *Journal*, September 30, 1915.

23. Barry interview with Fred and Charlie Huggins, December 28, 1974; Barry Manuscript; Barry interview with Pollard, July 1970.

24. Barry Manuscript; Barry interview with Pollard, July 1970.

25. For details on Pollard's changing attitude toward Brown in his declining years see chapter 13.

26. Barry Manuscript; Barry interview with Pollard, July 1970.

27. Barry interview with Pollard, July 1970; *Brown Daily Herald*, October 5, 1915.

28. *Brown Daily Herald*, October 11, 1915.

29. Barry interview with Pollard, July 1970.

30. Ibid.; Barry interview with Fred and Charlie Huggins, December 28, 1974; *Brown Daily Herald*, October 18, 1915.

31. *Brown Daily Herald*, October 22, 25, and 27, 1915. Stealing opponents signals was relatively easy in an era before the huddle, when quarterbacks shouted out plays at the line of scrimmage.

32. Allison Danzig, *The History of American Football: Its Great Teams, Players, and Coaches* (Englewood Cliffs: Prentice-Hall, 1956), 306-7; Barry interview with Pollard, July 1970; *Brown Daily Herald*, November 1, 1915.

33. *Brown Daily Herald*, November 6, 1915; New York *Times*, November 6, 1915.

34. *Brown University Football Program*, November 15, 1972, 69-70, Brown University Archives; *Brown Daily Herald*, November 1, 1915.

35. William M. Ashby, "Black Yale, Circa 1915," undated article, Brown University Archives. Yale traditionally admitted a small number of African-American students to its School of Religion. The New Haven college did not allow African Americans on its football team.

36. Ron Rapoport, "Fritz Pollard Remembers," Los Angeles *Times*, July 6, 1976; New York *Times*, November 7, 1915.

37. Ashby, "Black Yale."

38. *Brown Daily Herald*, November 8, 1915; New York *Age*, November 11, 1915.

39. Ashby, "Black Yale"; *Brown Daily Herald*, November 8, 1915; author interview with Wardwell Leonard, July 22, 1987; Barry and Mitchell, *A Tale of Two Centuries*, 127.

40. *Brown University Football Program*, November 15, 1972, 69-70; *Brown Daily Herald*, November 12, 1915. On the importance of the Harvard-Yale game to the two schools, see Thomas Bergin, *The Game: The Harvard-Yale Football Rivalry, 1875–1983* (New Haven: Yale University Press, 1984).

41. *Brown Daily Herald*, November 15, 1915.

42. Ibid.

43. Chicago *Defender*, August 13, 1927.

44. Robert W. Wheeler, *Jim Thorpe: World's Greatest Athlete* (Norman: University of Oklahoma Press, 1979), 29-47, 137; Allison Danzig, *Oh, How They Played the Game: The Early Days of Football and the Heroes Who Made It Great* (New York: Macmillan, 1971), 157-76; Danzig, *American Football*, 221-24.

45. John S. Steckbeck, *Fabulous Redmen: The Carlisle Indians and Their Famous Football Teams* (Harrisburg: J. Horace McFarland, 1951), 6-7, 85, 130; *Brown Daily Herald*, November 26, 1915.

CHAPTER 5. THE TOURNAMENT OF ROSES

1. Frederick W. Marvel as told to Joe Nutter, "Forty-Four Years of Brown Sports," Providence *Journal*, April 28, 1934; "Wallace Wade: No One Begrudged Him His Triumphs in Football," *Brown Alumni Monthly*, November 1970, 47.

2. *Brown Daily Herald*, November 17, 1915; Barry interview with Pollard, July 1970.

3. Fred Russell and George Leonard, *Big Bowl Football: The Great Postseason Classics* (New York: Ronald Press, 1963), 3-6; "A. Manton Chace Memorandum," Brown University Archives, Providence, Rhode Island.

4. Russell and Leonard, *Big Bowl Football*, 9-12.

5. Ibid.; "Chace Memorandum"; Frank Bianco, "For Brown the Wrong Shoe Was on the Foot in the '16 Rose Bowl Game," *Sports Illustrated*, November 24, 1980, 112-14. On the rise and fall of Rugby-style football on the West Coast, see Roberta J. Park, "From Football to Rugby—and Back, 1906–1919: The University of California-Stanford Response to the 'Football Crisis of 1905'," *Journal of Sport History* 11 (Winter 1984): 10-18.

6. *Brown Daily Herald*, November 26–December 21, 1915; Barry interview with Fred and Charlie Huggins, December 28, 1974.

7. Marvel, "Forty-Four Years of Brown Sports"; John Hanlon, "When Brown Played in the Rose Bowl," *Brown Alumni Monthly*, December 1985–January 1986, 29-30, 46; *Brown Daily Herald*, December 22, 1915. Several other eastern teams had played on the West Coast in addition to Michigan. The University of Chicago had played Stanford on Christmas Day 1894, and Syracuse made a trip to the Pacific Northwest to play three games in 1915.

8. Barry interview with Pollard, July 1970; Hanlon, "When Brown Played in the Rose Bowl," 29-30.

9. Barry interview with Fred and Charlie Huggins, December 28, 1974; Watson Smith to author, February 28, 1987; Barry interview with Pollard, July 1970.

10. Marvel, "Forty-Four Years of Brown Sports"; "Fritz Pollard Memorandum on the Rose Bowl Trip," Brown University Archives; Jay Barry, "Back to the Rose Bowl," *Brown Alumni Monthly*, December 1965, 6-8, 20; *Brown Daily Herald*, October 30, 1969.

11. Hanlon, "When Brown Played in the Rose Bowl," 29-30; "Pollard Memorandum on the Rose Bowl Trip"; Marvel, "Forty-Four Years of Brown Sports," Providence *Journal*.

12. Marvel, "Forty-Four Years of Brown Sports"; Barry interview with Pollard, July 1970.

13. Marvel, "Forty-Four Years of Brown Sports"; "Pollard Memorandum on the Rose Bowl Trip."

14. John C. Ewers, "Five Strings to His Bow: The Remarkable Career of William (Lone Star) Dietz," *Montana: The Magazine of Western History* 27 (January 1977): 2-13; Russell and Leonard, *Big Bowl Football*, 13-14; John C. Hibner, "Lone Star Dietz," *College Football Historical Society* 1 (August 1988): 1-4.

15. Bianco, "For Brown the Wrong Shoe," 112-14.

16. Russell and Leonard, *Big Bowl Football*, 14.

17. Ibid., 16, 68.

18. *Rose Bowl Football Program*, January 1, 1956 and assorted materials on the 1916 Tournament of Roses Parade, Brown University Archives; Marvel, "Forty-Four Years of Brown Sports"; Bianco, "For Brown the Wrong Shoe," 112-14.

19. Seth Moseley 2d, "Fritz Pollard, All-American," Westchester *Standard-Star*, January 7, 1979; Marvel, "Forty-Four Years of Brown Sports."

20. *Brown Daily Herald*, January 5, 1916; New York *Times*, January 2, 1916.

21. "Pollard Memorandum on the Rose Bowl Trip"; Hanlon, "When Brown Played in the Rose Bowl," 29-30, 46; *Rose Bowl Football Program*, January 1, 1956.

22. Bianco, "For Brown the Wrong Shoe," 112-14; William E. Sprackling to Jay Barry, October 23, 1970, Brown University Archives.

23. Bianco, "For Brown the Wrong Shoe," 112-14.

24. Ibid.; *Rose Bowl Football Program*, January 1, 1956.

25. "Pollard Memorandum on the Rose Bowl Trip"; Moseley, "Fritz Pollard," Westchester *Standard-Star*, January 7, 1979; Barry interview with Fred and Charlie Huggins, December 28, 1974; *State College of Washington Evergreen*, January 12, 1916.

26. Hanlon, "When Brown Played in the Rose Bowl," 30, 46; "Jay Barry Memorandum on Rose Bowl Stories," Brown University Archives; New York *Times*, January 2, 1916; Jay Barry and Wheaton Holden tape recording for a film on Fritz Pollard, in possession of Wheaton Holden.

27. Hanlon, "When Brown Played in the Rose Bowl," 30, 46; Marvel, "Forty-Four Years of Brown Sports."

28. A note on Pollard's grades is in the Brown University Archives; undated article from the Providence *Journal*, in the Brown University Archives.

29. Barry interview with Pollard, July 1970.

CHAPTER 6. AN ALL-AMERICA SEASON

1. Harry T. Sampson, *Blacks in Black and White: A Source Book on Black Films* (Metuchen: Scarecrow Press, 1974), 56-59; Anthony Slide, *The American Film Industry: A Historical Dictionary* (Westport: Greenwood Press, 1986), 104; Thomas Cripps, *Slow Fade to Black: The Negro in American Film, 1900–1942* (New York: Oxford University Press, 1977), 80, 83-84, 172, 175.

2. Sampson, *Blacks in Black and White*, 56-59.

3. Barry interview with Pollard, July 1970; author interview with Mary Jennings, July 27, 1987.

4. Barry interview with Pollard, July 1970; Shirley Graham, *Paul Robeson: Citizen of the World* (Westport: Negro Universities Press, 1971), 67, 70-71; author interview with Mary Jennings, July 27, 1987; author interview with Andrew Buni, June 14, 1988.

5. Author interview with Wardwell Leonard, July 22, 1987; Jay Mayo Williams Folder, Brown University Archives, Providence, Rhode Island; author interview with Lance Trusty, May 28, 1989.

6. Author interview with Fritz Pollard, Jr., June 12, 1987; "Notes on the 1916 Football Season," Brown University Archives. Fritz Pollard, Jr.'s comments are supported by author interview with Mary Jennings, July 27, 1987, and author interview with Mable Abrams, July 28, 1987.

7. William E. Sprackling to Jay Barry, October 20, 1970, Brown Uni-

versity Archives; author interview with Fritz Pollard, Jr., June 12, 1987; author interview with Leslie Keeling and Eleanor Towns, July 17, 1987. Also see Pollard's comments on the 1950–51 college basketball scandal in the New York *Amsterdam News*, February 24, 1951. Pollard maintained that "no, the boys shouldn't have taken the money, but I can certainly understand the temptation they were faced with. . . . Maybe a fund should be set up out of the Garden gross receipts for basketball players. Then they would reap a little of the profit of their labors."

8. *Brown Daily Herald*, October 2, 1916; Allison Danzig, *The History of American Football: Its Great Teams, Players, and Coaches* (Englewood Cliffs: Prentice-Hall, 1956), 71.

9. *Brown Daily Herald*, October 2, 1916.

10. Ibid., October 9, 1916.

11. Author interview with Wardwell Leonard, July 22, 1987.

12. *Brown Daily Herald*, October 16, 1916.

13. Providence *Journal*, October 17, 1916; *Brown Daily Herald*, October 19, 28, 1916. A student poll indicated that Brown men preferred Hughes by a margin of 3–1.

14. *Brown Daily Herald*, October 23, 1916; "Notes on Robinson Stories," Brown University Archives.

15. Barry interview with Fred and Charlie Huggins, December 28, 1974.

16. Ibid.

17. *Brown Daily Herald*, October 28, 1916; Barry interview with Fred and Charlie Huggins, December 28, 1974.

18. Taped interview with Wallace Wade, February 23, 1985.

19. *Brown Daily Herald*, October 28, 1916.

20. Ibid., October 30, 1916; New York *Times*, October 29, 1916.

21. Barry interview with Pollard, July 1970; *Brown Daily Herald*, October 30, 1916.

22. Ibid.

23. Ibid., November 2 and 6, 1916.

24. Neil Wilkof, "Pollard Paces Brown Comeback," *Yale Daily News*, October 10, 1968; Tim Cohane, *The Yale Football Story* (New York: Putnam's Sons, 1951), 200-203.

25. *Brown Daily Herald*, November 13, 1916; Wilkof, "Pollard Paces Brown Comeback"; Barry interview with Pollard, July 1970. The best volume on Robinson is Jules Tygiel, *Baseball's Great Experiment: Jackie Robinson and His Legacy* (New York: Oxford University Press, 1983).

26. *Brown Daily Herald*, November 13, 1916; New York *Times*, November 12, 1916; "Yale versus Brown, 1916: A Play by Play Summary," Brown University Archives.

27. "Yale versus Brown, 1916"; *Brown Daily Herald*, November 13, 1916.

28. "Yale versus Brown, 1916"; New York *Times*, November 12, 1916; the *Yale Alumni Weekly* comment is reprinted in the *Crisis*, January 1917, 139.

29. "Yale versus Brown, 1916"; *Brown Daily Herald*, November 13, 1916.

30. John McCallum, *Ivy League Football since 1872* (New York: Stein and Day, 1977), 71, 77.

31. New York *Times*, November 12, 1916; Providence *Journal*, November 12, 1916; New York *Evening Sun*, November 13, 1916; New York *Age*, November 23, 1916.

32. *Brown Daily Herald*, November 13 and 15, 1916.

33. Providence *Journal*, November 16 and 18, 1916.

34. Ibid., November 18, 1916; *Brown Daily Herald*, November 15, 1916.

35. "Harvard versus Brown, 1916: A Play by Play Summary," in the Brown University Archives; New York *Times*, November 19, 1916.

36. "Harvard versus Brown, 1916"; Providence *Journal*, November 19, 1916.

37. "Harvard versus Brown, 1916"; New York *Times*, November 19, 1916; Barry interview with Fred and Charlie Huggins, December 28, 1974.

38. *Brown Daily Herald*, November 20, 1916; "Harvard versus Brown, 1916."

39. New York *Times*, November 19, 1916.

40. *Brown Daily Herald*, November 21, 1916.

41. Ibid., November 22 and 25, 1916; Ronald A. Smith, *Sports and Freedom: The Rise of Big-Time College Athletics* (New York: Oxford University Press, 1988), 154-64.

42. "Notes on Robinson Stories"; Barry interview with Fred and Charlie Huggins, December 28, 1974; Barry interview with Pollard, November 23, 1974.

43. Author interview with Wardwell Leonard, July 22, 1987; New York *Times*, December 1, 1916; Ellery C. Huntington, ed., *50 Years of Colgate Football, 1890-1940* (Hamilton: Republican Press, 1940), 116-17.

44. New York *Times*, December 1, 1916; Barry interview with Fred and Charlie Huggins, December 28, 1974.

45. Barry interview with Fred and Charlie Huggins, December 28, 1974; *Brown Daily Herald*, December 1, 1916; Barry interview with Pollard, July 1970.

46. Bill Libby, *Champions of College Football* (New York: Hawthorn Books, 1975), 63, 186; Barry interview with Pollard, November 23, 1974;

Herbert Aptheker, ed., *A Documentary History of the Negro People in the United States, 1910-1932* (Secaucus: Citadel Press, 1977), 142-44; John Hope Franklin and Alfred A. Moss, Jr., *From Slavery to Freedom: A History of Negro Americans*, 6th ed. (New York: Alfred A. Knopf, 1988), 291-93.

47. New York *Times*, December 10, 26, 1916. On Camp and the origin of All-America selections, see Danzig, *History of American Football*, 31-32, 124-28. Camp is quoted in Arthur R. Ashe, Jr., *A Hard Road to Glory*, vol. 1: *A History of the African-American Athlete, 1619-1918* (New York: Warner Books, 1988), 102-3, and the *Brown Daily Herald*, January 3, 1917.

48. Barry interview with Pollard, November 23, 1974. The Chicago *Herald* editorial is reprinted in the *Brown Alumni Monthly*, March 1917, 212-13.

CHAPTER 7. WAR AND TRANSITION

1. Pollard to Jay Barry, January 13, 1969, Brown University Archives, Providence, Rhode Island.

2. Ibid.

3. Author interview with St. Clair T. Bourne, Sr., May 25, 1988; New York *Age*, 1915-16.

4. Pollard to Barry, January 13, 1969; Barry interview with Pollard, November 23, 1974.

5. Ibid.; *Brown University Financial Records*, 1915-17, Brown University Archives; file card relating to Frederick D. Pollard, November 25, 1918, in the Rockefeller Archive Center, North Tarrytown, New York. The Brown University records show that Pollard occupied rooms 19 and 40 in Hope College during 1917. The total yearly cost of these rooms was $127. It is not clear whether or not Rockefeller paid for one or both rooms in addition to the pressing equipment.

6. *Brown Daily Herald*, November 21, 1916, January 5, 1917; Barry interview with Pollard, November 23, 1974. At the time, professionalism was defined more strictly than it is today and payment of room, board, or tuition would have been considered a violation of amateur standing. See Marc S. Maltby, "The Origins and Early Development of Professional Football, 1890-1920," Ph.D. diss., Ohio University, 1987, 82.

7. Barry interview with Pollard, July 1970; *Brown Daily Herald*, December 13, 1915, March 12, 19, 27, and 28, 1917.

8. New York *Age*, February 8, 15, and 22, 1917; *Crisis*, March 1917, 249. Also see Pollard's comments about playing for the St. Christopher Club in the New York *Amsterdam News*, March 13, 1937.

9. New York *Age*, 1917-21, see especially February 22 and March 15,

1917 and December 4, 1920; Ocania Chalk, *Black College Sport* (New York: Dodd, Mead, 1976), 77; Arthur R. Ashe, Jr., *A Hard Road to Glory*, vol. 1: *A History of the African-American Athlete, 1619–1918* (New York: Warner Books, 1988), 106.

10. New York *Age*, April 5 and 19, 1917; Chalk, *Black College Sport*, 308-10; author interview with Fritz Pollard, Jr., June 12, 1987.

11. Wilson is quoted in Robert A. Divine et al., *America: Past and Present* (Glenview: Scott, Foresman, 1984), 699; *Brown Daily Herald*, March 27, 1917.

12. Gerald W. Patton, *War and Peace: The Black Officer in the American Military, 1915–1941* (Westport: Greenwood Press, 1981), 36-38; Arthur E. Barbeau and Florette Henri, *The Unknown Soldiers: Black American Troops in World War I* (Philadelphia: Temple University Press, 1974), 12-14. Also see John Hope Franklin and Alfred A. Moss, Jr., *From Slavery to Freedom: A History of Negro Americans*, 6th ed. (New York: Alfred A. Knopf, 1988), 293-98.

13. *Brown Daily Herald*, April 30 and May 15, 1917.

14. Ibid., May 16, 1917.

15. The New York *Evening Mail* account is reprinted in the New York *Age*, May 24, 1917; Jay Barry's note on Pollard's grades is in the Brown University Archives.

16. *Brown Daily Herald*, September 27 and 29, 1917; Barry's note on Pollard's grades.

17. *Brown Daily Herald*, September 29, 1917; Barry interview with Fred and Charlie Huggins, December 28, 1974; author interview with Pearce Johnson, March 17, 1988; Jay Mayo Williams Folder, Brown University Archives.

18. *Brown Daily Herald*, February 12, 1918; New York *Age*, September 28, 1918; Jack W. Berryman, "Early Black Leadership in Collegiate Football: Massachusetts as a Pioneer," *Historical Journal of Massachusetts* 9 (June 1981): 17-28.

19. Barbeau and Henri, *Unknown Soldiers*, 23-26. For a detailed account of the East St. Louis riot, see Elliott M. Rudwick, *Race Riot at East St. Louis* (Carbondale: Southern Illinois University Press, 1964).

20. Patton, *War and Peace*, 64, 162-65; Barbeau and Henri, *Unknown Soldiers*, 26-31. For a detailed account of the Houston Riot, see Robert V. Haynes, *A Night of Violence: The Houston Race Riot of 1917* (Baton Rouge: Louisiana State University Press, 1976).

21. Patton, *War and Peace*, 65-67.

22. Ibid., 9, 181-85; Barbeau and Henri, *Unknown Soldiers*, 60-69, 141-45; William C. Matney, ed., *Who's Who Among Black Americans*, 4th ed. (Lake Forest: Educational Communications, 1985), 675.

23. Patton, *War and Peace*, 38-44; Barbeau and Henri, *Unknown Soldiers*, 68.

24. Patton, *War and Peace*, 83-84; Barbeau and Henri, *Unknown Soldiers*, 60-61; W. E. B. Du Bois, "Close Ranks," *Crisis*, July 1918, 118. The 92nd Division's combat record in France was not nearly as good as that of the Negro 93rd Division which was made up of National Guard units and fought with the French army. After the war, the 92nd came under heavy criticism from the army and other sources. Its record was probably no worse than many other American divisions. In fact, the majority of African-American soldiers in France did not see combat, but were assigned to service detachments. Many white officers did not deem blacks fit for combat. For more on the 92nd and 93rd Divisions in France, see Barbeau and Henri, *Unknown Soldiers*, chaps. 7-8.

25. Barry interview with Pollard, July 1970; Philadelphia *Tribune*, June 1, 1918; Barbeau and Henri, *Unknown Soldiers*, 57.

26. Patton, *War and Peace*, 137-38; Barbeau and Henri, *Unknown Soldiers*, 63; Philadelphia *Tribune*, October 19, 1918.

27. Horace Mann Bond, *Education for Freedom: A History of Lincoln University, Pennsylvania* (Princeton: Princeton University Press, 1976), 4-5, 348-52; Herbert Aptheker, ed., *A Documentary History of the Negro People in the United States, 1910–1932* (Secaucus: Citadel Press, 1977), 136-39.

28. Horace Mann Bond, *The Education of the Negro in the American Social Order* (New York: Octagon Books, 1966), 370-71; author interview with Leslie Keeling and Eleanor Towns, July 17, 1987.

29. Carl Nesfield, "Pride Against Prejudice: Fritz Pollard, Brown's All-American Pre-World War I Vintage," pt. 2, *Black Sports*, December 1971, 61; Horace Mann Bond, "The Story of Athletics at Lincoln University," an unpublished chapter of *Education for Freedom*, Special Collections, Langston Hughes Memorial Library, Lincoln University, Oxford, Pennsylvania. On the transition from student control of athletics to administrative control at predominantly white universities, see Ronald A. Smith, *Sports and Freedom: The Rise of Big-Time College Athletics* (New York: Oxford University Press, 1988), 147-64.

30. Bond, "Story of Athletics"; *Lincoln University Herald*, January 1919; Philadelphia *Tribune*, October 19, 1918.

31. Philadelphia *Tribune*, November 2, 1918; Bond, "Story of Athletics."

32. Philadelphia *Tribune*, November 9 and 16, 1918; Barry interview with Pollard, July 1970; Bond, "Story of Athletics."

33. New York *Age*, November 16, 1918; *Lincoln University Herald*, January 1919.

34. Bond, "Story of Athletics"; Philadelphia *Tribune*, December 7, 1918.

35. Nesfield, "Pride Against Prejudice," pt. 2, *Black Sports*, December 1971, 61; author interview with Leslie Keeling and Eleanor Towns, July 17, 1987; file card relating to Frederick D. Pollard, November 25, 1918, in the Rockefeller Archive Center. The file card indicates that another file on Pollard has been destroyed. Also see the Philadelphia *Tribune*, 1918–21 for articles on Edward C. Brown.

36. New York *Age*, December 21, 1918; Bond, "Story of Athletics"; Philadelphia *Tribune*, 1918–21. On the history of college basketball, see Neil D. Issacs, *All the Moves: A History of College Basketball* (Philadelphia: J. B. Lippincott, 1975), 30-37, and Joe Jares, *Basketball: The American Game* (Chicago: Follett Publishing, 1971), 33-37. On early black participation in the sport, see Chalk, *Black College Sport*, 72-85, and Ashe, *Hard Road to Glory*, vol. 1, 104-9.

CHAPTER 8. THE MAKING OF A PRO

1. New York *Times*, February 26, 1919; Barry interview with Pollard, July 1970; *Brown Daily Herald*, April 14, 1919.

2. Kenan Heise, "Football Legend 'Fritz' Pollard," Chicago *Tribune*, May 14, 1986; Benjamin G. Rader, *American Sports: From the Age of Folk Games to the Age of Spectators* (Englewood Cliffs: Prentice-Hall, 1983), 176-77; William J. Baker, *Sports in the Western World* (Totowa: Rowman and Littlefield, 1982), 209-10; Ocania Chalk, *Black College Sport* (New York: Dodd, Mead, 1976), 311-12.

3. John Hope Franklin and Alfred A. Moss, Jr., *From Slavery to Freedom: A History of Negro Americans*, 6th ed. (New York: Alfred A. Knopf, 1988), 313-18; Arthur I. Waskow, *From Race Riot to Sit-In, 1919 and the 1960s: A Study in the Connections Between Conflict and Violence* (Garden City: Anchor Books, 1967), 208, 305. On the Chicago riot, see William M. Tuttle, Jr., *Race Riot: Chicago in the Red Summer of 1919* (New York: Atheneum, 1970). For an overview of the Red Scare, see Robert K. Murray, *Red Scare: A Study in National Hysteria, 1919–1920* (Minneapolis: University of Minnesota Press, 1955).

4. Carl Nesfield, "Pride Against Prejudice: Fritz Pollard, Brown's All-American Pre-World War I Vintage," pt. 2, *Black Sports*, December 1971, 61; Philadelphia *Tribune*, October 18, 1919.

5. Ibid., October 11 and November 1 and 8, 1919, December 11, 1920; *Lincoln University Herald*, January 1920; Horace Mann Bond, "The Story of Athletics at Lincoln University," Langston Hughes Memorial Library, Lincoln University, Oxford, Pennsylvania; Akron *Beacon Journal*, November 11, 1919; Jay Barry longhand notes of an interview with Pollard,

undated, Brown University Archives, hereafter cited as Barry Longhand Notes. The football historian Marc S. Maltby maintains that Clair Purdy contacted Pollard in Pennsylvania, see "The Origins and Early Development of Professional Football, 1890–1920," Ph.D. diss., Ohio University, 1987, 325-26.

6. *Lincoln University Herald*, January 1920; Barry Longhand Notes; Akron *Beacon Journal*, September 19, 1919.

7. Ibid., November 8, 1919. For background on the Ohio professional teams, see Maltby, "Professional Football," 231-84.

8. Akron *Beacon Journal*, November 10 and 13, 1919; Barry Longhand Notes; Carl Nesfield, "Pride Against Prejudice," pt. 1, *Black Sports*, November 1971, 10.

9. David S. Neft and Richard M. Cohen, *Pro Football: The Early Years, an Encyclopedic History, 1895–1959* (Ridgefield: Sports Products, 1987), 11-12. Maltby, "Professional Football," 219-22, includes an excellent outline of the various kinds of teams associated with pro football in the early twentieth century and rightly points out that some teams developed from the athletic club tradition.

10. George Halas, *Halas by Halas: The Autobiography of George Halas* (New York: McGraw-Hill, 1979), 59; Robert L. Wheeler, "That Old Steam Roller," Providence *Journal*, undated, Brown University Archives; Mike Rathet and Don R. Smith, *Their Deeds and Dogged Faith* (New York: Balsam Press, 1984), 22. Maltby provides other reasons why football for pay did not catch on as well as professional baseball, see "Professional Football," 365-78.

11. Neft and Cohen, *Pro Football*, 11-12; Rathet and Smith, *Their Deeds*, 21-22; Barry interview with Pollard, July 1970; Robert W. Wheeler, *Jim Thorpe: World's Greatest Athlete* (Norman: University of Oklahoma Press, 1979).

12. Joe Horrigan, "Follis Led Early Black Pioneers in Pro Football," *Game Day* program, National Football League, October 16, 1988; Rathet and Smith, *Their Deeds*, 214-17.

13. Ibid., 217-20.

14. Akron *Beacon Journal*, November 18, 19, 20, and 22, 1919.

15. Ibid., November 24, 1919; Bob Carroll, "Bulldogs on Sunday: Pro Football in the 1920s"; [Professional Football Researchers Association], *Coffin Corner*, 8, no. 6 [1986?]: 6.

16. Akron *Beacon Journal*, November 28, 1919; Bond, "Story of Athletics."

17. Bond, "Story of Athletics"; Philadelphia *Tribune*, November 29, 1919.

18. Bond, "Story of Athletics"; Akron *Beacon Journal*, November 28, and December 2, 1919.

19. Bob Carroll, "Bulldogs on Sunday," *Coffin Corner*, 8, no. 7 [1986?]: 11-12 and 8, no. 8 (1986): 16; Halas, *Halas*, 90-91; Maltby, "Professional Football," 338-59.

20. Akron *Beacon Journal*, October 4, 11, 18, and 25, 1920; Seth H. Moseley II, "Coach of a Different Color," *Game Day* program, vol. 14, no. 11, 1983, Professional Football Hall of Fame, Canton, Ohio; Ron Rapoport, "Fritz Pollard Remembers," Los Angeles *Times*, July 6, 1976.

21. Nesfield, "Pride Against Prejudice," pt. 2, 62, 77; Frank Mac-Donnell, "Gus Dorais Tells Story of Courage on Gridiron," Detroit *Times*, November 29, 1933.

22. Richard Lechner, letter to the sporting editor, New York *Times*, June 22, 1986.

23. Nesfield, "Pride Against Prejudice," pt. 2, 62-63; Akron *Beacon Journal*, September–October 1919; author interview with Pearce Johnson, June 13, 1988.

24. Lechner to New York *Times*; Philadelphia *Tribune*, November 6, 1920; Barry interview with Pollard, July 1970; Charlie Powell, "Pollard Recalls First Canton Trip," undated newspaper clipping, Brown University Archives; author interview with Al Harvin, June 29, 1987. There is no evidence that Thorpe was racially prejudiced, at least any more so than other players in the league. The harsh words between the two players may have resulted from the sensational newspaper stories on their impending clash. According to Pollard, they later became friends. Photographic evidence indicates that Pollard's assertion was not true that Thorpe was as black as he.

25. Pittsburgh *Gazette Times*, November 1, 1920; Akron *Beacon Journal*, November 1, 1920; Barry interview with Pollard, July 1970.

26. Harry A. March, *Pro Football: Its "Ups" and "Downs"* (Albany: J. B. Lyons, 1934), 152; Pittsburgh *Gazette Times*, November 1, 1920; Barry interview with Pollard, July 1970. March's history of pro football is notoriously inaccurate, but the story may have some substance because Pollard also recalled the incident. It is doubtful that the Indians "particularly hated Pollard," but they may have tried to intimidate the rival star.

27. New York *Age*, November 13, 1920; Bond, "Story of Athletics."

28. Bob Carroll, "Bulldogs on Sunday," *Coffin Corner*, vol. 8, no. 9, 19-20; Canton *Daily News*, November 26, 1920.

29. Bond, "Story of Athletics"; Philadelphia *Tribune*, December 25, 1920.

30. New York *Age*, December 25, 1920.

31. Bond, "Story of Athletics"; Barry interview with Pollard, July 1970.

32. Bond, "Story of Athletics."

33. New York *Age*, December 25, 1920; Powell, "Pollard Recalls First Canton Trip"; Neft and Cohen, *Pro Football*, 14; Halas, *Halas*, 66-67.

34. Dayton *Journal*, November 29, 1920; Buffalo *Express*, December 6, 1920.

35. Philadelphia *Tribune*, December 11, 1920; Nesfield, "Pride Against Prejudice," pt. 2, 63; Rapoport, "Pollard Remembers."

36. Akron *Beacon Journal*, December 13, 1920; Decatur *Review*, December 13, 1920; Halas, *Halas*, 65-66.

37. Nesfield, "Pride Against Prejudice," pt. 2, 63; Decatur *Review*, December 13, 1920; Rapoport, "Pollard Remembers."

38. Halas, *Halas*, 66; Neft and Cohen, *Pro Football*, 15, 20; March, *Pro Football*, 68; Barry interview with Pollard, July 1970 and November 23, 1974. An account of a game between Akron and the Conn All-Stars of Los Angeles appears in the Cleveland *Gazette*, February 5, 1921.

CHAPTER 9. A FOOTBALL ODYSSEY

1. Philadelphia *Tribune*, September 10, 1921; New York *Age*, February 19, 1921.

2. Philadelphia *Tribune*, August 20, 1921; Cleveland *Gazette*, November 19, 1921. Recent historians dispute the notion that Cleveland was a mecca for African Americans in the early 1920s. See Kenneth L. Kusmer, *A Ghetto Takes Shape: Black Cleveland, 1870-1930* (Urbana: University of Illinois Press, 1976), and Russell D. Davis, *Black Americans in Cleveland from George Peake to Carl B. Stokes, 1796-1969* (Washington, D.C.: Associated Publishers, 1972). It seems likely that Pollard was employed in Cleveland by either the Empire Savings and Loan Company or the Starlight Realty Company. See the Cleveland *Gazette*, March 19, 1921.

3. David S. Neft and Richard M. Cohen, *Pro Football: The Early Years, An Encyclopedic History, 1895-1959* (Ridgefield: Sports Products, 1987), 22; Akron *Beacon Journal*, October 3 and 10, 1921.

4. Ibid., October 10, 1921; Ocania Chalk, *Black College Sport* (New York: Dodd, Mead, 1976), 167-70; author interview with Andrew Buni, June 14, 1988; undated newspaper clipping on Pollard introducing Robeson to Florence Mills, Brown University Archives, Providence, Rhode Island.

5. Detroit *Free Press*, October 17, 1921; Canton *Daily News*, October 24, 1921.

6. Carl Nesfield, "Pride Against Prejudice: Fritz Pollard, Brown's All-American Pre-World War I Vintage," pt. 2, *Black Sports*, December 1971, 62; Buffalo *Express*, November 14, 1921; Akron *Beacon Journal*, November 21, 1921.

7. Dayton *Journal,* November 21, 1921; Akron *Beacon Journal,* November 21 and 25, 1921.

8. Author interview with Bob Carroll, December 2, 1988; Akron *Beacon Journal,* November 25, 1921; Ron Rapoport, "Fritz Pollard Remembers," Los Angeles *Times,* July 6, 1976.

9. Buffalo *Express,* December 4, 1921; Neft and Cohen, *Pro Football,* 20-22; Akron *Beacon Journal,* December 5, 1921.

10. Author interview with Bob Carroll, December 2, 1988; Cleveland *Gazette,* April 1, 1922; Barry Longhand Notes; George Halas, *Halas by Halas: The Autobiography of George Halas* (New York: McGraw-Hill, 1979), 91; Carl Nesfield, "Pride Against Prejudice," pt. 2, 63; Barry interview with Pollard, July 1970.

11. Milwaukee *Journal,* September 20 and October 2 and 9, 1922; author interview with Andrew Buni, June 14, 1988.

12. Milwaukee *Journal,* October 16, 1922; Racine *Journal-News,* October 16, 1922.

13. Milwaukee *Journal,* October 16, 1922; Nesfield, "Pride Against Prejudice," pt. 2, *Black Sports,* December 1971, 63.

14. Milwaukee *Journal,* October 23, 1922; Green Bay *Press-Gazette,* October 23, 1922; Milwaukee *Sentinel,* October 30, 1922.

15. Milwaukee *Journal,* November 3, 5, and 6, 1922. Plunkett's recruits Joe Alexander and Al Weltman, another former Syracuse star, never played for the Badgers.

16. A game in nearby Green Bay between the Blues and Columbus was played, but not enough rain fell for Green Bay to collect under its rain insurance policy. See Larry D. Names, *The History of the Green Bay Packers: The Lambeau Years, Part One* (Wautoma: Angel Press, 1987), 84. It seems likely that Rock Island did not have a guarantee or a share of the gate receipts for the game. Bob Carroll to author, February 7, 1989.

17. Milwaukee *Journal,* November 17, 19, and 20, 1922; Milwaukee *Sentinel,* November 20, 1922.

18. Milwaukee *Journal,* November 27, 1922; Racine *Journal-News,* December 1, 1922; Canton *Daily News,* December 4, 1922. Bob Carroll, an expert on professional football, has suggested that Pollard might have made $1,500 a game if he had been cut in for a share of the Milwaukee game receipts. Bob Carroll to author, February 7, 1989.

19. Chicago *Defender,* December 16, 1922 and February 9, 1924. The *Defender* states that the white all-star team was led by Ralph King of Harvard. King was actually a lineman from the University of Chicago. The *Defender* evidently confused Ralph King with Dick King, who was an All-America at Harvard in 1915 and Pollard's teammate at Milwaukee in 1922 until he was released at midseason.

20. Barry Longhand Notes; Brian S. Butler, "The Role of the Road Team in the N.F.L.: The Louisville Brecks," in *P.F.R.A. Annual 1988*, ed. Bob Braunwart (North Huntingdon, Pa.: Professional Football Researchers Association, 1988), 29-47; Lance Trusty, "From Prairie Ball to the NFL: The Hammond, Indiana Pros, 1917–1926," paper delivered at the North American Society of Sports Historians Convention, Clemson, South Carolina, May 28, 1989; author interview with Pearce Johnson, June 13, 1988; author interview with Bob Carroll, December 2, 1988; author interview with H. N. Young, December 2, 1988.

21. Barry Longhand Notes; Al Harvin, "Pollard at 84, Reflects on His Days of Glory," New York *Times*, February 7, 1978; author interview with H. N. Young, December 2, 1988; Dayton *Journal*, October 8, 1923. Some histories of the NFL list Pollard as coach of Hammond in 1923 and 1925, but not in 1924; see Neft and Cohen, *Pro Football*, 38. The position of quarterback was usually not as important then as it is today. In the double-wing or short-punt formations, the quarterback might be a blocking back, a running back, or the signal caller.

22. Chicago *Defender*, October 20 and November 10, 1923, and February 16, 1924; Barry Longhand Notes; author interview with H. N. Young, December 2, 1988.

23. McAlister Coleman, *Men and Coal* (New York: Farrar and Rhinehart, 1943), 30-31; Victor R. Greene, *The Slavic Community on Strike: Immigrant Labor in Pennsylvania Anthracite* (Notre Dame: University of Notre Dame Press, 1968), xiii, 2-6, 100; Donald L. Miller and Richard E. Sharpless, *The Kingdom of Coal: Work, Enterprise and Ethnic Communities in the Mine Fields* (Philadelphia: University of Pennsylvania Press, 1985), 182, 197-98, 211-12; author interview with John Klem, June 22, 1988.

24. Author interview with John Sullivan, June 23, 1988; author interview with Bill O'Brien, September 28, 1987; Richard Pagano, "Robert 'Tiny' Maxwell," *College Football Historical Society Bulletin* 1, no. 4 (1988): 1-3; Joe Zagorski, "The Day the Fans Took Over at Pottsville," *Coffin Corner*, 10, nos. 9–10 (1988): 14-15.

25. Author interview with John Sullivan, June 23, 1988.

26. Barry interview with Pollard, July 1970; author interview with John Klem, June 22, 1988; Bill O'Brien to author, February 14, 1989.

27. Shenandoah *Evening Herald*, October 15, 1923; Mahanoy City *Record-American*, October 15, 22, 23, and 29, 1923; Barry interview with Pollard, July 1970.

28. Mahanoy City *Record-American*, November 5, 13, 19, and 21, 1923; Shenandoah *Evening Herald*, November 19, 1923.

29. Author interview with John Sullivan, June 23, 1988; Nesfield, "Pride Against Prejudice," pt. 2, 77.

30. Shenandoah *Evening Herald*, November 23, 26, and 30, 1923; Mahanoy City *Record-American*, November 26, 1923.

31. Barry interview with Pollard, July 1970; Barry Longhand Notes; Nesfield, "Pride Against Prejudice," pt. 2, 77.

32. Mahanoy City *Record-American*, December 10 and 12, 1923; Shenandoah *Evening Herald*, December 10, 1923.

33. Author interview with Fritz Pollard, Jr., June 12, 1987; author interview with John Sullivan, June 23, 1988; Nesfield, "Pride Against Prejudice," pt. 2, 77.

34. Joe Zagorski, "The Anthracite Football League," in *P.F.R.A. Annual, 1987*, ed. Bob Braunwart (North Huntingdon, Pa.: Professional Football Researchers Association, 1987), 31-38; Shenandoah *Evening Herald*, October 10, 1924.

35. Mahanoy *Press*, October 2, 1924; Shenandoah *Evening Herald*, October 13, 1924; Pottsville *Republican*, October 13, 1924.

36. Author interview with John Sullivan, June 23, 1988. Smyth and Grigg were known as Symthe and Griggs in the Schuylkill County newspapers; it is unclear if they were trying to disguise themselves or the papers simply misspelled their names.

37. Shenandoah *Evening Herald*, October 14, 16, and 17, 1924; author interview with John Sullivan, June 23, 1988.

38. Shenandoah *Evening Herald*, October 20 and 27, 1924; Mahanoy *Press*, October 23, 1924.

39. Shenandoah *Evening Herald*, October 20 and 30, 1924; Mahanoy *Press*, November 7, 1924. The Thanksgiving Day game between Pottsville and Shenandoah was halted as fans rushed onto the field in the fourth period. See Zagorski, "The Day the Fans Took Over," 14-15.

40. Shenandoah *Evening Herald*, November 3 and 12, 1924; Mahanoy *Press*, November 12, 1924.

41. Shenandoah *Evening Herald*, November 15 and 17, 1924; Mahanoy *Press*, November 17, 1924.

42. Shenandoah *Evening Herald*, November 28, 1924; Mahanoy *Press*, November 28, 1924. Pottsville fans continue to maintain that the Maroons won the 1925 NFL championship. See the Pottsville *Republican*, March 7, 1985.

CHAPTER 10. RIDING A WHIRLWIND

1. Pollard Alumni Record Form, 1924, Brown University Archives, Providence, Rhode Island; Abram L. Harris, *The Negro as Capitalist: A*

Study of Banking and Business Among American Negroes (College Park: McGrath Publishing, 1968), 126.

2. Armand J. Thieblot, *The Negro in the Banking Industry* (Philadelphia: University of Pennsylvania Press, 1970), 180-83; Harris, *Negro as Capitalist*, 46, 84-85.

3. Philadelphia *Tribune*, May 24, 1919 and August 7, 1920; Harris, *Negro as Capitalist*, 125-43.

4. Carl Nesfield, "Pride Against Prejudice: Fritz Pollard, Brown's All-American Pre-World War I Vintage," pt. 2, *Black Sports*, December 1971, 63; Donald Steel et al., *The Encyclopedia of Golf* (New York: Viking, 1975), 127; Roy Damer, "Golf Loses a Link with the Past," Chicago *Tribune*, February 9, 1979; Chicago *Tribune*, February 10, 1979.

5. Pollard Alumni Record Form, 1924; Nesfield, "Pride Against Prejudice," pt. 2, 63; Barry interview with Pollard, July 1970; Chicago *Defender*, May 31, 1924.

6. Author interview with Leslie Keeling and Eleanor Towns, July 17, 1987; author interview with Fritz Pollard, Jr., June 12, 1987.

7. Author interview with Fritz Pollard, Jr., June 12, 1987; Pollard Alumni Record Form, 1924.

8. Author interview with Leslie Keeling and Eleanor Towns, July 17, 1987.

9. Author interview with Fritz Pollard, Jr., June 12, 1987; author interview with Leslie Keeling and Eleanor Towns, July 17, 1987.

10. Author interview with Fritz Pollard, Jr., June 12, 1987.

11. Green Bay *Gazette*, September 21, 1925; Barry Longhand Notes.

12. Akron *Beacon Journal*, September 28 and October 5, 1925; Buffalo *Express*, October 12, 1925; Canton *Repository*, October 19, 1925.

13. Detroit *Free Press*, October 26, 1925; Akron *Beacon Journal*, October 26, 1925.

14. Ibid., November 2, 1925; author interview with Pearce Johnson, June 13, 1988.

15. Philadelphia *Inquirer*, November 8, 1925; Philadelphia *Public Ledger*, November 8, 1925; Chicago *Defender*, November 14, 1925.

16. Akron *Beacon Journal*, November 9, 1925; Pottsville *Republican*, November 9, 1925.

17. Author interview with Pearce Johnson, June 13, 1988; Robert L. Wheeler, "That Old Steam Roller," Providence *Journal*, undated newspaper clipping, Brown University Archives.

18. Dick Reynolds, *The Steam Roller Story* (Providence: privately published, 1988), 5; Providence *Journal*, November 30 and December 7, 1925.

19. New York *Times*, November 27 and December 6 and 7, 1925; Harold E. Grange as told to Ira Morton, *The Red Grange Story: The*

Autobiography of Red Grange (New York: G. P. Putnam's Sons, 1953), 92.

20. Earl Loftquist, "Inside-Out," Providence *Journal*, undated newspaper clipping provided by Pearce Johnson; Providence *Journal*, December 9 and 10, 1925; Wheeler, "That Old Steam Roller," 24.

21. Providence *Journal*, December 10, 1925; Grange, *Red Grange Story*, 103-4.

22. Providence *Journal*, December 10, 1925.

23. Ibid., December 11 and 14, 1925. For other criticism of Grange and professional football, see Herbert Reed, " 'De-Granging' Football," *Outlook*, January 20, 1926, 102-3; *Literary Digest*, December 26, 1925, 24-25, 32-34.

24. David S. Neft and Richard M. Cohen, *Pro Football: The Early Years, An Encyclopedic History, 1895–1959* (Ridgefield: Sports Products, 1987), 54-57; Philadelphia *Inquirer*, September 26, 1926; Philadelphia *Bulletin*, September 26, 1926.

25. Buffalo *Courier-Express*, September 27, 1926; Akron *Beacon Journal*, September 27, 1926.

26. Ibid., October 4, 1926; Canton *Daily News*, October 4, 1926.

27. Akron *Beacon Journal*, October 11, 1926; newspaper clipping dated October 24, 1926, Brown University Archives.

28. Joe Horrigan, "Follis Led Early Black Pioneers in Pro Football," *Game Day* program, National Football League, October 16, 1988; Chicago *Defender*, November 6, 1926.

29. Frank Young, "A Few Words to the Sporting Editor of Chicago *American*," Chicago *Defender*, February 9, 1924.

30. Mahanoy City *Record-American*, October 18, 28, and 30, 1926; author interview with John Sullivan, June 23, 1988.

31. Mahanoy City *Record-American*, November 6, 8, and 12, 1926; author interview with John Sullivan, June 23, 1988.

32. Author interview with John Sullivan, June 23, 1988; Mahanoy City *Record-American*, 22 and 23, 1926.

33. Ibid., November 26, 1926; author interview with John Sullivan, June 23, 1988.

34. Mahanoy City *Record-American*, December 6, 1926.

35. Barry interview with Pollard, July 1970; Ron Rapoport, "Fritz Pollard Remembers," Los Angeles *Times*, July 6, 1976.

36. Barry Longhand Notes; Chicago *Defender*, October 27, 1928 and August 27, 1932; Barry interview with Pollard, July 1970.

37. Author interview with Fritz Pollard, Jr., June 12, 1987; Chicago *Defender*, September 10, 1927, June 11, 1932, and January 28, 1933.

38. Author interview with Fritz Pollard, Jr., June 12, 1987; Chicago *Defender*, December 24, 1932.

39. Author interview with Leslie Keeling and Eleanor Towns, July 17, 1987; Edwin B. Jourdain Folder, Evanston Historical Society, Evanston, Illinois.

40. Author interview with Fritz Pollard, Jr., June 12, 1987; Chicago *American*, March 19, 1931.

41. Nesfield, "Pride Against Prejudice," pt. 2, 80. On Binga, see the Chicago *Defender*, March 14, 1931, and Harris, *Negro as Capitalist*, 153-64.

CHAPTER 11. A NEW BEGINNING

1. Author interview with Fritz Pollard, Jr., June 12, 1987.

2. Carl Nesfield, "Pride Against Prejudice: Fritz Pollard, Brown's All-American Pre-World War Vintage," pt. 2, *Black Sports*, December 1971, 80; author interview with Joseph Mahood, March 20 and 22, 1989; author interview with Fritz Pollard, III, June 20, 1989; author interview with Fritz Pollard, Jr., June 12, 1987.

3. Roi Ottley and William J. Weatherby, eds., *The Negro in New York: An Informal Social History, 1626-1940* (New York: Praeger, 1967), 249-50; Cab Calloway and Bryant Rollins, *Of Minnie the Moocher and Me* (New York: Thomas Y. Crowell, 1976), 90-91, 116-17. For background on the Harlem or Negro Renaissance, see David Levering Lewis, *When Harlem Was in Vogue* (New York: Alfred A. Knopf, 1981), Jervis Anderson, *This Was Harlem* (New York: Farrar, Straus, Giroux, 1982), and Nathan Irwin Huggins, *Harlem Renaissance* (New York: Oxford University Press, 1971).

4. Ottley and Weatherby, eds., *Negro in New York*, 265-78; Gilbert Osofsky, *Harlem: The Making of a Ghetto* (New York: Harper and Row, 1966), 186-87.

5. New York *Age*, March 11, 1933; Barry interview with Pollard, July 1970; Edward Kennedy Ellington, *Music Is My Mistress* (New York: Doubleday, 1973), 234-36.

6. New York *Amsterdam News*, March 8 and May 17, 1933; New York *Age*, May 20, 1933; Martin Bauml Duberman, *Paul Robeson* (New York: Alfred A. Knopf, 1988), 167-68. Duberman states that Robeson received a salary of $15,000 plus traveling expenses for six weeks' work.

7. Barry interview with Pollard, July 1970; New York *Age*, May 20, 1933; New York *Amsterdam News*, July 19, 1933; William Lundell interview with Paul Robeson, undated copy, Brown University Archives,

Providence, Rhode Island; Duberman, *Robeson*, 621-22 *n*25, describes Pollard as Robeson's dresser.

8. New York *Amsterdam News*, September 27, 1933; New York *Age*, September 23, 1933; Peter Noble, *The Negro in Films* (Port Washington: Kennikat Press, 1969), 56-58; Thomas Cripps, *Slow Fade to Black: The Negro in American Films, 1900–1942* (New York: Oxford University Press, 1977), 216-17. The *Time* review of September 25, 1933 is quoted in Harvard Sitkoff, *A New Deal for Blacks: The Emergence of Civil Rights as a National Issue*, vol. 1: *The Depression Decade* (New York: Oxford University Press, 1979), 205.

9. Joe Nutter, "Fritz Pollard, Jr., Making Mark in Prep School Sport," Providence *Journal-Bulletin*, May 14, 1931; author interview with Fritz Pollard, Jr., June 12, 1987.

10. Author interview with Fritz Pollard, Jr., June 12, 1987; Joe Nutter, " 'Fritz' Pollard Returns to Brown Football Fields," Providence *Journal-Bulletin*, September 13, 1933.

11. Author interview with Leslie Keeling, July 18, 1987; author interview with Fritz Pollard, Jr., June 12, 1987; author interview with Joseph Mahood, March 20 and 22, 1989. The official name of the Carnegie Report of 1929 was Carnegie Foundation for the Advancement of Teaching, Bulletin 29, on *American College Athletics*.

12. Brown *Daily Herald*, October 13, 1933 and March 5, 1934; Providence *Journal*, February 20, 1934; Jay Barry's note of Fritz Pollard, Jr.'s grades in the Brown University Archives.

13. Author interview with Leslie Keeling and Eleanor Towns, July 17, 1990.

14. Barry interview with Pollard, July 1970; author interview with Joseph Mahood, March 20 and 22, 1989; author interview with Fritz Pollard, Jr., June 12, 1987.

15. The *Independent News* was first known as the New York *Independent*. Roi Ottley, *"New World A-Coming": Inside Black America* (Boston: Houghton Mifflin, 1943), 274-75; Claude McKay, *Harlem: Negro Metropolis* (New York: Harcourt, Brace, Jovanovich, 1968), 94-95.

16. Author interview with St. Clair T. Bourne, Sr., May 25, 1988; McKay, *Harlem*, 96.

17. Barry interview with Pollard, July 1970. There is no complete set of copies of the New York *Independent News*. An assortment of copies for the years 1935 and 1939–41 are in the Brown University Archives. There is no confirmation of Pollard's estimate of the paper's circulation.

18. New York *Independent News*, 1939–41. Pollard's article "The Athlete and the Actor" is in the Brown University Archives.

19. New York *Independent News*, 1939–41. On the "Don't Buy Where

You Can't Work" campaign see Sitkoff, *A New Deal for Blacks*, vol. 1, 258, 263.

20. Author interview with Pearce Johnson, June 13, 1988; Gerald R. Gems, "Shooting Stars: The Rise and Fall of Blacks in Professional Football," *P.F.R.A. Annual 1988* (North Huntingdon, Pa.: Professional Football Researchers Association, 1988), 11-15. Also see Thomas G. Smith, "Outside the Pale: The Exclusion of Blacks from the National Football League, 1934-1946," *Journal of Sport History* 15 (Winter 1988): 255-81, esp. 257 for statements by Halas and Rooney that there was no agreement to exclude blacks.

21. Gems, "Shooting Stars," 12; author interview with Joe Horrigan, June 26, 1989; author conversation with C. Robert Barnett, May 28, 1989; Mike Rathet and Don R. Smith, *Their Deeds and Dogged Faith* (New York: Balsam Press, 1984), 209.

22. New York *Amsterdam News*, February 23, 1935. Fritz, Jr., actually had three years of eligibility remaining.

23. New York *Amsterdam News*, August 31 and September 21 and 28, 1935; New York *Age*, October 26, 1935.

24. Barry interview with Pollard, July 1970; New York *Amsterdam News*, September 21, 1935.

25. Ibid., October 19 and 26, 1935. Montgomery's team had recently lost a closely contested exhibition game to the NFL New York Giants.

26. Ibid., November 2, 9, 16, and 23, and December 7, 1935; Providence *Journal*, December 6, 1935.

27. Author interview with Fritz Pollard, Jr., June 12, 1987; New York *Amsterdam News*, July 4 and 18 and August 1, 8, 15, and 22, 1936. Also see Richard D. Mandell, *The Nazi Olympics* (New York: Macmillan, 1971), and William J. Baker, *Jesse Owens: An American Life* (New York: Free Press, 1986).

28. New York *Amsterdam News*, September 26, October 10, 17, 24, 31, November 7, 14, 21, and December 5, 1936.

29. Ibid., September–December 1937, see esp. September 25, October 9, and November 13 and 20.

30. J. Wayne Burrell, "Sports Whirl," New York *Amsterdam News*, July 30, 1938.

31. New York *Amsterdam News*, August 7, 1938; Barry interview with Pollard, July 1970. On Pompez and the connection between black professional sports and crime figures, see Donn Rogosin, *Invisible Men: Life in Baseball's Negro Leagues* (New York: Atheneum, 1983), 105-8, 110-13.

32. Associated Negro Press news clipping, October 8, 1934, Claude A. Barnett News Releases, Chicago Historical Society. Simmons was referred to as either Ozzie or Oze by the black press.

33. New York *Amsterdam News*, January 8, 1938; Associated Negro Press news clipping, December 2, 1936, Claude A. Barnett News Releases. Simmons maintained that one of the owners who talked to him about a contract was George Halas. Author conversation with C. Robert Barnett, May 28, 1989. The presence of University of Illinois coach Bob Zuppke on the board of five coaches who picked the "official" All-America team may have been a factor in Simmons's failure to be selected. After dropping out of Brown, Fritz, Jr., wanted to play at Illinois but was told that Zuppke did not allow blacks on the Illinois team. Author interview with Fritz Pollard, Jr., June 12, 1987.

34. On black players in the 1930s at predominantly white colleges, see Smith, "Outside the Pale," 255-71. On black college players in the 1930s, see Arthur R. Ashe, Jr., *A Hard Road to Glory*, vol. 2: *A History of the African-American Athlete, 1919-1945* (New York: Warner Books, 1988), 102-6 and Ocania Chalk, *Black College Sport* (New York: Dodd, Mead, 1976), 266-77.

35. Smith, "Outside the Pale," 269; Washington is quoted in Rathet and Smith, *Their Deeds*, 209; Barry interview with Pollard, July 1970. Smith points out that the black all-star team had less than two weeks to practice and that its line was weak. Coach Kemp, who had not played pro ball since 1933, toiled nearly the whole game at tackle.

36. Letter from Herschel "Rip" Day to Dan Burley, New York *Amsterdam News*, January 10, 1942, December 6, 1941.

37. New York *Independent News*, May 27, 1939. On Pollard's articles for the *Amsterdam News*, see the issues for December 7, 1935, February 27, 1937, and March 7 and 13, 1937.

38. Barry interview with Pollard, July 1970. On Harper, see Bruce Kellner, ed., *The Harlem Renaissance: A Historical Dictionary for the Era* (New York: Methuen, 1987), 157. On the background of Suntan Studios, see Julius J. Adams, "Pollard Inherited Sun Tan Studio After Producer Died," New York *Amsterdam News*, September 10, 1949.

CHAPTER 12. ANOTHER WAR AND PEACE

1. Richard Dalfiume, "The 'Forgotten Years' of the Negro Revolution," in *The Black Man in America: Since Reconstruction*, ed. David Reimers (New York: Thomas Y. Crowell, 1970), 217-31.

2. John Patrick Diggins, *The Proud Decades: America in War and Peace, 1941-1960* (New York: W. W. Norton, 1988), 27-31 and Geoffrey Perrett, *Days of Sadness, Years of Triumph: The American People, 1939-1945* (Baltimore: Penguin Books, 1973), 310-24; Dalfiume, "The 'Forgotten Years,'" 218.

3. New York *Amsterdam News*, April 11 and 18, 1942; author interview with Fritz Pollard, Jr., June 12, 1987 and June 13, 1989.

4. Carl Nesfield, "Pride Against Prejudice: Fritz Pollard, Brown's All-American Pre-World War I Vintage," pt. 2, *Blacks Sports*, December 1971, 80; Roi Ottley, *"New World A-Coming": Inside Black America* (Boston: Houghton Mifflin, 1943), 275-76; Barry interview with Pollard, June 1981; author interview with St. Clair T. Bourne, Sr., May 25, 1988. It seems most likely that "the man" refers to Adam Clayton Powell, Jr., editor of the *People's Voice*.

5. New York *Mirror*, March 30, 1942; Dan Burley, "Confidentially Yours," New York *Amsterdam News*, April 11, 1942; Jules Tygiel, *Baseball's Great Experiment: Jackie Robinson and His Legacy* (New York: Oxford University Press, 1983), 23-24, 84-90; Donn Rogosin, *Invisible Men: Life in Baseball's Negro Leagues* (New York: Atheneum, 1983), 103-17. On Negro baseball during the war, see Rob Ruck, *Sandlot Seasons: Sport in Black Pittsburgh* (Urbana: University of Illinois Press, 1987), 173-76.

6. Rogosin, *Invisible Men*, 102-3; Barry interview with Pollard, July 1970. On Pollard's reputation as an entertainment promoter, see the New York *Amsterdam News*, February 12, 1938.

7. Barry interview with Pollard, July 1970; Jay Barry, "Fritz," *Brown Alumni Monthly*, October 1970, 33; Barry interview with Pollard, November 23, 1974.

8. Barry interview with Pollard, July 1970, November 23, 1974, June 1981.

9. Julius J. Adams, "Pollard Inherited Sun Tan Studio After Producer Died," New York *Amsterdam News*, September 10, 1949; "Juke-Box Movie War," *Business Week*, May 18, 1940, 52-53; "Jimmy's Got It Again," *Look*, November 19, 1940, 12-14.

10. Thomas M. Pryor, "Pot Shots at the News," New York *Times*, April 7, 1940; "Jimmy's Got It Again," 12-14; New York *Times*, October 31, 1940 and October 21, 1941; Anthony Slide, *The American Film Industry: A Historical Dictionary* (Westport: Greenwood Press, 1986), 320.

11. New York *Amsterdam News*, August 15, 1942; Barry interview with Pollard, July 1970; Arnold Shaw, *Honkers and Shouters: The Golden Years of Rhythm and Blues* (New York: Macmillan, 1978), 78; Thomas Cripps, *Slow Fade to Black: The Negro in American Film, 1900–1942* (New York: Oxford University Press, 1977), 234 and *Black Film as Genre* (Bloomington: Indiana University Press, 1978), 42-43.

12. Author interview with Leslie Keeling and Eleanor Towns, July 17, 1987.

13. Barry interview with Pollard, July 1970; Cripps, *Slow Fade to Black*,

234-35, 417 *n*37. For some lesser-known black artists who appeared in Soundies, see the New York *Amsterdam News*, August 21, 1943.

14. Al Laney, "Fritz Pollard, Football Legend, Now Books Talent in Harlem," New York *Herald Tribune*, January 1, 1944; Slide, *American Film Industry*, 320; Cripps, *Slow Fade to Black*, 234-35.

15. Barry interview with Pollard, July 1970; Adams, "Pollard Inherited Sun Tan," New York *Amsterdam News*, September 10, 1949.

16. For a brief overview of the integration of professional sports in the postwar era, see William W. MacDonald, "The Black Athlete in American Sports," in *Sports in Modern America*, ed. William J. Baker and John M. Carroll (St. Louis: River City Publishers, 1981), 97-98.

17. Dan Burley, "Confidentially Yours," New York *Amsterdam News*, June 28, 1947. Few black sportswriters even knew for whom Pollard played in the NFL, much less that he was a coach and brought in other black players. See, for example, the New York *Amsterdam News*, November 17, 1945.

18. Burley, "Confidentially Yours"; New York *Amsterdam News*, November 29, 1947; Barry interview with Pollard, July 1970. Those who followed Pacific Coast League football were not surprised by the popularity of black players because Kenny Washington and others were star gate attractions during the war.

19. Author interview with Leslie Keeling and Eleanor Towns, July 17, 1987; author interview with Andrew Buni, June 14, 1988; author interviews with several people from Harlem who wish to remain anonymous; author interview with Leslie Keeling, July 18, 1987.

20. Willie Hamilton, "Mrs. Mary Ella Pollard, 'Voice of the Amsterdam News,'" undated newspaper clipping, Brown University Archives, Providence, Rhode Island; author interview with Leslie Keeling, July 18, 1987; author interview with Fritz Pollard, Jr., June 12, 1987.

21. Author interview with Major Robinson, May 24, 1988; author interview with Pat Patterson, May 24, 1988; author interview with St. Clair T. Bourne, Sr., May 2, 1988. The only recorded comment Pollard made on his relationship with the Rockefellers in later years was at the time of Nelson Rockefeller's inauguration as governor of New York in 1959. He wrote Jay Barry: "Just returned from Rockefeller's Inauguration. What a GREAT SHOW they put on. Just like the Installation of a King. This man is our next President of U.S." Pollard to Barry, undated letter, Brown University Archives.

22. In his biography of Robeson, Martin Duberman implies that Pollard and Robeson were not close after their football-playing days. In writing the biography, however, Duberman relies heavily on the voluminous correspondence and writings of Eslanda Robeson because Paul Robeson wrote

letters infrequently and seldom answered his mail. Pollard indicates in his July 1970 interview with Jay Barry that he often met Robeson on the street and they would stop off at a saloon, where Pollard would sometimes play the piano and Robeson would sing. Fritz Pollard, Jr., has also emphasized the close relationship between his father and Robeson. Commentary on Robeson's Paris speech is in Martin Bauml Duberman, *Paul Robeson* (New York: Alfred A. Knopf, 1988), 341-59.

23. New York *Age*, April 30, 1949; Fritz Pollard as told to Major Robinson, "Greatest Negro Football Players of All Time," *Our World*, November 1949, 54-57. Pollard also included Marion Motley, William H. Lewis, Kenny Washington, Ed Gray, and Charles West among his top ten. As Robeson's political difficulties worsened in the 1950s, Pollard saw Robeson less frequently or not at all. In 1958, Eslanda Robeson sent a New Year's greeting to Pollard. See Pollard to Eslanda and Paul Robeson, January 29, 1958, Robeson Family Archives, Howard University, Washington, D.C., and Duberman, *Robeson*, 454. In 1976, Pollard said about Robeson: "We kept in touch till he died. I was a pallbearer at his funeral." See Ron Rapoport, "Fritz Pollard Remembers," Los Angeles *Times*, July 6, 1976.

24. Nesfield, "Fritz Pollard," pt. 2, 81; Barry interview with Pollard, July 1970.

25. Barry interview with Pollard, July 1970; Pollard to Jay Barry, December 9, 1958 and February 20, 1959, Brown University Archives; author interview with Fritz Pollard, Jr., June 12, 1987.

26. Brochure on the Negro Athlete Hall of Fame sent to Federal Bureau of Investigation director J. Edgar Hoover, October 28, 1952, Frederick Douglass Pollard File, Federal Bureau of Investigation Records; Bob Cordasco, "Acceptance a Problem for Black Sports Hall?" New York *Post*, June 29, 1973; New York *Times*, June 29, 1973.

27. Pollard to Eisenhower, October 10, 1952, Box 398; Eisenhower to Pollard, October 18, 1952, draft letter, and Eisenhower to Pollard, October 20, 1952, revised version, both in Box 398; Elmer Q. Oliphant to Eisenhower, March 7, 1955, Box 712; all in the Dwight D. Eisenhower Records as President, Dwight D. Eisenhower Library, Abilene, Kansas.

28. Pollard to Eisenhower, January 22, 1953, Box 1297; Oliphant to Eisenhower, March 7, 1955, Box 712, all in Eisenhower Records as President, Eisenhower Library.

29. Eisenhower to Oliphant, March 11, 1955, Box 712; Eisenhower to Pollard, November 15, 1956, Box 2468; all in the Eisenhower Records as President, Eisenhower Library; author interview with Fritz Pollard, Jr., June 12, 1987.

30. Earl Lofquist, "Inside Out," Providence *Sunday Journal*, November

7, 1954; "The Ten Greatest Negro Athletes of All Time," *Ebony*, August 1949, 34-35; John Hanlon, "Hall-Enshrined Pollard Heaps Credit on Team," Providence *Sunday Journal*, November 7, 1954; transcript, "Fritz Pollard Luncheon," November 6, 1954, Brown University Archives. Along with Pollard, the *Ebony* poll listed Jesse Owens, Joe Louis, Jackie Robinson, Satchel Paige, Sam Langford, Henry Armstrong, Joe Gans, Harrison Dillard, and Jack Johnson.

31. Providence *Sunday Journal*, January 1, 1956; Providence *Evening Bulletin*, January 23, 1956; Earl Lofquist, "After Forty Years, Back to the Rose Bowl," Providence *Sunday Journal*, January 1, 1956.

CHAPTER 13. BITTERSWEET YEARS

1. Barry interview with Pollard, July 1970.

2. "Feature Review of *Rockin' the Blues*," October 1957, newspaper clipping, Brown University Archives, Providence, Rhode Island; New York *Age*, October 20, 1956; Bruce Kellner, ed., *The Harlem Renaissance: A Historical Dictionary for the Era* (New York: Methuen, 1987), 243-44, 249-50; Cleveland *Call and Post*, October 27, 1956.

3. Cleveland *Call and Post*, October 27, 1956; Claude A. Barnett New Releases, Associated Negro Press, November 17, 1956, Chicago Historical Society; Barry interview with Pollard, July 1970; "Feature Review of *Rockin' the Blues*."

4. New York *Amsterdam News*, March 7, 1964. Pollard's sports articles appeared in the *Amsterdam News* as well as many small southern black newspapers; clippings of his 1960s articles are in the Brown University Archives.

5. Watson Smith to author, January 30, 1987.

6. Pollard to Barry, December 9, 1958 and Pollard to Frank Finney, December 19, 1958, Brown University Archives; New York *Amsterdam News*, June 14, 1969.

7. Various letters between Pollard and Barry written in the 1970s, a book outline, a film synopsis, and a film contract, Brown University Archives; New York *Amsterdam News*, February 15, 1975.

8. Jay Barry manuscript, "Fritz Pollard, Negro All-American," February 20, 1970; transcript of "Fritz Pollard Luncheon," November 6, 1954; both in the Brown University Archives.

9. Author interview with Fritz Pollard III, June 20, 1989.

10. Providence *Journal*, May 5, 1967; author interview with Fritz Pollard III, June 20, 1989; John Hanlon, "Another Fritz Pollard at Brown," Providence *Journal*, May 4, 1973.

11. Author interview with Fritz Pollard, Jr., June 12, 1987; Pollard to

Barry, January 1, 1972; Ralph A. Mateka to Pollard, December 6, 1972; Richard F. Seaman to Pollard, August 31, 1973; all in the Brown University Archives.

12. Hanlon, "Another Fritz Pollard"; author interview with Fritz Pollard III, June 20, 1989; Jay Barry notes of a conversation with Fritz Pollard III, undated, Brown University Archives. On the race question at Brown during the early 1970s, see David Temkin, "Times of Tension," *Brown Alumni Monthly*, June-July 1989, 24-31.

13. Jay Barry, "Fritz Pollard: Breaking the Barrier of Race," *Issues*, December 1976, 26; Bruce Warren, "Pollard Remembers the Old Days," undated newspaper clipping, Brown University Archives; Ron Rapoport, "Pollard Died Hating Halas," Chicago *Sun-Times*, May 16, 1986.

14. Author interview with Fritz Pollard, Jr., June 12, 1987.

15. Telegram, Pete Rozelle to Pollard, May 4, 1976, Brown University Archives.

16. New York *Times* sportswriter Al Harvin, who did several articles on Pollard, was more sensitive and accurate than many other writers. See, for example, Harvin, "Pollard at 84," New York *Times*, February 7, 1978. Joe Jares, "The Wrong Man Behind the Mike," *Sports Illustrated*, May 12, 1980, 45; James A. Michener, *Sports in America* (New York: Random House, 1976).

17. Jerry Izenberg, "A Genuine Unknown Hero," New York *Post*, April 11, 1978.

18. Author interview with Joe Horrigan, June 26, 1989; Jim Campbell, "Pro! Talk: A Conversation with Fritz Pollard," September 11, 1977, Brown University Archives; Carl Nesfield, "Pride Against Prejudice: Fritz Pollard, Brown's All-American Pre-World War I Vintage," pt. 2, *Black Sports*, December 1971, 81.

19. Despite being the greatest end Walter Camp ever saw, Robeson still has not been inducted into the National Collegiate Football Hall of Fame. Ron Rapoport, "Fritz Pollard Remembers," Los Angeles *Times*, July 6, 1976.

20. Rapoport, "Pollard Remembers."

21. Author interview with Leslie Keeling and Eleanor Towns, July 17, 1987; author interview with Fritz Pollard, Jr., June 12, 1987; author interview with Fritz Pollard III, June 20, 1989.

22. Chicago *Tribune*, April 3, 1979; Barry interview with Pollard, June 1981; author interview with Fritz Pollard, Jr., June 12, 1987.

23. Author interview with Fritz Pollard, Jr., June 12, 1987; New York *Times Biographical Service*, May 1986, 705.

24. Author interview with Fritz Pollard III, June 20, 1989; Rapoport,

"Pollard Died Hating Halas"; author interview with Leslie Keeling and Eleanor Towns, July 17, 1989.

EPILOGUE

1. An excellent work on the importance of the civil rights movement on the grass-roots level is Robert J. Norrell, *Reaping the Whirlwind: The Civil Rights Movement in Tuskegee* (New York: Alfred A. Knopf, 1985).

2. Arthur R. Ashe, Jr., *A Hard Road to Glory*, vol. 1: *A History of the African-American Athlete, 1619-1918* (New York: Warner Books, 1988), ix.

3. Author interview with Fritz Pollard, Jr., June 12, 1987; Ashe, *Hard Road to Glory*, vol. 1, ix.

4. E. Franklin Frazier, *Black Bourgeoisie: The Rise of a New Middle Class* (New York: Free Press, 1957). Harry Edwards, *The Revolt of the Black Athlete* (New York: Free Press, 1969), gives a similar interpretation of the black middle class. Author interview with Leslie Keeling and Eleanor Towns, July 17, 1987.

5. Barry interview with Pollard, November 23, 1974; author interview with Fritz Pollard, Jr., June 12, 1987.

6. Author interview with Pearce Johnson, June 13, 1988; author interview with Fritz Pollard, Jr., June 12, 1987.

BIBLIOGRAPHIC NOTE

This note is intended to aid the reader in further study of the various aspects of American life in which Fritz Pollard participated during the twentieth century. It is not intended to be a list of materials consulted or used in the writing of *Fritz Pollard: Pioneer in Racial Advancement*. Because of the relative scarcity of sources on some aspects of Pollard's career, I have relied heavily on oral interviews. This work could not have been completed in its present form without the extensive interviews that Brown alumnus Jay Barry did with Pollard in the 1970s. Barry also collected three boxes of materials relating to Pollard's career, which were very helpful. Oral interviews, at best, present many problems relating to faltering memory and point of view. When the interviews are conducted by another person and involve a seventy-five-year old man recalling events of fifty years before or more, they must be used with caution. Beyond that, I was aware that Pollard gave different interpretations of events to white as opposed to African-American interviewers. Thus, I made every effort to check Pollard's recollection and interpretation of events against other sources. I made a particular point of interviewing a sizable number of African Americans who knew Pollard or were familiar with his career. The interviews with Pollard's children and grandson were useful, but other interviews conducted in Chicago and the New York City area also proved to be important in this study.

The best archival source on Pollard's career is the Brown University Archives, Providence, Rhode Island. In addition to materials collected by Barry, the Brown Archives contain newspaper clippings and assorted other materials pertaining to Pollard's life and times. The Schomburg Collection of the New York Public Library contains much background material on

Pollard's career. Also helpful were collections at the Chicago Historical Society, regional branches of the Chicago Public Library, the Evanston Historical Society, the Lincoln University Archives, and the Dartmouth College Archives. I was able to obtain Federal Bureau of Investigation records pertaining to Pollard under the Freedom of Information Act. Records at the Dwight D. Eisenhower Presidential Library in Abilene, Kansas, were important in tracing Pollard's involvement in national political affairs.

Pollard's public career can be best followed in the African-American newspapers of his day; the Chicago *Defender*, New York *Age*, New York *Amsterdam News*, Philadelphia *Tribune*, Cleveland *Gazette*, and Pittsburgh *Courier* were most helpful. White dailies were less valuable except with regard to football game accounts and for Pollard's later career; the most useful were the New York *Times*, Chicago *Tribune*, and Providence *Journal*. African-American periodicals which provided accounts of Pollard's career and important background material included *Crisis*, *Our World*, *Opportunity*, *Ebony*, and *Black Sports*.

There is no biography of Pollard. One can learn much about the struggle of the African-American athlete in the early twentieth century, however, by consulting a number of fine biographies of other prominent black sportsmen. Some of the best are Randy Roberts, *Papa Jack: Jack Johnson and the Era of White Hopes* (New York, 1983), Martin Bauml Duberman, *Paul Robeson* (New York, 1988), William J. Baker, *Jesse Owens: An American Life* (New York, 1986), and Jules Tygiel, *Baseball's Great Experiment: Jackie Robinson and His Legacy* (New York, 1983). Many articles about Pollard are superficial and marred by inaccuracies. One of the best and most revealing is a two-part account by the black sportswriter Carl Nesfield, "Pride Against Prejudice: Fritz Pollard Brown's All-American Pre-World War I Vintage," *Black Sports*, November 1971, 16–20, 31, 53 and December 1971, 60–63, 77, 80–81. Other generally reliable articles are Jay Barry, "Fritz," *Brown Alumni Monthly*, October 1970, 30–33 and Seth H. Moseley 2d, "Fritz Pollard, All-American," Westchester *Standard-Star*, January 7, 1979.

For Pollard's family background and upbringing in Chicago, an indispensable source is Luther J. Pollard, "Luther Pollard Family Notes" in the Brown University Archives. Other works that provided valuable information on turn-of-the-century Chicago were: "Anniversary, Township of Rogers Park Annexation to the City of Chicago," *Lerner Home Newspapers*, April 3, 1968, in the Chicago Historical Society; Michael H. Ebner, *Creating Chicago's North Shore: A Suburban History* (Chicago, 1988); Bessie Louise Pierce, *A History of Chicago*, vol. 3: *The Rise of a Modern City, 1871–1893* (Chicago, 1975); Illinois Commission on Race Relations, *The Negro in Chicago: A Study of Race Relations and a Race Riot* (Chicago, 1922);

Allan H. Spear, *Black Chicago: The Making of a Negro Ghetto, 1890–1920* (Chicago, 1967); and St. Clair Drake and Horace R. Cayton, *Black Metropolis: A Study of Negro Life in a Northern City*, vol. 1 (New York, 1962).

Pollard's career at Brown University can be best traced through the plentiful array of sources in the Brown University Archives, including the Jay Barry material. There are numerous studies of college football covering the early twentieth century. I found the following works useful: Alexander M. Weyland, *The Saga of American Football* (New York, 1955); Ocania Chalk, *Black College Sport* (New York, 1976); Arthur R. Ashe, Jr., *A Hard Road to Glory*, vol. 1: *A History of the African-American Athlete, 1619–1918* (New York, 1988); Allison Danzig, *The History of American Football: Its Great Teams, Players and Coaches* (Englewood Cliffs, 1956); Ronald A. Smith, *Sports and Freedom: The Rise of Big-Time College Athletics* (New York, 1988); Jack W. Berryman, "Early Black Leadership in Collegiate Football: Massachusetts as a Pioneer," *Historical Journal of Massachusetts* 9 (1981): 17–28; Fred Russell and George Leonard, *Big Bowl Football: The Great Postseason Classics* (New York, 1963); and John McCallum, *Ivy League Football since 1872* (New York, 1977). For background on Pollard's World War I service, see Gerald W. Patton, *War and Peace: The Black Officer in the American Military, 1915–1941* (Westport, 1981) and Arthur E. Barbeau and Florette Henri, *The Unknown Soldiers: Black American Troops in World War I* (Philadelphia, 1974). In addition to the Philadelphia *Tribune*, the best source on Pollard's coaching career at Lincoln University is Horace Mann Bond, "The Story of Athletics at Lincoln University," in the Special Collections, Langston Hughes Memorial Library, Lincoln University, Oxford Pennsylvania.

Many books and articles dealing with early professional football and the fledgling National Football League contain inaccuracies. The *Coffin Corner* and *P.F.R.A. Annual*, publications of the Professional Researchers Association, are two of the more reliable sources. The Professional Football Hall of Fame in Canton, Ohio, provides a wealth of information about the early game. Among published works, I found the following to be valuable: David S. Neft and Richard M. Cohen, *Pro Football: The Early Years, An Encyclopedic History, 1895–1959* (Ridgefield, 1987); Marc S. Maltby, "The Origins and Early Development of Professional Football, 1890–1920," Ph.D. diss., Ohio University, 1987; Mike Rathet and Don R. Smith, *Their Deeds and Dogged Faith* (New York, 1984); Joe Horrigan, "Follis Led Early Black Pioneers in Pro Football," *Game Day* program, National Football League, October 16, 1988; George Halas, *Halas by Halas: The Autobiography of George Halas* (New York, 1979); Larry D. Names, *The History of the Green Bay Packers: The Lambeau Years, Part*

One (Wautoma, 1987); Robert Curran, *Pro Football's Rag Days* (Engle-wood Cliffs, 1969); Jack Cusak, *Pioneer in Pro Football* (Ft. Worth, 1963); and Allison Danzig, ed., *Oh, How They Played the Game: The Early Days of Football and the Heroes Who Made It Great* (New York, 1971). On Pennsylvania Coal Region football, the area's newspapers are the best source. Also see Donald L. Miller and Richard E. Sharpless, *The Kingdom of Coal: Work, Enterprise and Ethnic Communities in the Mine Fields* (Philadelphia, 1985).

On Pollard's Harlem years, I found the following studies to be helpful: David Levering Lewis, *When Harlem Was in Vogue* (New York, 1981); Jervis Anderson, *This Was Harlem* (New York, 1982); Roi Ottley and William J. Weatherby, eds., *The Negro in New York: An Informal Social History, 1626-1940* (New York, 1967); Nathan Irwin Huggins, *Harlem Renaissance* (New York, 1971); Gilbert Osofsky, *Harlem: The Making of a Ghetto* (New York, 1956); Cab Calloway and Bryant Rollins, *Of Minnie the Moocher and Me* (New York, 1976); and Bruce Kellner, ed., *The Harlem Renaissance: A Historical Dictionary for the Era* (New York, 1987).

Much of the commentary on Pollard's multifaceted business career is based on his own testimony. For background on the African-American banking industry, see Abram L. Harris, *The Negro as Capitalist: A Study of Banking and Business Among American Negroes* (College Park, 1968) and Armand J. Thieblot, *The Negro in the Banking Industry* (Philadelphia, 1970). On the African-American newspaper business, I relied on oral in-terviews with a number of former black newspaper writers. I also found Roi Ottley, *"New World A-Coming": Inside Black America* (Boston, 1943) and Claude McKay, *Harlem: Negro Metropolis* (New York, 1968) helpful on the status of black weeklies in New York during the 1930s.

Pollard's career in the film and entertainment industries was wide-rang-ing. The following works were important in providing the background for his endeavors: Edward Kennedy Ellington, *Music Is My Mistress* (New York, 1973); Arnold Shaw, *Honkers and Shouters: The Golden Years of Rhythm and Blues* (New York, 1978); Julius J. Adams, "Pollard Inherited Sun Tan Studios After Producer Died," New York *Amsterdam News*, September 10, 1949; Peter Noble, *The Negro in Films* (Port Washington, 1969); Thomas Cripps, *Slow Fade to Black: The Negro in American Films, 1900-1942* (New York, 1977); and Anthony Slide, *The American Film Industry: A Historical Dictionary* (Westport, 1986).

Finally, Pollard's career can only be placed in perspective by reading widely in African-American history. Ralph Ellison, *The Invisible Man* (New York, 1947) remains invaluable in attempting to understand the problems that blacks face living in a white-dominated culture. William E. B. Du Bois, *The Souls of Black Folk* (Chicago, 1903) provides the backdrop for twentieth-century African-American history. Other important works are: George M. Frederickson, *The Black Image in the White Mind: The Debate on Afro-American Character and Destiny, 1817–1914* (New York, 1971); August Meier, *Negro Thought in America, 1880–1915: Racial Ideologies in the Age of Booker T. Washington* (Ann Arbor, 1963); and Leon F. Litwack, *Been in the Storm So Long: The Aftermath of Slavery* (New York, 1979). Robert J. Norrell, *Reaping the Whirlwind: The Civil Rights Movement in Tuskegee* (New York, 1985) provides insights into the civil rights movement at the grass roots level. E. Franklin Frazier, *Black Bourgeoisie: The Rise of a New Middle Class* (New York, 1957) and Harry Edwards, *The Revolt of the Black Athlete* (New York, 1969) outline the problems and responsibilities of the African-American middle class. W. Lloyd Warner, Buford H. Junker, and Walter A. Anderson, *Color and Human Nature: Negro Personality Development in a Northern City* (Westport, 1970) study the question of skin color in the African-American community during the early twentieth century. Harvard Sitkoff, *A New Deal for Blacks: The Emergence of Civil Rights as a National Issue*, vol. 1: *The Depression Decade* (New York, 1979) and Richard Dalfiume, "The 'Forgotten Years' of the Negro Revolution," in *The Black Man in America: Since Reconstruction* David Reimers, ed. (New York, 1970) provide useful insights into the origins of the modern civil rights movement. Lawrence Levine, *Black Culture and Black Consciousness: Afro-American Folk Thought from Slavery to Freedom* (New York, 1977) is an indispensable guide to the emerging African-American culture of the twentieth century.

INDEX

283

A Note on the Author

JOHN M. CARROLL is a native of Warwick, Rhode Island. He received a Bachelor of Arts degree from Brown University, a Master of Arts in history from Providence College, and a Ph.D. in history from the University of Kentucky. He is a professor of history at Lamar University. He has edited six books and written more than twenty-five scholarly articles.

	DATE DUE	
NOV 12 2000		
DEC 15 2000		